QUEER LIBRARY ALLIANCE

This book is number seven in the Series on Gender and Sexuality in Information Studies, Emily Drabinski, series editor.

Also in the series:

Queers Online: LGBT Digital Practices in Libraries, Archives, and Museums, edited by Rachel Wexelbaum

Ephemeral Material: Queering the Archive, by Alana Kumbier

Feminist and Queer Information Studies Reader, edited by Rebecca Dean and Patrick Keilty

Feminist Pedagogy for Library Instruction, by Maria Accardi

Make Your Own History: Documenting Feminist and Queer Activism in the 21st Century, edited by Lyz Bly and Kelly Wooten

Out Behind the Desk: Workplace Issues for LGBTQ Librarians, edited by Tracy Nectoux

QUEER LIBRARY ALLIANCE: GLOBAL REFLECTIONS AND IMAGININGS

Rae-Anne Montague and Lucas McKeever,
Editors

LIBRARY JUICE PRESS
SACRAMENTO, CA

Copyright respective authors, 2017

Published in 2017 by Library Juice Press

Library Juice Press
PO Box 188784
Sacramento, CA 95822

http://libraryjuicepress.com/

This book is printed on acid-free, sustainably-sourced paper.

Library of Congress Cataloging-in-Publication Data

Names: Montague, Rae-Anne, editor. | McKeever, Lucas, editor.
Title: Queer library alliance : global reflections and imaginings / Rae-Anne Montague and Lucas McKeever, editors.
Description: Sacramento, CA : Library Juice Press, 2017. | Series: Series on gender and sexuality in information studies ; number 7 | Includes bibliographical references and index.
Identifiers: LCCN 2017030855 | ISBN 9781634000314 (acid-free paper)
Subjects: LCSH: Libraries and sexual minorities.
Classification: LCC Z711.92.S49 Q44 2017 | DDC 027.6/3--dc23
LC record available at https://lccn.loc.gov/2017030855

Contents

Acknowledgements ix

Introduction - *Rae-Anne Montague and Lucas McKeever* xi

Part One: Reflections - Developing Library Services to Meet LGBTQ Users' Needs

Chapter 1. "Disruption Is Not Pleasant But Sometimes It Produces Results": Michael McConnell, Pioneer of Same Sex Marriage and Intellectual Freedom of Librarians in the United States - *Noriko Asato and Andrew B. Wertheimer* 1

Chapter 2. "We Have Made a Start but There is a Long Way to Go": Public Library LGBTQ* Provision to Children and Young People in the Current UK Context - *Elizabeth L. Chapman* 21

Chapter 3. In the Democratic Republic of the Congo, a Defiant LGBTQ Community Flourishes: Collaborating to Preserve their Memory Despite the DRC's Archives Act - *Louis Kamwina Nsapo* 77

Chapter 4. Universal Decimal Classification: A Universal Discriminative Classification - *Gregory Toth* 101

Part Two: Imaginings - Queering Professional Practice

Chapter 5. Rural and Urban Queering Alliances Out of the Library towards Legal Protection of Lesbian, Gay, Bisexual, Transgender, and Questioning People in India - *Bharat Mehra and Lisette Hernandez*   125

Chapter 6. "What is It We Do Not Know?" - LGBTQ and Library Staff - *Ragnhild Brandstedt*   171

Chapter 7. From Gay Surfers to Old Lesbians Organizing for Change: Developing an LGBT Initiative at a State University in Florida - *Matthew Knight*   189

Chapter 8. Global Promotion of LGBTQ Library Resources and Services through Social Media - *Rachel Wexelbaum*   209

About the Contributors   239

Index   247

Acknowledgements

This book would not be possible without the contributors. Thank you all for the amazing work you each are doing and for your willingness to share your experiences with others across the world. This collection is a direct result of the founding and ongoing imaginings of what the LGBTQ Users Special Interest Group (SIG) of the International Federation of Library Associations and Institutions (IFLA) can be. As we finalize the collection, the SIG is in the middle of its fourth year and we would be remiss to not thank those who have made it all possible: Thaddeus Andracki, Francisco Arrais Nascimento, Fabio Assis Pinho, Raphaëlle Bats, Ragnhild Brandstedt, Jamie Campbell Naidoo, Ana Elisa de Campos Salles, Anders Cato, Thomas Chaimbault, Elizabeth L. Chapman, José Augusto Chaves Guimarães, Philippe Colomb, Thomas Colombéra, Anna Culbertson, John DeSantis, Christer Edeholt, Barbara Ford, Bruna Gisele Motta, Gilberto Gomes Cândido, Gabriel Gomez, Laverne Gray, Joseph Hafner, Louis Kamwina Nsapo, Lisa Lamont, Maria Lindgren, Bharat Mehra, Martin Morris, Heather Moulaison Sandy, Miriam Nauri, Ann Okerson, Josche Owerkerk, Anne Reddacliff, K.R. Roberto, Miriam Säfström, Eduardo da Silva Alentejo, Noémi Somorjai, Stephen Stratton, Julie Ann Winkelstein, Joanne Yeomans, and countless others have made and continue to make the SIG possible. Thank you all for your ongoing support!

We cannot thank Emily Drabinski enough. Her thoughtful feedback and support throughout this process has been key to making this project successful. 　　　　-- *Rae-Anne Montague and Lucas McKeever*

Introduction

Rae-Anne Montague and Lucas McKeever

> The relationship between story and survival is really important for queer and trans people. - Michael Erickson, Glad Day Bookshop[1]

Queer identities are complex. They are embedded in a web of intersectionality and are often challenging to fully define.[2] Sometimes queerness shines like a beacon and this radiance is captured in media. Sometimes it is more subtle. Often it is invisible.

Promoting understanding and visibility are primary goals of this anthology. The text draws inspiration from many sources, including the IFLA LGBTQ Users SIG, the Queer Library Alliance, and our ongoing interest in probing queer representation.

The International Federation of Library Associations and Institutions (IFLA) describes itself as "the leading international body representing the interests of library and information services and their users... - the global voice of the library and information profession."[3] In 2013, a small group of conference attendees came together at the annual meeting in Singapore.[4] They noted that, aside from social gatherings of LGBTQ-identified professionals at the conference, no structured or sustained discussions of issues related to library services for lesbian, gay, bisexual, transgender, queer/questioning (LGBTQ) community members had taken place within IFLA during its eighty-year history. With a burst of collective energy, the LGBTQ Users Special Interest Group (SIG) emerged. The SIG serves as a platform to promote visibility and dialogue around queer issues of importance to librarians globally. In its first three years, the SIG has provided a space for fifteen presentations to be given to audiences made up of information professionals from around the world. The idea to develop this anthology emerged at the first meeting of the SIG in August 2014 in Lyon, France as a way to make these conversations accessible to a broader audience.[5]

Our international lens draws upon our individual and collective experiences. The first part of our title, Queer Library Alliance (QLA), is the namesake of a student group that emerged at the University of Illinois at Urbana-Champaign (UIUC) Graduate School of Library and Information Science (GSLIS).[6] Students from this program have been involved for many years in attending, organizing for, volunteering with, and presenting at the Midwest Bisexual, Lesbian, Gay, Transgender, and Ally College Conference (MBGLTACC), a regional, student-led gathering that began in Iowa in 1993.[7] In February 2008, UIUC hosted MGBLTACC. Having the conference on the campus afforded new opportunities for student involvement and the participation of GSLIS students subsequently increased. QLA officially emerged from that time. MGBLTACC participation included the planning and facilitation of group presentations and the hosting of exhibits designed to explore queer-library and information science intersections, such as information access, cataloging and classification, collection development, special collections, and children and youth services. Some of this work complemented efforts of members of the Progressive Librarians Guild student group.[8] Collaborative conference involvement spawned new interest in promoting queer advocacy, exploring professional and academic issues, and developing varied social activities. These included a book club, participation in campus and local queer events, and work with national organizations such as the Gay, Lesbian, Bisexual, and Transgender Round Table of the American Library Association (GLBTRT) and the Society of American Archivists Lesbian and Gay Archives Roundtable (LAGAR), as well as field trips to LGBTQ libraries and archives. Both of the editors of this volume were involved in QLA at GSLIS.[9]

The latter half of our title stems from the esteemed scholarship in Judith Butler's seminal text, *Bodies that Matter*. Butler eloquently invites us to consider where we have been and where we might go. In the context of connecting LGBTQ issues with library and information science (LIS), this plethora of possibilities is critical at this time in our history.

> If the term "queer" is to be a site of collective contestation, the point of departure for a set of historical reflections and futural imaginings, it will have to remain that which it is, in the present, never fully owned, but always and only redeployed, twisted, queered from a prior usage and in the direction of urgent and expanding political purposes.[10]

Intersectional Realities

It's a queer world. Imagine. In LIS terms, this means that there has been queer content since there has been content. Even so, it is clear that much of our story has not been recorded or recognized. In fact, we have been and still are frequently disregarded and misrepresented. Might this be due to inadequacies in language, or taxonomy, or human creativity, or some combination? Queer complexities are unintelligible within simple systems.[11] Does this lead to confusion and fear? As library professionals who create, utilize, and make accessible systems for organization and classification of information, intersectionality must remain a clear objective in addressing these historical absences. While discussing the tension that exists between choosing what materials are acceptable or unacceptable to archive, Tim Dean explains that "Just as archives include certain things by excluding others, so they also routinely exclude particular classes of witness to what they include."[12] For information professionals, this points to the inevitability that the very processes we engage with every day will remain exclusionary in one way or another. Rather than becoming discouraged, acknowledging this shortcoming can remind us that achieving equity in library services is an ongoing process rather than a project with an end date.

In 2015, the UN High Commissioner for Human Rights, Zeid Ra'ad Al Hussein, issued a report on "Discrimination and violence against individuals based on their sexual orientation and gender identity." The report concludes that:

The overall picture remains one of continuing, pervasive, violent abuse, harassment and discrimination affecting LGBT and intersex persons in all regions. These constitute serious human rights violations, often perpetrated with impunity, indicating that current arrangements to protect the human rights of LGBT and intersex persons are inadequate.[13]

As of May 2015, there were 118 countries where same sex sexual acts between adults in private are legal, seventy-five countries where same-sex sexual acts are still illegal, and sixty-two countries where discrimination in employment based on sexual orientation was prohibited.[14] In June 2016, the UN Human Rights Council voted to appoint an independent expert to monitor and report on levels of violence and discrimination against LGBT people.[15] In tandem with this official recognition, many activists are bringing issues to light and making efforts to end discrimination around the globe.[16]

We advocate for queer rights and representation grounded in social justice and intersectionality.

> With an intersectional lens, activists, human rights defenders, policy makers, and stakeholders can also uncover how political, economic and social structures such as patriarchy, capitalism and neo-liberalism generate and perpetuate social inequality in all spaces of societies. It can show how the State's institutions produce and replicate systems of oppression based on gender, sexuality, class, race, religion, ability, amongst others, all of which play in simultaneous ways and affect particularly the most marginalised individuals and groups.[17]

How are librarians, archivists and other LIS professionals contributing to socially just and intersectionally-grounded policies and practices? This is the root of what we seek to better understand via the IFLA LGBTQ Users SIG and through contributions to this anthology. We were very pleased to receive many responses to the call for contributions based on topics of contemporary importance to librarians serving LGBTQ users around the world. We ultimately selected eight areas to develop as chapters. These topics represent some of our efforts to respond to challenges, address critical needs, and serve as essential forces against systematic oppression across service areas, library types, and borders.

Part 1: Reflections - Developing Library Services to Meet LGBTQ Users' Needs

> Culturally sensitive catalogue headings are not a quirky, unnecessary luxury but proof of our commitment to the truth and accuracy.
> - Sanford Berman[18]

The first section of this collection of essays looks at how we are developing understanding and library services that reflect and are responsive to LGBTQ user needs.

Noriko Asato and Andrew Wertheimer start off with an exploration of the highly influential Michael McConnell case. The case of McConnell, whose offer to work as a librarian at the University of Minnesota in 1970 was rescinded after he openly revealed his homosexual identity, reverberated throughout the profession and prompted changes within libraries, the ALA, and beyond. This early and essential disruption eventually led to a happy ending when the Jean-Nickolaus Tretter Collection in GLBT Studies received the Baker-McConnell papers over forty years later.

Elizabeth Chapman's contribution considers the state of LGBTQ public library services to children in the United Kingdom. She examines current policy and reveals several "patchy" areas, including lack of awareness and knowledge. The need for more training is also discussed.

In the third chapter, Louis Kamwina Nsapo offers an analysis of difficulties faced while archiving personal materials in the Democratic Republic of the Congo. Public rhetoric surrounding homosexuality and the lingering effects of imperialism present activists with unique challenges in their efforts to preserve the cultural memory of DRC's LGBTQ community.

In chapter four, Gregory Toth reviews biases inherent in the Library of Congress, Dewey Decimal, and Universal Decimal Classification systems with an emphasis on retrieval problems for LGBTQ topics. He urges all librarians to advocate for changes to improve cataloging practices.

Part 2: Imaginings - Queering Professional Practice

The second part of this collection emphasizes opportunities and approaches for augmenting queer professional practice, which ultimately benefits all library users.

Bharat Mehra and Lisette Hernandez's chapter offers content analysis of news items from *The Times of India* and proposes library alliances at economic, educational, legal, political, and social levels to promote lawful protection of sexual minorities in India. Librarian voices are an essential force in progressive change.

In the sixth chapter, Ragnhild Brandstedt describes the process of awareness-making at Mariestad Public Library in Sweden through collaboration between the public library and LGBTQ advocates. This action-based research, conducted in 2012-2013, has led to education for the entire library staff, certification, and numerous improvements in service.

Matthew Knight's contribution describes the process of developing a queer academic collection at the University of South Florida featuring monographs, archives, oral histories, and research materials. Key issues include access, community engagement, and resource allocation.

In the final chapter, Rachel Wexelbaum reviews concerns over inequitable access and calls on librarians to review spaces and services available to vulnerable users. She offers suggestions for using social media to increase safe spaces and reliable information services for LGBTQ users, in collaboration with community members.

Context and Limits

Most of the contributors to this anthology have been involved with the IFLA LGBTQ Users SIG. We hail from, reside in, and study issues from several countries around the world including Canada, Democratic Republic of Congo, England, Hungary, India, Japan, Sweden, and the United States. We are a queer collective. That said, we also recognize that there are biases inherent in our perspectives. For example, during the development of this anthology, both editors lived in the United States. For the editors and others guided by Western perspectives, our conceptions of queer worlds are limited. Our understanding and by extension our writing, is biased by our particular experiences and positions in the world. We encourage readers to consider additional works by queer people of color, indigenous scholars, and other diverse authors.

As referenced above, the ALA GLBTRT was founded in 1970 as the ALA's Task Force on Gay Liberation, the first national gay, lesbian, bisexual, and transgender professional organization. The GLBTRT strives to serve the information needs of the GLBT professional library community, and the GLBT information and access needs of individuals at large. It supports the free and necessary access to information, as reflected by the missions of the ALA and democratic institutions.[19] Organized professionals concerned with our stories occupy themselves around the world to enable varied access to queer history and culture.[20] Some operate boldly. Others persist quietly

The initial period of the development of this book took place in 2015, forty-five years after the founding of the first GLBT professional library organization. This was a gleeful time for many individuals and families in the United States, because on June 26, during the ALA Annual Meeting in San Francisco, the Supreme Court of the United States recognized the fundamental right of same-sex couples to marry.[21] While not all LGBTQ people advocate for marriage, many viewed this event with joy and celebrations abounded during the ALA gathering.

Sadly, as we approached publication in 2016, another queer-focused event took place in the United States. On June 12, there was a mass shooting inside a gay nightclub in Orlando, Florida that left fifty people dead. This mind-numbing event occurred in the middle of PRIDE month, in the city where ALA would soon be gathering for our annual meeting. It was a stark reminder of our marginality and the need for increased understanding and justice. As thoughtful leaders like Avram Dinkelstein and Angela Davis have stated,"freedom is a constant struggle."[22] As librarians, archivists, and other information professionals committed to facilitating access and high-quality services for LGBTQ- and other marginalized users, there is much more to consider and do.

Endnotes

1. Erickson is co-owner of the Glad Day Bookshop. Established in 1970 in Toronto, Glad Day is the oldest LGBTQ bookshop in the world. http://www.gladdaybookshop.com/pages/history.

2. See for example, see: Gloria Anzaldúa, *Borderlands/La Frontera: The New Mestiza* (San Francisco: Aunt Lute Books, 1987); Niko Besnier and Kalissa Alexeyeff, eds., *Gender on the Edge: Transgender, Gay, and Other Pacific Islanders* (Honolulu: University of Hawai'i Press, 2014); Sokari Ekine and Ahkima Abbas, eds., *Queer African Reader* (Nairobi: Pambazuka Press, 2013); Scott Siraj al-Haqq Kugle, *Living Out Islam: Voices of Gay, Lesbian, and Transgender Muslims* (New York: NYU Press, 2013); Audrey Yue and Jun Zubillaga-Pow, eds., Queer Singapore: Illiberal Citizenship and Mediated Cultures (Hong Kong: Hong Kong University Press, 2012).

3. About IFLA, http://www.ifla.org/about. Accessed November 12, 2016.

4. Male homosexual activity is illegal in Singapore. http://www.equaldex.com/region/singapore.

5. Rae-Anne Montague, "Leading and Transforming Library Services," paper presented at IFLA WLIC, 2015. http://library.ifla.org/1288/1/128-montague-en.pdf.

6. In 2016, the GSLIS became the School of Information Sciences.

7. The Midwest Bisexual, Lesbian, Gay, Transgender, Ally College Conference (MBLGTACC). http://lgbt.wikia.com/wiki/Midwest_Bisexual_Lesbian_Gay_Transgender_Ally_College_Conference.

8. The Progressive Librarians Guild (PLG) was founded in New York City in 1990. PLG does not accept the notion of librarianship as a neutral profession and asserts that "cataloging, indexing, acquisitions policy and collection development, the character of reference services, library automation, library management, and virtually every other library issue embody political value choices." http://www.progressivelibrariansguild.org/content/purpose.shtml

9. QLA: Queer Library Alliance. https://ischool.illinois.edu/events/2013/02/18/qla-queer-library-alliance.

10. Judith Butler . *Bodies that Matter: On the Discursive Limits of "Sex"* (New York: Psychology Press, 1993), 228.

11. "It is a fundamental of taxonomy that nature rarely deals with discrete categories. Only the human mind invents categories and tries to force facts into separated pigeon-holes. The living world is a continuum in each and every one of its aspects." Alfred. C. Kinsey, Wardell B. Pomeroy, and Clyde E. Martin, *Sexual Behavior in the Human Male* (Philadelphia: W.B. Saunders Co. 1948).

12. Tim Dean, "Introduction: Pornography, Technology, Archive," in *Porn Archives*, ed. Tim Dean, Steven Ruszczycky, and David Squires (Durham, NC: Duke University Press, 2014), 4.

13. United Nations, Human Rights Council, "Discrimination and Violence against Individuals Based on their Sexual Orientation and Gender Identity,"(May 4, 2015), 20, http://www.ohchr.org/EN/HRBodies/HRC/RegularSessions/Session29/Documents/A_HRC_29_23_en.doc.

14. Aengus Carroll and Lucas Paoli Itaborahy, *State Sponsored Homophobia 2015: A World Survey of Laws: Criminalisation, Protection and Recognition of Same-Sex Love* (Geneva; ILGA, 2015), 25-28, 33-36. http://old.ilga.org/Statehomophobia/ILGA_State_Sponsored_Homophobia_2015.pdf.

15. UN News Centre, "UN agrees to appoint human rights expert on protection of LGBT," July 1, 2016, http://www.un.org/apps/news/story.asp?NewsID=54385#.V4PxBZMrLaY.

16. For example, the website "Where Love is Illegal" documents and shares stories of discrimination from around the world: http://whereloveisillegal.com. Another intriguing national example is Ladlad, a Filipino LGBT political party: http://ladladpartylist.blogspot.com.

17. Fernando D'Elio with Neha Sood, "Intersections," in Carroll and Itaborahy, *State Sponsored Homophobia*, 2015, 21.

18. Listen to Sanford Berman discuss his ideas in more detail in an interview available through the A. Arro Smith "Capturing our Stories" Oral Histories Program RS 97/1/70. http://archives.library.illinois.edu/alaarchon/index.php?p=collections/controlcard&id=8511.

19. Gay, Lesbian, Bisexual, and Transgender Round Table of the American Library Association (GLBTRT). http://www.ala.org/glbtrt.

20. In fall 2016, there were forty-three LGBTQ libraries, archives, and special collections included in the Wikipedia listing. https://en.wikipedia.org/wiki/Libraries_and_the_LGBTQ_community.

21. Obergefell et al. v. Hodges, Director, Ohio Department of Health, et al., Supreme Court of the United States Syllabus No. 14–556, http://www.supremecourt.gov/opinions/14pdf/14-556_3204.pdf.

22. Avram Dinkelstein co-founded the "Silence=Death" Project in 1986. He reflects on the process here: http://www.silenceopensdoors.com/2010/04/04/silencedeath-2. Angela Y. Davis is a political activist, scholar, author, and speaker. Her most recent book is *Freedom is a Constant Struggle: Ferguson, Palestine, and the Foundations of a Movement* (Chicago: Haymarket Books, 2016).

Bibliography

Anzaldúa, Gloria. *Borderlands/La Frontera: The New Mestiza*. San Francisco: Aunt Lute Books, 1987.

Besnier, Niko and Kalissa Alexeyeff, eds. *Gender on the Edge: Transgender, Gay, and Other Pacific Islanders*. Honolulu: University of Hawai'i Press, 2014.

Butler, Judith. *Bodies that Matter: On the Discursive Limits of "Sex."* New York: Psychology Press, 1993.

Carroll, Aengus and Lucas Paoli Itaborahy. *State Sponsored Homophobia 2015: A World Survey of Laws: Criminalisation, Protection and Recognition of Same-Sex Love.* Geneva; ILGA, 2015. http://old.ilga.org/Statehomophobia/ILGA_State_Sponsored_Homophobia_2015.pdf.

Dean, Tim. "Introduction: Pornography, Technology, Archive." In *Porn Archives,* edited by Tim Dean, Steven Ruszczycky, and David Squires, 1-28. Durham, NC: Duke University Press, 2014.

D'Elio, Fernando, with Neha Sood, "Intersections." In Carroll and Itaborahy, *State Sponsored Homophobia,* 18-22. Geneva: ILGA, 2015

Ekine, Sokari and Ahkima Abbas, eds. *Queer African Reader.* Nairobi: Pambazuka Press, 2013.

Kugle, Scott Siraj al-Haqq. *Living Out Islam: Voices of Gay, Lesbian, and Transgender Muslims.* New York: NYU Press, 2013.

Kinsey, Alfred. C., Wardell B. Pomeroy, and Clyde E. Martin. *Sexual Behavior in the Human Male.* Philadelphia: W.B. Saunders Co., 1948.

Montague, Rae-Anne. "Leading and Transforming Library Services." Paper presented at IFLA WLIC, 2015. http://library.ifla.org/1288/1/128-montague-en.pdf.

Obergefell et al. v. Hodges, Director, Ohio Department of Health, et al. Supreme Court of the United States, Syllabus No. 14–556. http://www.supremecourt.gov/opinions/14pdf/14-556_3204.pdf.

UN News Centre. "UN agrees to appoint human rights expert on protection of LGBT." July 1, 2016, http://www.un.org/apps/news/story.asp?NewsID=54385#.V4PxBZMrLaY.

United Nations, Human Rights Council. "Discrimination and Violence against Individuals Based on their Sexual Orientation and Gender Identity." May 4, 2015. http://www.ohchr.org/EN/HRBodies/HRC/RegularSessions/Session29/Documents/A_HRC_29_23_en.doc.

Yue, Audrey and Jun Zubillaga-Pow, eds. *Queer Singapore: Illiberal Citizenship and Mediated Cultures*. Hong Kong: Hong Kong University Press, 2012.

PART ONE:
REFLECTIONS - DEVELOPING LIBRARY SERVICES TO MEET LGBTQ USERS' NEEDS

Chapter 1

"Disruption Is Not Pleasant But Sometimes It Produces Results": Michael McConnell, Pioneer of Same Sex Marriage and Intellectual Freedom of Librarians in the United States

Noriko Asato and Andrew B. Wertheimer

Introduction

One month before the United States Supreme Court ruled that it was unconstitutional to bar same-sex marriage, the *New York Times* profiled two men who helped to overturn discriminatory laws that codified marriage as only being between one man and one woman. The front-page article mentioned that one-half of the pioneering couple was a retired public librarian in Minnesota named Michael McConnell.[1] The article explained that he had originally moved to the state in order to be with his lover, Jack Baker, and to accept a position at the University of Minnesota's St. Paul campus library. It also stated that before he could start his new position, the University Regents rescinded the job offer because he and Baker had publicly declared their intention to marry. McConnell and Baker became pioneers in a struggle to extend equality in marriage laws, and in the process McConnell also became a pioneer in extending protection for lesbian, gay, bisexual, transgender, and queer (LGBTQ) librarians who were just starting to come out of the closet. He took his case to the American Library Association (ALA), which was expanding its defense of intellectual freedom and had established a mechanism to investigate the cases of librarians fired by administrators who disagreed with their thoughts or conduct. In the years that followed, ALA would have a major conflict over whether McConnell's firing or "non-hiring" was an intellectual freedom case. This struggle took place at the same time that gay and lesbian American librarians were organizing one of the first gay/lesbian professional associations, the Gay Liberation Task Force, within the Social Responsibilities Round Table, an activist section within ALA. As this chapter will show, the ALA failed to defend McConnell's employment, but his case helped demonstrate the complexities involved with defending librarians' employment rights and the parameters of free speech as individuals. For LBGTQ librarians, especially outside North America, the McConnell case is an important case study of how a librarian activist was able to change social attitudes within and beyond the profession.

The McConnell Case Overview

On April 27, 1970, Michael McConnell received an offer letter for the position of cataloging department head at the University of Minnesota (U of M) St. Paul campus library. University librarian Ralph Hopp wrote that "we are looking forward to having you join our staff."[2] McConnell immediately accepted the offer. Although the University's Board of Regents' formal approval of the hiring had not yet been issued, he did not foresee any problems and resigned his position at Park College in Kansas City. He relocated to Minesota to be with his lover, Jack Baker, who was a U of M law student. Three weeks later, they applied for a marriage license at the Hennepin County clerk's office, attracting statewide media attention since they openly admitted that they were homosexuals.[3] On June 24th, the University Regents withdrew his appointment on the grounds that "his personal conduct, as represented in the public and University news media, is not consistent with the best interest of the University."[4]

The Minnesota Civil Liberties Union subsequently filed a suit on McConnell's behalf in Federal District Court, accusing the University of violating his constitutional rights—breaching his contract solely on the basis of his public pronouncement of homosexuality. The court ruled that the "plaintiff does not have an inalienable right to be employed by the University but he has a right not to be discriminated against under the Fourteenth Amendment due process clause," and issued an injunction restraining the University from refusing his employment.[5] On October 18, 1971, the US Court of Appeals for the Eighth Circuit overturned the decision and recognized the Regents' authority over university administration, which limited the intervention of judicial review.[6] The US Supreme Court denied a writ to review the case on April 3rd, 1972. McConnell and Baker found themselves in court several times in the following years as they tried to force the court to recognize their marriage and the injustice of Minnesota's sodomy laws. Our focus in this chapter, however, will be on the manner in which the ALA responded to McConnell's struggles as a gay librarian.

McConnell's Appeal to the American Library Association

On January 11, 1971, after the University Regents took their case to Appeals Court, McConnell contacted the ALA's Program of Action in Support of the Library Bill of Rights (henceforth, Program of Action). Established at the ALA's 1969 annual conference in Atlantic City, the Program of Action was a long-awaited defense scheme set up by ALA after a number of librarians lost their positions as a result of their courageous battles against local censorship groups. The Program of Action was administered by the Intellectual Freedom Committee (IFC), which investigated cases alleging violations of the Principle of Intellectual Freedom and enacted various censures if infringements were found.[7] In his letter, McConnell referred to a 1946 ALA document, *Tenure in Libraries: A Statement of Principles of Intellectual Freedom and Tenure for Librarians*. Articles (2) and (4) of the *Principles* state that "appointments and promotions [be] based solely on merit without interference from political, economic, religious, or other groups," and that the workplace should provide "the opportunity for the librarian to devote himself to the practice of his profession without fear of undue interference or dismissal and provides freedom from discharge for political, religious, racial, or other unjust reasons."[8]

The 1971 Midwinter Conference in Los Angeles

Beyond simply filing paperwork to request action on his case, McConnell also spoke at the 1971 ALA midwinter conference to share his story. He addressed the ALA Task Force on Gay Liberation, then an ALA SRRT sub-group. Outgoing SRRT Task Force Coordinator Israel Fishman called McConnell "our martyr in residence."[9] His partner, Jack Baker, received a big round of applause when he stood up to greet the group. McConnell began his presentation with a brief overview of his situation, explaining that his attempt to have a resolution in support of his claim passed by the Minnesota Library Association at their conference had succeeded, with over 400 in support and only ten against. He had called on the ALA-IFC to investigate his complaint to consider whether the University of Minnesota Regents should be censured. McConnell explained that the regents had privately told reporters that "it would not be a good precedent to approve my appointment." Regent Marjorie Howard had said she would rather "face a lawsuit than the wrath of the public and legislature."[10] McConnell concluded these statements showed that the Regents' actions violated the ALA's Principle of Intellectual Freedom.

In the same talk, McConnell suggested that Gay librarians should be active in the following ways:
1. Create bibliographies that are not biased against homosexuality
2. Create Gay Pride Week library displays with facts and positive information
3. Subscribe to Gay-Lesbian periodicals for the 10 million unrepresented homosexuals
4. Build quality collections. He explained that libraries are full of biased information about homosexuality, and that new materials should be considered carefully

5. Support the Gay Liberation Task Force (GLTF) with money and manpower
6. Notify the GLTF with all examples of job discrimination or items unfairly excluded from collections
7. Offer professional assistance to local Gay Liberation groups

He further called on the audience to suggest other ways that they could work together. Beyond that he asked, "What can we expect from our association?" Telling the audience about his experience in dealing with ALA, he exclaimed:

> If you want anything from ALA, you are going to have to demand it. Our association is very reluctant to act, especially quickly... six months, I've been waiting for action. It took disruption. Disruption is not pleasant, but sometimes it produces results. I would like to say the Gay-lib[eration] movement has not been taken seriously in the association. ... We intend to not back down until we get what we want from this association.

At the same conference, a less favorable reception was evident as the IFC reviewed McConnell's letter, along with sixteen pages of documents and 127 attachments. The IFC decided that the case fell outside the parameters of the Library Bill of Rights, which was the fundamental principle behind the Program of Action. IFC Chair David Berninghausen, who also worked at the U of M, explained to McConnell that while his case was indeed subject to the 1946 policy, the jurisdiction and procedures were unspecified.[11] Enraged by the IFC's evasive attitude, the Task Force on Gay Liberation appealed to the ALA president stating, "the IFC decision seems to be a clear attempt to hide this obscene incident."[12] The case was then forwarded to the Association of College and Research Libraries (ACRL), which claimed that the case was in its jurisdiction. After investigating, the ACRL denounced the U of M Regents and implored them to rescind their decision and employ McConnell.[13] However, it failed to push the ALA to press the decision on behalf of the entire association. Not surprisingly, this tepid response failed to move the Regents.

Program of Action for Mediation, Arbitration, and Inquiry

It is important to understand McConnell's experience within the historical context of ALA's efforts to defend intellectual freedom. As early as 1939, Phillip Keeney, the former head librarian at Montana State University, had called on the ALA to defend librarians such as himself who lost their positions defending intellectual freedom.[14] Many members were very proud to finally witness the establishment of the Office for Intellectual Freedom (1967), the Freedom to Read Foundation (1969), and the Leroy C. Merritt Humanitarian Fund (1970). The Office, Foundation, and Fund were meant to be the profession's arsenal to defend librarians fired for following their ethical and professional mandates. Especially important was the 1969 "Program of Action in Support of the Library Bill of Rights" which gave the IFC executive powers to investigate cases of IF violations, which at the time seemed to be an almost revolutionary mechanism for action. However, many cases brought to the Program of Action, such as McConnell, T. Ellis Hodgin (1969), and Zoia Horn (1972),[15] troubled the IFC charged with evaluating them, since they were not traditional cases involving a librarian fired for defending library materials. This precise point became a major point of contention between leaders of the ALA IFC who were worried about maintaining a narrow window of cases they felt the association could afford to defend. This contrasted greatly with the position of the profession's activists, especially those in the Social Responsibility Round Table (SRRT). They demanded that ALA provide institutional support and job security for librarians' own intellectual freedom—even when it related to speech practiced outside of the workplace.[16]

In 1971, thanks to pressure from SRRT activists, ALA Council (its legislative body) recognized the limitations of the old Program of Action to deal with cases like McConnell's. At the 1971 annual conference in Dallas, Texas, ALA Council passed (with a vote of 214 for and only two opposed) a new "Program of Action for Mediation, Arbitration, and Inquiry" (PAMAI) to cover librarian's employment and tenure issues. It was also intended to deal with status, fair employment practices, and due process; to interpret pertinent ALA policies; and to determine appropriate courses of action, such as formal or informal mediation, arbitration, filing a brief, or inquiry. If these actions did not produce a solution, the Staff Committee on Mediation, Arbitration, and Inquiry (SCMAI) was to appoint a fact-finding subcommittee to investigate the case and produce a written report for the ALA's Executive Director. The report would be effective following Executive Board approval.[17] The PAMAI was specifically designed to correct the shortfall of the previous "Program of Action," in that it was equipped with detailed procedures and means to carry out the action. It seemed like a perfect scheme, except for one serious limitation—OIF Director Judith Krug insisted on adding the clause "no formal inquiry will be made into cases which are in litigation."[18] This would not be the first time that activists butted heads with Krug, but her insistence was designed to keep ALA from loosing its non-profit tax-exempt status and to limit its liability.

The First Report (1972)

The PAMAI "no interference while in court" clause proved problematic in McConnell's case. His request for action officially came under PAMAI's charge after the Dallas annual conference in June 1971. However, PAMAI did not begin to consider his case until the Supreme Court denied McConnell's writ for review on April 3, 1972. This meant the decision of the Appeals Court that the University Regents had the authority to choose employees suitable to the institution and had not abused their power in refusing McConnell's employment was left standing.[19]

On August 7, 1972, the first SCMAI draft report on the McConnell Case was reviewed by the Krug and two other SCMAI members. In addition, three ALA members, including Barbara Gittings, a leader of SRRT's Task Force on Gay Liberation, were appointed to assist the review. However, the report was widely leaked during the 1973 ALA Midwinter meeting in Washington DC. before being submitted to the Executive Board. The Board discussed it in closed session and immediately sent it back to SCMAI for revision.[20] ALA President Katherine

Laich, who sensed an air of discontent among membership and Council, announced that the report was rejected for further study. *Library Journal* wrote that, in the unofficially circulated SCMAI report, the committee had identified its job as "to determine what standards are currently prevailing" but not to "become an advocate of change."[21] The magazine questioned the role of SCMAI and ridiculed its report under the headline, *"SCMAI Strikes Out."*[22]

The SRRT Action Council boasted that their political tactics had successfully caused the report to be rejected and appealed its unfairness to ALA Council.[23] SRRT's Action Council also sent a telegram to pressure the Executive Board.[24]

The Second Report (1973)

Instead of collecting materials on its own, the SCMAI conducted its second investigation of McConnell's case only by reviewing court documents, since it claimed that "all the pertinent facts had been gathered during the judicial process."[25] It concluded that because the University had never officially employed McConnell, SCMAI was "precluded from taking any meaningful action toward mediation or arbitration of the case." Thus, the committee concluded that by adopting the court decision, the University had the right to rescind McConnell's contract and reject his claim. On November 1, 1973, the ALA Executive Board received and approved this second report.[26]

After reading SCMAI's second report in *American Libraries* (January 1974), the Minnesota SRRT immediately called for SCMAI to re-investigate the case. On January 24, 1974, during the midwinter meeting in Chicago, ALA-SRRT endorsed the Minnesota SRRT's action and resolved that "SCMAI has made no formal inquiry into McConnell's request for action since the conclusion of litigation, particularly with regard to the University of Minnesota's bad faith conduct;" therefore, their statement that SCMAI "has been precluded from taking meaningful action . . . is not supported by said report of the facts." It further resolved that "McConnell's request for action be referred back to SCMAI for immediate formal inquiry into all issues that affect fundamental fairness in accordance with the principles of Intellectual Freedom."[27] The next day, ALA Council passed an "Equal Employment Opportunity (EEO)" policy to back up efforts to press its agenda to SCMAI. It was written to assure "a policy of equality of opportunity for all library employees, or applicants for employment, regardless of race, color, creed, sex, age, individual life style, or national origin."[28]

At the 1974 ALA annual conference in New York City, SRRT activists continued their campaign, leading Council to pass a motion referring McConnell's case once again back to SCMAI. They demanded the committee conduct a formal investigation based on the new EEO policy. Responding to the pressure from Council, SCMAI established a new Fact-Finding Committee foe McConnell's appeal on August 29. Thus, after ten months of persistent efforts orchestrated by SRRT and others, the case was re-opened once again to call for action from the professional association.[29]

The Final Report (1975)

Finally, in October 1975, five years after the University rescinded its job offer, the "Report of the Fact-Finding Committee (FFC), ALA Staff Committee on Mediation, Arbitration, and Inquiry (SCMAI), concerning J. Michael McConnell" was published in *American Libraries*. The committee had taken a full year to investigate. The three-column, three-page report detailed the original request, development of past events and investigations, and added a chronology. Seemingly ignoring Council's expectations, the FFC approached the case with a review of information already obtained, including McConnell's Request for Action, correspondence, and court records. Surprisingly, the Committee resisted SRRT and Council criticisms and once again looked only at the same limited sample of evidence. However, the subcommittee also consulted with SCMAI members and ALA's legal counsel, and revisited the provisions of PAMAI. They learned in the document that SCMAI's review and actions were limited to issues raised by the complainant, meaning

SCMAI's intervention was constrained on the basis of McConnell's original formal request. In essence, McConnell's (initial) demands were for a public apology by the University of Minnesota; for a change in employment policies; and for ALA to take a firm stance on intellectual freedom cases.[30] The ALA Fact-Finding Committee Report (1975) explains why his request to the Program of Action was short of what a victim of discrimination would normally want. In addition, he said that ALA lacked a reputation for taking strong political stances, so instead of wishing to secure his position or charge the University with a violation of due process, the alternative courses of action expressed in his request for action would be the only realistic and attainable ones.[31] ALA used McConnell's original stance of reluctance and reconciliation to justify not investing resources in the case.[32]

The report explained that after the Supreme Court denied McConnell's appeal for review, the ruling by the Eighth Circuit Court of Appeal supporting the University's action remained in effect; thus the Regents' actions were found legal, and they "had no obligation whatever to any investigatory body of the ALA." SCMAI realized that "ALA had no power or legal grounds to force those involved to discuss the case or to reveal facts they would not wish to disclose." The subcommittee supported SCMAI's earlier judgment that "a formal inquiry is not warranted," since it found no violation of ALA policies by the Regents.[33] In the report, the subcommittee reprimanded Council for making a hasty and drastic move by rejecting SCMAI's second report without verifying facts or considering alternatives, while the SCMAI was also criticized for its inability to effectively communicate with Council. Finally, FCC recommended that the McConnell case be closed.

Dissolution of SCMAI

SCMAI's final report on McConnell's case, compiled by the Fact-Finding Committee, clearly demonstrated a major problem inherent in ALA's defense system. Basically, ALA lacked any authority or practical means to deal with those who violated its codes or principles. Since its 1971 establishment, SCMAI had received forty-six cases and seven inquiries for information over two years. The breakdown of these cases is: seven on tenure and academic status; seventeen on unfair employment; fifteen regarding due process; two concerning unethical procedures; three related to intellectual freedom; and two classified as "others."[34] These numbers indicate that most of the cases were related to employment issues, and only a few were in the traditional realm of intellectual freedom. Although PAMAI replaced the Program of Action in order to expand the ALA's investigational purview, the disproportional number of employment disputes must have been a disappointing and exhausting experience for SCMAI members. When the statistics were reported in 1973, only a few ALA staff members were allocated to work for SCMAI, and they were already dealing with sixteen cases in addition to their other duties. Judith Krug, Director of OIF and a SCMAI member, commented on this in a 2006 interview:

> They [LeRoy Merritt Humanitarian Fund board] wanted to deal with discrimination also and we did not believe that that was our goal. You know, very often, discriminatory actions can be interpreted as involving intellectual freedom principles but (pause) you have to be careful with interpretations. I think that the Foundation Board's feeling, and certainly my feeling, was that we had a huge mouthful that we were trying to chew and we honestly didn't need anything else, nor could we accommodate anything else. [35]

SCMAI encountered many problems and was eventually dismantled in 1988. The following year, the Standing Committee on Review, Inquiry and Mediation (SCRIM) replaced SCMAI. In 1991 it was abolished as well, after dealing with another twelve cases.[36]

Conclusion

This paper has focused primarily on issues related to the way ALA handled the University of Minnesota Regents discriminatory overturning of Michael McConnell's employment offer in the early 1970s. There are many ways that one could examine this important case, since it ripped the Association apart. By 1975, McConnell despaired over ALA's inaction. When ALA's Gay Liberation Task Force Coordinator Barbara Gittings wrote to McConnell to see if he wanted to be part of a newly formed advisory committee to the ALA Office for Library Personnel Resources "to give the gay viewpoint" on the newly passed Equal Employment Opportunity Subcommittee, McConnell was quick to decline. He wrote:

> Frankly, I don't give a flying fuck about that bigoted bureaucracy. I have no intention of involving myself in any of its committee work period. If you detect bitterness it is purely intentional. I intend to devote my energies strictly at the Minnesota State level. At least the bigots here make themselves known and can be dealt with. The goody, goody liberals and closet cases in ALA may continue their meaningless game playing, but I'll not be on the team... It is obvious to me that ALA really doesn't want to do anything meaningful for Gays. The bureaucracy in reality ignores Gays except for a few words stuck here and there to keep us off their backs. They ignore requests of membership, and lie in print about their actions. My own case is but one of the few examples quotable in this context. They are very effective at playing one "minority" off another with Gays coming off on the losing end.[37]

He was exasperated by ALA, adding that he had "spent close to $10,000 of my own money to help combat the bigotry in Minnesota and at ALA." He concluded that efforts in Minnesota, where legal protection was extended to almost two million people, had been far more profitable. At the same time, he found that "ALA has added rhetoric to their policy statements," but not protected anyone, adding that, "The one case they did take (mine) they handled with lies and extreme immorality." Gittings wrote back to reassure McConnell that she understood his bitterness about ALA, but added: "don't underestimate your impact just because you didn't get the visible return of support for your case." She pointed out that the talks he gave at three ALA conferences had growing audience numbers, and that he "surely touched hundreds of gays in ALA."[38]

Beyond its effect on Gays and Lesbians within ALA, we can see that McConnell's determination to take his fight public in the court system, as well as in the court of public opinion helped to raise awareness within the field of how denial of same-sex marriage rights was a denial of rights. Thus, it was not surprising that the *New York Times* ran a long piece on McConnell in 2015 when the U.S. Supreme Court overturned state laws banning same sex marriage.

McConnell and Baker pursued their legal and personal battles on many fronts over five decades, and will be publishing a book about their experiences next year with the University of Minnesota Press. It will be exciting not only as a personal memoir and a document of their activism, but also as a form of redress for the wrongs committed against McConnell by that same university. The couple was also an inspiration for the establishment of the U of M Gay, Lesbian, Bisexual, Transgender, Ally (GLBTA) Programs Office. The Office set up a booth at a public event for the 40th anniversary of Twin Cities Pride, not only to celebrate GLBTA rights but also to reflect on the history of struggles. In a news release, U of M President Eric Kaler apologized, saying that the university's treatment of McConnell was "reprehensible" and not consistent with the university's present practice.[39] On hearing the long overdue apology that the couple had fought so hard for, McConnell said, "For me, that wipes the slate completely clean." They proceeded to donate eighty boxes of files to the U of M Jean-Nickolaus Tretter Collection in GLBT Studies.[40]

From the international perspective suggested by this book, we can see that some countries are ahead of the United States in terms of offering safe environments for lesbian, gay, bisexual, transgender, and queer individuals and communities in terms of personal and professional identities. Many others, where one can still be arrested for simply the vague charge of "promoting homosexuality" as in Russia or Uganda, remain far behind,.[41] It is especially for readers in those countries that we hope McConnell's story will be inspiring in terms of how one can promote sexual equality as individuals and as librarians, archivists, or information professionals. From that perspective, it is amazing how many of the suggestions McConnell offered in 1971 echo today in terms of what LGBTQ information professionals can do to fight discrimination, although we might add digital libraries, digital archives, metadata, social media, and information privacy to the list of environments where the issue can be moved forward. Readers living in repressive regimes should remember that current progress has largely been thanks to the efforts of LGBTQ activists like McConnell and Baker, who risked so much to advance social understanding. It is our hope that this struggle can be seen more clearly when we recall that these two not only risked their careers, but could also have been imprisoned in many American states (including Minnesota) simply for cohabitating in 1970.

Endnotes

1. Erik Eckholm, "The Same-Sex Couple Who Got a Marriage License in 1971," *New York Times*, May 16, 2015, accessed September 25, 2015, http://www.nytimes.com/2015/05/17/us/the-same-sex-couple-who-got-a-marriage-license-in-1971.html.

2. Jenna Ross, "Same-sex couple who filed historic case donate papers to U collection," *Star Tribune*, Oct. 26, 2015, accessed Nov. 2, 2015, http://www.startribune.com/same-sex-couple-who-filed-historic-case-donate-papers-to-u-collection/337328891/

3. James Michael McConnell v. Elmer R. Anderson et al., 1970.

4. "Report of the Fact-Finding Committee, ALA Staff Committee on Mediation, Arbitration, and Inquiry (SCMAI), concerning J. Michael McConnell," *American Libraries* 6 (1975): 549; James Michael McConnell v. Elmer R. Anderson et al., 1970.

5. Ibid.

6. James Michael McConnell v. Elmer R. Anderson et al., 1971.

7. For librarians' censorship battles and ALA's development of the policies, see Noriko Asato, "Librarians' Free Speech: The Challenge of Librarians' Own Intellectual Freedom to the American Library Association,1946-2007," *Library Trends* 63 (2014): 75-105; Noriko Asato, "The Origins of the Freedom to Read Foundation: Public Librarians' Campaign to Establish a Legal Defense Against Library Censorship," *Public Library Quarterly* 30 (2011): 286-306.

8. American Library Association, "Tenure in Libraries: A Statement of Principles of Intellectual Freedom and Tenure for Libraries," in

Personnel Organization and Procedure: A Manual Suggested for Use in College and University Libraries, (Chicago: American Library Association, 1952), 42-43.

9. Michael M. McConnel, [Recording ALA 1971 Midwinter Conference Task Force on Gay Liberation Talk]. Barbara Gittings and Kay Tobin Lahusen Gay History Papers and Photographs, 1855-2009 [bulk 1963-2007]. New York Public Library Manuscripts and Archives Division. Coll. 6397. II.A. American Library Association's Task Force, 1966-2006. Box 21. Folder 5, Correspondence, 1970s."

10. Ibid.

11. Ken Bronson, *A Quest for Full Equality* (2004), 17, accessed September 20, 2015, https://www.qlibrary.org/wordpress/wp-content/uploads/2014/04/QuestforFull_Equality.pdf .

12. Ibid., 17.

13. American Library Association, "Annual Conference Highlights," *American Libraries* 2 (1971): 865.

14. Phillip Keeney, "The Next Case," *Wilson Library Bulletin* 13 (1939): 663-666. For more on Keeney, see Rosalee McReynolds, Louise S. Robbins, *The Librarian Spies: Philip and Mary Jane Keeney and Cold War Espionage* (Westport, CT: Praeger Security International, 2009).

15. T. Ellis Hodgin, director of the Martinsville (Virginia) public library, was dismissed after joining a lawsuit against his daughter's public elementary school, which required students to attend weekly religious education classes sponsored by a local church group during school hours. Zoia Horn (1972) was jailed for protecting the privacy of an Anti-Vietnam War activist. For more on these cases, see Asato "Librarians' Free Speech" (2014).

16. The details of library activists organizing the Social Responsibility Round Table (SSRT) in the late 1960s and 1970s have been researched. Louise Robbins's (1996) *Censorship and the American library: The American Library Association's Response to Threats to Intellectual Freedom, 1939-1969*, and Toni Samek's (2001) *Intellectual Freedom and Responsibility in American Librarianship, 1967-1974*.

17. "Program of Action for Mediation, Arbitration, and Inquiry," *American Libraries* 2 (1971): 828-831.

18. Ibid., 830; "Action Council Resolutions," *SRRT Newsletter* 29, January 2-6 (1974): 4.

19. "ALA Report: Request for Action," *American Libraries* 5 (1974): 44.

20. Lillian N. Gerhardt and Patricia Glass Schuman, "ALA Midwinter: A Cautious Optimism," *Library Journal* 98 (1973): 980.

21. "A New Management Mood," *Library Journal* 98 (1973): 830.

22. Gerhardt and Schuman, "ALA Midwinter," 979.

23. "A New Management Mood," 832.

24. Tyron Emerick, "Midwinter," *SRRT Newsletter* 24 (1973): 2.

25. "ALA Report," 44.

26. "ALA Report," 43.

27. "Action Council Resolutions," *SRRT Newsletter* 29 (1974): 4.

28. "Draft: ALA Equal Opportunity Policy," *College Libraries News* 34 (1973): 261.

29. "Report of the Fact-Finding Committee," 549.

30. Report of the Fact-Finding Committee," 550.

31. Ibid.

32. The authors observed that since McConnell filed a Request for Action to the IFC, his stance gradually became more of an assertive demand for social justice over time, as he experienced ALA's unsupportive attitudes and a reverse in the courts. We look forward to reading McConnell's own account of his and Jack's inner development as activists to promote LGBT rights in their upcoming book, which will be published by the University of Minnesota Press in January 2016.

33. Ibid.

34. "SCMAI Report to ALA Membership," *American Libraries* 4 (1973): 370.

35. April Gage, "Speaking freely: An oral history of the Freedom to Read Foundation" (Master's Thesis, San José State University, 2006): 112.

36. "Special Presidential TF on the Status of Librarians Final Report," American Library Association, accessed Sept. 22, 2015, http://www.ala.org/educationcareers/employment/resources/statusoflibrnfinalrpt

37. Letter, Michael McConnel to Barbara Gittings, Sept. 16, 1975. Barbara Gittings and Kay Tobin Lahusen Gay History Papers and

Photographs, 1855-2009 [bulk 1963-2007]. New York Public Library Manuscripts and Archives Division. Coll. 6397. II.A. American Library Association's Gay Task Force, 1966-2006. Box 21. Folder 5, Correspondence, 1970s."

38. Letter, Barbara Gittings to Michael McConnel to, Jan. 2, 1976. Barbara Gittings and Kay Tobin Lahusen Gay History Papers and Photographs, 1855-2009. Box 21. Folder 5, Correspondence, 1970s."

39. "Marking the 40th Anniversary of Twin Cities Pride, University of Minnesota Reflects on Its GLBT History" Discovery, University of Minnesota, June 22, 2012, accessed Nov. 2, 2015, http://discover.umn.edu/news/arts-humanities/marking-40th-anniversary-twin-cities-pride-university-minnesota-reflects-its

40. Ross, "Same-sex couple."

41. For an overview of human rights abuses to LGBTQ and allies, see updates and reports from Amnesty International. http://www.amnestyusa.org/our-work/issues/lgbt-rights

Bibliography

"A New Management Mood." *Library Journal* 98 (1973): 827-33.

"Action Council Resolutions." *SRRT Newsletter* 29, January 2-6 (1974): 2-6.

"ALA Report: Request for Action." *American Libraries* 5 (1974): 43-44.

American Library Association. "Annual Conference Highlights." *American Libraries* 2 (1971): 861-75.

American Library Association. "Tenure in Libraries: A Statement of Principles of Intellectual Freedom and Tenure for Libraries." In *Personnel Organization and Procedure: A Manual Suggested for Use in College and University Libraries*, 41-52. Chicago: American Library Association, 1952.

Barbara Gittings and Kay Tobin Lauren Gay History Papers and Photographs, 1855-2009 [bulk 1963-2007]. New York Public

Library Manuscripts and Archives Division. Coll. 6397. II.A. American Library Association's Gay Task Force, 1966-2006. Box 21. Folder 5, Correspondence, 1970s."

Bronson, Ken. A Quest for Full Equality. 2004. Accessed September 20, 2015. https://www.qlibrary.org/wordpress/wp-content/uploads/2014/04/QuestforFull_Equality.pdf

"Draft: ALA Equal Opportunity Policy." *College Libraries News* 34 (1973): 261-63.

Eckholm, Erik. "The Same-Sex Couple Who Got a Marriage License in 1971." *New York Times*, May 16, 2015. Accessed September 25, 2015. http://www.nytimes.com/2015/05/17/us/the-same-sex-couple-who-got-a-marriage-license-in-1971.html.

Emerick, Tyron. "Midwinter." *SRRT Newsletter* 24 (1973): 1-2.

Gage, April. "Speaking Freely: An Oral History of the Freedom to Read Foundation." (Master's thesis, San José State University, 2006).

Gerhardt, Lillian N. and Patricia Glass Schuman. "ALA Midwinter: A Cautious Optimism." *Library Journal* 98 (1973): 979-85.

James Michael McConnell v. Elmer R. Anderson et al., 1970.

James Michael McConnell v. Elmer R. Anderson et al., 1971.

Keeney, Phillip. "The Next Case." *Wilson Library Bulletin* 13 (1939): 663-66.

"Marking the 40th Anniversary of Twin Cities Pride, University of Minnesota Reflects on Its GLBT History" Discovery, University of Minnesota, June 22, 2012. Accessed Nov. 2, 2015. http://discover.umn.edu/news/arts-humanities/marking-40th-anniversary-twin-cities-pride-university-minnesota-reflects-its

"Program of Action for Mediation, Arbitration, and Inquiry." *American Libraries* 2 (1971): 828-31.

"Report of the Fact-Finding Committee, ALA Staff Committee on Mediation, Arbitration, and Inquiry (SCMAI), concerning J. Michael McConnell." *American Libraries* 6 (1975): 549-51.

Ross, Jenna. "Same-Sex Couple Who Filed Historic Case Donate Papers to U Collection," *Star Tribune*, Oct. 26, 2015. Accessed Nov. 2, 2015. http://www.startribune.com/same-sex-couple-who-filed-historic-case-donate-papers-to-u-collection/337328891/

"SCMAI Report to ALA Membership." *American Libraries* 4 (1973): 370-71.

"Special Presidential TF on the Status of Librarians Final Report." American Library Association. Accessed Sept. 22, 2015. http://www.ala.org/educationcareers/employment/resources/statusoflibrnfinalrpt

Chapter 2

"WE HAVE MADE A START BUT THERE IS A LONG WAY TO GO": PUBLIC LIBRARY LGBTQ* PROVISION TO CHILDREN AND YOUNG PEOPLE IN THE CURRENT UK CONTEXT

Elizabeth L. Chapman

A Note on Terminology

In this chapter, I have opted to use the umbrella term "LGBTQ*" to refer to lesbian, gay, bisexual, trans*, and other queer or questioning identities. The asterisk is intended to be inclusive of all groups, including those who are sometimes marginalized within the wider queer community, such as intersex and asexual people. When discussing secondary literature, however, I sometimes use the terms employed by the sources in question.

There is an ongoing debate within the trans* community as to whether an asterisk should be used after the word trans(*).[1] Those in favor of its use argue that it explicitly broadens the term to include those who might otherwise feel excluded from the trans umbrella, such as non-binary people (i.e., people who do not identify with a binary male or female gender).[2] Meanwhile, others argue that it is important to fight for the word "trans" (without the asterisk) as a non-exclusionary and disruptive term in its own right.[3] I have opted to include the asterisk in this chapter because I feel that, as a cisgender woman, the term "trans*" is not mine to criticize[4] and I wish to be as inclusive as possible. In future work,

I will be guided in my use of terminology by the consensus emerging from within trans* communities.

Legislative and Policy Context

The current legislative environment in the UK is broadly supportive of LGBTQ* people. Discrimination on the grounds of sexual orientation or gender reassignment status is prohibited in the UK under the Equality Act 2010,[5] although there is uncertainty as to whether these protections are extended to non-binary trans* people.[6] Trans* people may apply for a Gender Recognition Certificate recognizing their true gender under the Gender Recognition Act 2004, subject to a diagnosis of gender dysphoria from a medical practitioner;[7] however, again, it can be very difficult for non-binary people to apply for a GRC.[8] Same-sex couples have been able to jointly adopt children since the Adoption and Children Act came into force in December 2005,[9] and the number of children adopted by same-sex couples almost doubled between 2009 and 2013.[10] More recently, same-sex marriage became legal in the UK (excluding Northern Ireland) in 2014.[11]

Within recent memory, the legislative environment has not always been supportive of LGBTQ* people. The infamous Section 28 legislation stated that local authorities must not "intentionally promote homosexuality or publish material with the intention of promoting homosexuality" from 1988 until its repeal in 2003.[12] Owing to a lack of clarity in the legislation, there was uncertainty as to whether this included the provision of LGBTQ* materials in public libraries. Nonetheless, it does appear to have had a negative impact on library services for LGBTQ* people, due to self-censorship by librarians and local authorities.[13] Furthermore, diversity consultant and campaigner John Vincent notes that he has personally spoken to individuals working in the cultural sector who are under the impression that this legislation is still in force, or are uncertain as to whether or not this is the case.[14]

The 1997-2010 Labour government produced guidance recommending that libraries should provide materials that reflect a diverse society, including materials aimed at LGB people;[15] however, the DCMS guidance is no longer current. To the best of my knowledge, neither the 2010-2015 Conservative-Liberal Democrat coalition government[16] nor the current majority Conservative government have issued any comment on the subject. More generally speaking, there has been a shift away from the Labour government's social inclusion agenda.[17] Public libraries are still legally obliged to "meet the general requirements and any special requirements of both adults and children" under the Public Libraries and Museums Act.[18] As will subsequently be discussed, however, it would appear that some library services are failing to meet these obligations in an environment of severe cuts to government spending.

Although libraries are statutory services under the Public Libraries and Museums Act, spending on libraries is not ring-fenced.[19] Official statistics from the Chartered Institute of Public Finance and Accountancy (CIPFA) show that expenditure on books fell by 14% in 2013-14,[20] while the number of branches open ten hours or more per week has fallen by 9.8% since 1997.[21] In addition, public libraries have seen a sharp increase in the use of volunteers: the CIPFA statistics show that the number of full-time-equivalent volunteers has risen from 13,417 in 2007 to 35,813 in 2014.[22] Over the same period, the number of paid staff members has fallen from 25,769 (including 5,298 qualified professionals) in 2007 to 19,307 (including 3,106 qualified professionals) in 2014.[23]

Attitudes towards (Young) LGBTQ* People

Recent UK opinion poll data suggest that attitudes towards LGB people are becoming more positive. Research by LGB(T)[24] rights organisation Stonewall found that 90%+ of people support protections that are now part of the Equality Act and 91% said they would feel comfortable if a close friend were gay. However, a much lower 58% said they supported the Adoption and Children Act, which allows same-sex couples to adopt children, and three in five respondents felt that society in general was prejudiced against LGB people.[25] Research on attitudes to trans* people shows continuing prejudice among a substantial portion of the population,[26] with around half of survey respondents in Scotland and Wales saying they would be unhappy if a close relative formed a long-term relationship with a trans* person.[27]

Despite some apparent improvement in attitudes towards LGB people among the general population, the research evidence suggests that schools are still extremely homophobic, biphobic, and transphobic environments, with inevitable negative effects for the wellbeing of young LGBTQ* people.[28] Preliminary findings from the Youth Chances Survey, which surveyed over 7,000 young people aged 16-25 and is the largest UK survey of its kind to date, showed that 74% of LGBTQ* young people had been subjected to name-calling, 45% had experienced harassment or threats, and 23% had suffered physical assault.[29] Similar research in Scotland found that 69.1% of LGBT respondents between the ages of 13 and 25 had personally experienced homophobic or biphobic bullying in school, while 76.9% of trans* respondents had experienced homophobic, biphobic or transphobic bullying.[30] It can thus be argued that there is a pressing need for materials that can present young LGBTQ* people with positive images of their identities, and help to develop empathy among others.[31]

LGBTQ* People and Public Libraries

Public libraries in the UK do not have much of a history of LGBTQ* service provision. Long-standing diversity consultant and campaigner John Vincent recently published a monograph on LGBT service provision in the cultural sector since 1950; he notes that in the 1950s and 1960s, "libraries offered very little of LGBT relevance."[32] Despite some positive developments in the 1970s such as the "Other Award" for inclusive children's literature,[33] matters did not substantially begin to change until the late 1970s and early 1980s, when there began to be an increased focus on equalities work, including attention to the needs of lesbians and gay men.[34] Although by the mid-1980s, "some library services were developing good, positive provision for LGBT people,"

Vincent notes that "this was still small-scale".[35] A contemporary commentator observed that "within the profession the issue has been almost totally ignored."[36]

A blow was dealt to the progress in libraries by the passing of Section 28 in 1988 (discussed above) and by a backlash in some areas of the media against left-wing councils and a perceived excess of "political correctness."[37] Despite this, Vincent noted "A growing focus on LGBT issues" in certain parts of the public library sector from the mid-1990s onwards;[38] however, provision continued to be "extremely patchy" overall.[39]

In his book, Vincent goes on to discuss progress in public library service provision to LGBTQ* people over the ten years since the repeal of Section 28 (2004-2013). He identifies a number of examples of good practice, in areas such as collection development; information provision; promotional booklists; community consultation and engagement; participation in LGBT History Month and other cultural events; LGBT reading groups; and staff training events, seminars and conferences.[40] It is not immediately apparent, however, whether these examples are "typical," or whether they are remarkable for being unusual. Vincent goes on to observe that, despite many positive developments in the public library world, "there is still considerable progress to be made."[41] Moreover, even where he has identified examples of good practice, these have primarily focused on adult service provision, and he identifies materials for children and young people as an outstanding issue.[42]

There has been a general lack of attention to LGBTQ* service provision on the part of the profession as a whole in the UK, particularly when compared with the activities of the GLBT Round Table of the American Library Association.[43] The UK professional body, the Chartered Institute of Library and Information Professionals (CILIP), did produce some guidance on sexual orientation and libraries. This included a page on legislation protecting LGBT employees from discrimination in the workplace,[44] guidance on service provision for LGBT library users, including stock selection,[45] and suggestions for additional services.[46]

However, as noted by Waite,[47] this guidance has been removed from the website and continues to be absent at the time of writing in 2015.

There also appears to be little attention paid to LGBTQ* and broader social inclusion issues in UK LIS curricula. At the time of writing in 2007, Goldthorp noted that none of the professional training courses offered by Scottish universities addressed LGBT issues.[48] A close reading of the websites of UK-based LIS courses accredited by CILIP[49] did not identify any courses that offer modules on diversity, equality, or social inclusion. However, a minority of universities appear to address the issue within the context of broader modules. The postgraduate Information and Library Management course at the University of Northumbria addresses "aspects of social inclusion" as part of its "Collection Management" module,[50] while the optional "Services to Children and Young People" module, offered as part of the MA in Library & Information Studies at University College London, covers "the diverse user needs within this client group" and "how to promote services to diverse audiences."[51] Moreover, this course has in the past featured a visiting lecturer session on the provision of LGBTQ* fiction to children and young people.[52] Finally, the MA in Librarianship at the University of Sheffield addresses LGBTQ* issues, along with other aspects of diversity and social inclusion, within the elective "Public and Youth Library Services" module.[53] However, these courses appear to be very much in the minority, and it is difficult to ascertain the extent to which equality and diversity issues are actually addressed.

In the UK, accreditation of LIS courses is based on the CILIP Professional Knowledge and Skills base, which contains only a brief mention of "respect for diversity within society."[54] The Quality Assurance Agency Subject Benchmark for Library and Information Management, which sets out the expected standards and content for the discipline, does not include any mention of diversity or social inclusion.[55]

Research on Provision of LGBTQ* Materials and Services to Children and Young People in UK Public Libraries

The relatively small amount of extant research on public library provision of LGBTQ* materials and services to children and young people has primarily been carried out in the North American context.[56] To date, the issue has been neglected in the UK research literature, although a small number of studies have been carried out on school library provision[57] and a larger number on general LGBTQ* public library provision, with the primary focus on adults.[58] To my knowledge, the only extant UK study on LGBTQ* public library provision to children and young people is my own small-scale Master's dissertation.[59] In the following sub-sections, I will present some key findings from my doctoral research into the provision of LGBTQ* fiction to children and young people in public libraries.[60]

My study sought to investigate the extent of provision of LGBT-related fiction to children and young people in thirteen English public library authorities: how this material is procured and made available, staff attitudes to the material, and factors affecting provision. A mixed-methods approach, comprising a checklist study, questionnaires, and interviews, was used to address these questions. Questionnaire responses were received from thirteen stock team managers (a 100% response rate) and 28 stock team members (a 52% response rate). Subsequently, thirteen individuals from four of the participating authorities were interviewed, together with five pilot interviewees. Further methodological details are presented in the thesis.

Availability of LGBTQ* Fiction for Children and Young People in the UK

The study located 556 LGBT-related fiction titles aimed at children and young people that are readily available (in print) in the UK; however, the large majority of these (476 titles) were YA titles, with substantially fewer available for younger age groups (49 picture books, six early readers, and 25 books for junior school children). The complete checklist used for the study is available in an appendix to the thesis. Less than a third of the books (161 titles, or 29%) were produced by publishers domiciled in the UK. This is in line with Epstein's analysis, which confirms the dominance of US-published titles.[61]

Over half of the titles (288 books, or 51.8%) were available in e-book format in the UK. However, far fewer are available in other formats, as shown in **Figure 1**. This is consistent with broader research by the Royal National Institute of Blind People on the availability of titles in accessible formats.[62]

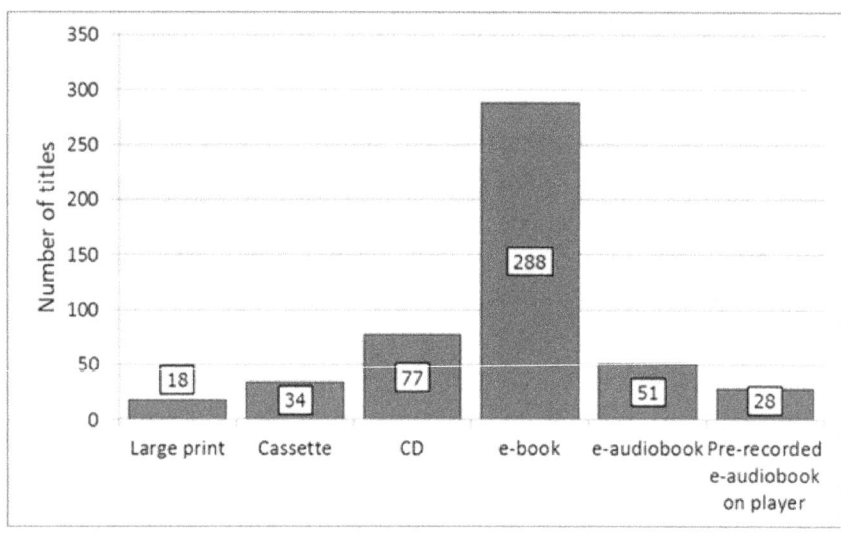

Figure 1: Availability of checklist titles in different formats

Library Stock Holdings of LGBTQ* Fiction for Children and Young People

Analysis of library holdings revealed room for improvement in the number of titles held by the participating authorities. As shown in **Figure 2** below, none of the participating authorities held more than

128 titles, or 23.0% of the total checklist titles. The authority on the far right-hand side of the chart had been purposively selected owing to its good reputation for LGBTQ* provision; its somewhat better performance is thus unsurprising. None of the other participating authorities held more than 18.2% of the checklist titles.

Holdings of picture books and early readers were particularly poor, with no authorities holding more than 16 titles, and one authority holding no titles at all. These data are pulled out in **Figure 3**.

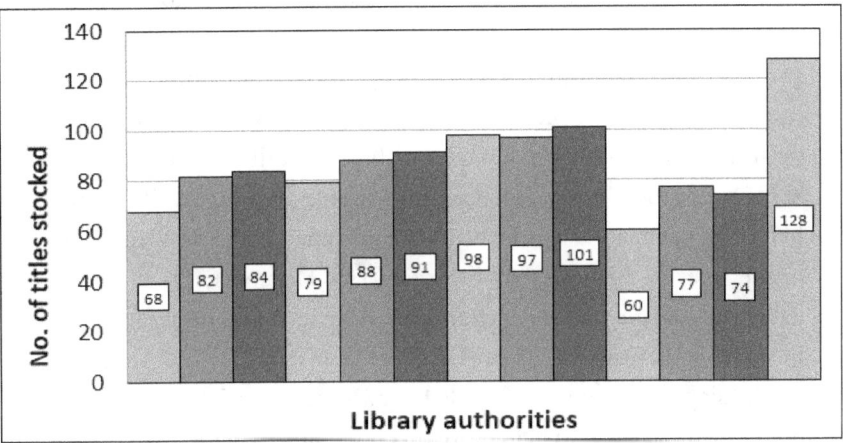

Figure 2: Library holdings of checklist titles

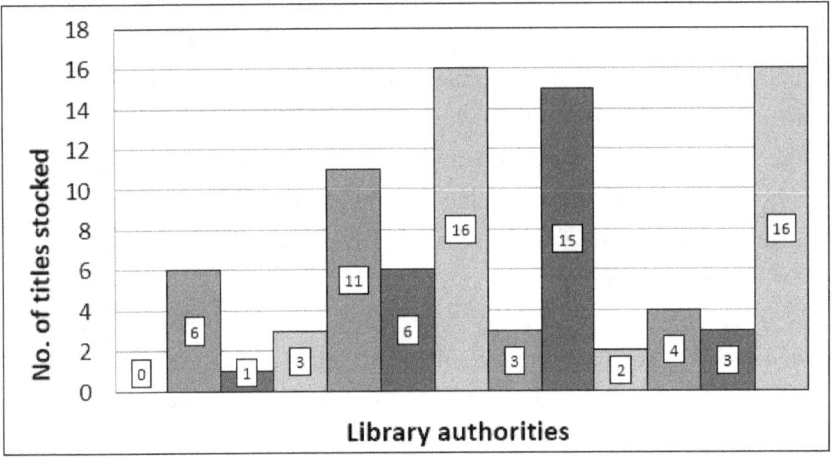

Figure 3: Library holdings of picture book and early reader titles

Three of the participating authorities were members of the London Libraries consortium (https://www.londonlibraries.gov.uk/). Users of these libraries thus have access to a broader range of titles via the other libraries which are partners in the consortium. Consortium membership substantially increased the range of titles available, with 213 titles (38.3% of the checklist) offered through the consortium. Thus, membership in a consortium functions as a useful way for authorities with smaller budgets to offer a wider range of diverse titles. However, providing access to LGBTQ* titles through a consortium should not be used as an excuse for failure to provide such titles within the authority. Martin and Murdock point out that every branch library, no matter how small, should have a core collection of LGBTQ* YA titles, so that a young person can walk into any library and find such titles on the shelves.[63] Some young people may not feel comfortable ordering LGBTQ* titles from other libraries if this involves an interaction with a staff member,[64] or they may be unaware that they can do so. Moreover, it is also potentially problematic if one authority abrogates its duties under the Public Libraries and Museums Act by shifting responsibility to other authorities.

Holdings of titles in accessible formats were very low. For example, none of the authorities held more than nine titles in large print or more than eleven titles on CD. As shown previously in Figure 1, only 18 of the checklist titles were available for libraries to stock in large print format, and holdings were thus constrained by the limited number of titles; however, 77 titles were potentially available on CD. Moreover, less than half of the participating libraries stocked any titles in either of the e-audiobook formats, and none of the authorities held any titles in e-book format. This may be due to a general lack of take-up of these formats on the part of the participating authorities, but this lay beyond the scope of the study.

There has been very little previous research on the levels of provision of LGBTQ* fiction aimed at children and young people in public library authorities in the UK. My own Master's dissertation research found room for improvement in the two case study authorities, particularly as regards picture books, and tentatively suggested that "provision may be limited in other authorities [across the UK]."[65] The present research appears to confirm this. In addition, studies from the US and Canada have also concluded that public library holdings of LGBTQ* fiction for children and young people are limited,[66] while UK research on school libraries has found a similar lack of LGBTQ* provision.[67]

Factors Affecting Provision

The study identified a number of factors that affected provision to a greater or lesser degree; key amongst these were lack of awareness on the part of librarians coupled with the mechanics of library supply.[68] In the UK, the majority of public library materials are procured from library suppliers, which are private companies. Birdi explains:

> The two principal methods of current stock selection for public libraries are supplier selection, where the library supplier selects the stock for the library in accordance with specifications drawn up by the library authority, and online approvals, where the library staff select materials from a list provided by the supplier's website.[69]

It is important to note that, in both cases, the list of materials available for librarians to choose from is pre-filtered by the supplier and often excludes materials from US publishing houses and small presses.[70] It is common practice for libraries to purchase certain materials, such as manga and graphic novels, outside the supplier contract, and nine out of the thirteen participating authorities said that they retained a portion of the children's and young people's stock budget to spend on specialist materials outside the contract. However, only four out of twenty-six stock team members who answered this question (15.4%) said that they used this money to purchase LGBTQ* materials for children and young people.

The study also revealed that only 150 titles (27.0% of the checklist titles) were classified as "Library Range" by the participating supplier, and only five picture books fell into this category. In other words, only a minority of titles would appear in supplier selections or on the pre-filtered list available to librarians via the supplier's website. This appeared to be due in part to the fact that so many of the extant titles were published in the US.[71]

The lack of provision through mainstream library suppliers was compounded by a lack of knowledge and awareness among many of the participating librarians, who thus did not make the additional effort necessary to purchase LGBTQ* fiction for children and young people from specialist sources. This lack of awareness and knowledge is discussed in more detail in the following sub-sections.

Lack of Awareness

A key theme emerging from the data was a lack of awareness of the need for provision of LGBTQ* materials to children and young people on the part of librarians. Nearly all of the research participants, in both the questionnaire and interview stages of the research, admitted that it was an area they had not addressed at all. Variations on the phrase "we just haven't thought about it" appeared repeatedly in the data as the reason for not promoting LGBT stock for children and young people and for not providing it in the first place:

> It's just not something that anybody's really thought of. (Pilot interviewee)

> Q: Do you put on displays of books with LGBT content aimed at children and young people?
> A: No. Mainly because we just haven't thought about it (Questionnaire respondent)

The overwhelming trend in the study was that librarians were positive about the idea of providing LGBTQ* fiction to children and young people,[72] but only when directly asked. This was summed up in a quotation from one of the pilot interviewees:

> I think [my colleagues are] very positive, I'm not sure if it ever becomes flagged up as an issue of discussion though, erm… I'm sure if they were asked about it, it would be, erm, kind of a positive

area [...] but, particularly, it doesn't come up particularly... (Pilot interviewee)

There was little evidence of proactivity among participants, with several commenting that they had never been asked to provide these materials:

> Have never been asked to [put on a display of books with LGBT content aimed at children and young people] and I suppose it's something we haven't really thought about. (Questionnaire respondent)

> I am not aware of any complaints regarding the lack of titles available for children & young people in our libraries. (Questionnaire respondent)

This linked with a perception on the part of a minority of individuals that there was little or no demand for LGBTQ* materials for children or young people in their area:

> Q: Do you make an effort to include books with LGBT content aimed at children and young people in displays on other themes? A: No. There is no such demand on the LGBT subject. (Questionnaire respondent)

In contrast, a small number of interviewees acknowledged that it is problematic to assume that there is no demand when dealing with an invisible minority who still experience stigma and oppression from many quarters:

> Don't presume, that because nobody mentions it, that you're not getting young lesbian and gay people in, it's invisible, you know, because people are questioning their sexuality. (Interviewee)

Two participants questioned whether LGBTQ* people do in fact want to read books specifically about LGBTQ* people:

> It's like, they're not different people, they're just people, like, they don't have, they don't, like, nobody gay or lesbian or transgender wants to read something different based on, you know? (Interviewee)

However, the research evidence suggests that many LGBTQ* individuals want to see themselves in at least some of the material they read.[73] Another interviewee, who self-identified as lesbian, highlighted the heteronormative nature of this assumption by flipping it:

> Yeah, it's like, it's like if that whole section was gay fiction, and there was three books for straight teenagers, what—how would that be perceived? You know. It's like, oh, well, do straight people *want* to ta—read about straight people? (Interviewee)

There was a particular lack of awareness among participants regarding the need for provision of LGBTQ* materials for children and young people specifically:

> I think people don't ever really think about children in these situations and it's, it's very interesting doing this re – being part of this research now because it's making me really question why have we ne – why have we never thought about it? Erm… I think there's so much work and awareness around adult, sort of, LGBT issues, that that's what we've possibly concentrated on, and never really given the children, children's area any thought." (Interviewee)

Some individuals acknowledged the need for LGBTQ* materials for teenagers, but questioned whether these materials would be relevant to younger children. Comments demonstrated a lack of awareness of both the existence of LGBTQ*-headed families, and the age at which children start to become aware of their own sexuality or gender identity:

> I can't see the relevance for children, but I do see there might be a place for promoting this category of fiction with teenagers. (Questionnaire respondent)

In fact, the Youth Chances survey found that over half of LGBQ respondents (53%) knew they were LGBQ by the age of 13, while a slightly higher proportion of trans* respondents (58%) knew they were trans* by the same age.[74] The Gender Identity Research and Education Society notes that "most gender dysphoric adults report experiencing gender variance from a very early age."[75] In addition, official statistics showed that in 2014 there were approximately 21,000 civil partner or co-habiting same-sex couples with dependent children in the UK,[76] up from 13,000 the previous year.[77] There is thus an identifiable need for LGBTQ*-inclusive materials for younger children.

Although the majority of participants were positive about LGBTQ* provision when asked, the lack of awareness of the need for provision, the assumption that no requests equate to no demand, the query as to whether LGBTQ* people want to read about LGBTQ* people, and the failure to recognize how LGBTQ* materials could be relevant to children, all point to entrenched hetero/cisnormative assumptions and heterosexual/cisgender privilege. Cisgender, heterosexual library users are not expected to "out" themselves as such in order to be able to access books that represent themselves or their families, but LGBTQ* library users appear to be invisible unless they do this. Given that previous studies have found that LGBTQ* people are often reluctant to ask for the materials they want,[78] a "vicious circle" can result:[79] the material is not provided; a homophobic climate persists in which (young) people feel unable to ask for materials; and the material is not provided.

Lack of Knowledge of Materials Available

The lack of awareness among library staff members extended to knowledge of the books themselves. Seven of the interviewees freely admitted their own lack of knowledge, and in some cases also identified a general lack of knowledge among the staff in the authority as well.

> I wish I could say I was surprised, but… knowledge of LGBT titles generally is… I've found to be shocking in the local authorities I've worked for, and specifically for young people, I mean my knowledge is very scant […] and I am fairly up-to-date on what's being published and what books are available, and I know next to nothing about LGBT publishing and the books that are there. (Pilot interviewee)

Seven interviewees made an explicit link between lack of knowledge and poor provision, and felt that greater awareness of the materials available would enable them to provide better service:

> I think it's probably, erm, that people are not very aware, that's probably more the issue than anything else, erm, they're not aware that this – I certainly wasn't [laughs] aware that there was this much material available, erm... (Interviewee)

A similar number of interviewees acknowledged that they did not know where to find such materials or information on the titles available:

> I think... we, we perhaps don't know enough about... smaller publishers, um, and also non-UK publishers. (Interviewee)

> Speaking as someone who hasn't sought it out, I wouldn't know where to start. (Pilot interviewee)

This is particularly concerning, given that a key part of a librarian's professional skills is the ability to research any given topic that may come up as an enquiry or reference question, regardless of whether they have any existing knowledge in the field—as detailed in the CILIP Professional Knowledge and Skills Base.[80] This was acknowledged by one of the pilot interviewees:

> You could actually sit down and seek it out. We are librarians, we're supposed to be able to do that! (Pilot interviewee)

Downey identifies the idea that "it's hard to find LGBT-themed books" as one of the "traps" that librarians may fall into. She goes on to point out:

> Librarians tend to take pride in knowing where to find information. It's an important part of our jobs. As I often tell my patrons, being a good librarian is mostly a matter of knowing where to look. Seeking out alternative sources is not nearly as difficult or time-consuming as we might fear, and it fits in well with our overall responsibilities.[81]

Training

The limited knowledge and awareness among participants may in part be due to a lack of training on LGBTQ* issues as they relate to libraries in general, and on stock procurement in particular. Only seven out of twenty-seven stock team members who answered this question (25.9%) said that they had received any training on LGBTQ* issues; a further seven said that they could not remember; and thirteen (or 48.1%) said that they had definitely not received any such training. Of the seven who had attended such training, only two said that stock procurement issues were covered.

Interviewees were also asked if they had received training on LGBTQ* issues as they relate to libraries. The majority of interviewees had not received any such training; however, one of the participating library authorities was unusual in that it provided LGBTQ* training for all staff members several times a year, according to the stock team manager. The course was run by an external consultant who specializes in equality and diversity issues; it included a strong focus on customer service, challenging preconceptions, and removing barriers to provision:

> It's just about, um, getting people to open up their minds to what different barriers or challenges people might bring. Like [...] how a lot of our forms or formal ways of doing things might make a lot of assumptions. Like, you know, the very first thing you're asked to do is to fill in a form and the first, very first question on that form is male, female. (Interviewee)

The interviewees at TC concurred that the regular LGBTQ* training provided at this authority was very useful. Five out of the six interviewees were extremely positive about it, with three commenting that it had a beneficial effect on staff attitudes in general, as well as being useful for them personally. However, the training did not cover issues relating to stock selection or procurement; it did highlight LGBTQ* authors, but these tended to be adult stock:

> It covered adult stock [...] Not specifically selection, because it's training that's provided to staff at all levels who won't have any control over stock selection, erm... So part of it was sort of awareness-raising of LGBT authors that, um, frontline library staff would be seeing as just mainstream authors. (Interviewee)

It is apparent once again that even when LGBTQ* materials and services are considered, there is a lack of attention to children and young people.

These findings are broadly in line with previous research, which suggests that little training on LGBTQ* issues is provided to library workers in the UK.[82] The "Right Man for the Job" research found that there was a need for more specialized and targeted social inclusion training in general.[83]

Conclusion

The provision of LGBTQ* materials and services to children and young people in public libraries has been a neglected area in both research and practice in the UK. On the surface, the current legislative and social environment in the UK would appear to be favorable to the provision of LGBTQ* materials in libraries. Recent legislation has permitted same-sex couples to marry and jointly adopt children, and discrimination on the grounds of sexual orientation or gender reassignment is illegal. However, young LGBTQ* people continue to face hostile environments in school, and negative attitudes toward trans* people persist among a substantial portion of the population. There is thus a need to provide library materials that will reflect the lives of marginalized young people, and help to build empathy among others.

Historically, the provision of materials and services to LGBTQ* people in UK public libraries has been extremely limited and patchy. The development of services was hampered by the infamous Section 28 legislation (in force between 1988 and 2003), which prevented local authorities from "promoting" homosexuality. Moreover, it has been suggested that some individuals working within the cultural sector believe that this legislation is still in force.

The study reported on in this chapter found that library holdings of LGBTQ* fiction aimed at children and young people were limited; provision of picture books and early readers was particularly poor. Very few items were available in accessible formats, although provision was constrained by the low numbers of titles published in certain formats (e.g., large print). Key factors affecting provision included the lack of materials available through mainstream library suppliers and the lack of knowledge and awareness on the part of librarians with responsibility for stock procurement. These factors worked in conjunction: since librarians had not considered the need to provide LGBTQ* materials for children and young people, they rarely made the effort to compensate for the limited supplier provision by purchasing such materials from specialist sources. Many participants also showed limited knowledge of the materials available or where to find them.

The lack of awareness on the part of librarians suggests that public libraries are deeply hetero/cisnormative environments. This situation is compounded by a lack of training; the majority of participants had not received any training within their library authorities on LGBTQ* issues as they relate to libraries. Moreover, there appears to be little attention paid to LGBTQ* issues or diversity more generally in UK LIS curricula, and the UK professional body, CILIP, no longer provides guidance on LGBTQ* provision in libraries. In addition, public libraries' ability to provide socially inclusive services has been hampered by substantial cuts to both staff numbers and book budgets in recent years.

Recommendations for Improving Provision

- Staff at all levels should be made aware of the need for provision of LGBTQ* materials aimed at children and young people, including materials for younger children.
- Budget cuts should not be used as an excuse for failure to provide LGBTQ* materials. Effort should be made to meet all needs within the overall context of the collection.
- A lack of requests for LGBTQ* materials should not be taken to indicate a lack of demand. Not everyone will feel comfortable asking for this material, and this may be particularly true of young people.

- LGBTQ* fiction aimed at children and young people may be available via your mainstream library supplier even if it does not appear on the buying lists. Make sure you are searching the supplier's entire database, or ask the supplier specifically for this material.
- In the event that your mainstream supplier does not provide an adequate selection of LGBTQ* fiction aimed at children and young people, it may be necessary to buy from a specialist bookshop such as Gay's the Word (www.gaystheword.co.uk) or Letterbox Library (www.letterboxlibrary.com). Most library authorities have a clause in their supplier contract allowing them to do this. Moreover, specialist bookshops have expertise in this area and will be able to advise on appropriate titles.
- Ensure that LGBTQ* materials aimed at children and young people are specifically mentioned in documentation such as collection development policies and supplier specifications.
- Librarians with responsibility for children's and young people's stock procurement should keep themselves up-to-date with new publications in this area. In addition, guidance or training on the procurement of LGBTQ* fiction aimed at children and young people should be provided to all staff members with responsibility in this area.
- LIS curricula should include a greater focus on diversity issues in general and LGBTQ* issues in particular, including provision of materials and services to children and young people.

Endnotes

1. Avery Tompkins, "Asterisk," *Transgender Studies Quarterly* 1, no. 1-2 (2014).
2. Sam Killermann, "What Does the Asterisk in 'Trans*' Stand For?," *It's Pronounced Metrosexual* (blog), March 4, 2015, http://itspronouncedmetrosexual.com/2012/05/what-does-the-asterisk-in-trans-stand-for/.
3. CN Lester, "Why I Use 'Trans' and Not 'Trans*'," *A Gentleman and a Scholar* (blog), 30 June, 2011, http://cnlester.wordpress.com/2011/06/30/why-i-use-trans-and-not-trans/; Natalie Reed, "So Let's Talk About the Fucking Asterisk," *A Natalie Reed Tumblr*, n.d., http://nataliereed84.tumblr.com/post/65412526336/so-lets-talk-about-the-fucking-asterisk, accessed June 7, 2015.
4. Nat Titman, "About That Often Misunderstood Asterisk," *Practical Androgyny* (blog), October 13, 2013, http://practicalandrogyny.com/2013/10/31/about-that-often-misunderstood-asterisk/.
5. Equality Act, 2010, c. 15 (UK).
6. Jade Fernandez, Kay Leacock, and Alex Hilton, "The Equality Act 2010 – Are Non-Binary People Protected?", *Beyond the Binary* (blog), February 8, 2015, http://beyondthebinary.co.uk/2015/02/08/the-equality-act-2010-are-non-binary-people-protected/.
7. Gender Recognition Act, 2004, c. 7 (UK).
8. Fernandez, Leacock, and Hilton, "The Equality Act 2010".
9. Adoption and Children Act, 2002, c. 38 (UK).
10. Chapman, "Provision of LGBT-Related Fiction to Children and Young People in English Public Libraries: A Mixed-Methods Study"; Department for Education, "Children Looked After in England, Including Adoption," (London: Department for Education, 2013), https://www.gov.uk/government/statistics/children-looked-after-in-england-including-adoption.
11. Marriage (Same Sex Couples) Act, 2013, c. 30 (England and Wales); Marriage and Civil Partnership Act (Scotland), asp 5.
12. Local Government Act, 1988, c. 9 (UK), section 28.

13. See for example Anne Curry, *The Limits of Tolerance: Censorship and Intellectual Freedom in Public Libraries* (Lanham, MD: Scarecrow Press, 1997), 79; John Vincent, "Lesbians, Bisexuals, Gay Men and Transgendered People," *Public Library Policy and Social Exclusion Working Papers 5* (Leeds: Leeds Metropolitan University, 2000), http://eprints.rclis.org/7121/1/vol3wp5.pdf; *LGBT People and the UK Cultural Sector: The Response of Libraries, Museums, Archives and Heritage since 1950* (Farnham, Surrey: Ashgate, 2014).

14. Vincent, *LGBT People and the UK Cultural Sector*.

15. DCMS, "Libraries, Museums, Galleries and Archives for All" (DCMS, 2001), http://webarchive.nationalarchives.gov.uk/+/http://www.culture.gov.uk/PDF/libraries_archives_for_all.pdf; IDeA, "Sexuality - the New Agenda: A Guide for Local Authorities on Engaging with Lesbian, Gay and Bisexual Communities," (London: Improvement and Development Agency, 2007), http://www.idea.gov.uk/idk/aio/6531483.

16. For readers unfamiliar with UK politics, Labour is a left-of-center political party, the Liberal Democrats are centrist, and the Conservatives are right-wing.

17. Biddy Casselden, Alison J. Pickard, and Julie McLeod, "The Challenges Facing Public Libraries in the Big Society: The Role of Volunteers, and the Issues That Surround Their Use In England," *Journal of Librarianship and Information Science* (2014), http://dx.doi.org/10.1177/0961000613518820.

18. Public Libraries and Museums Act, 1964, c. 75 (UK), section 7.

19. Culture Media and Sport Committee, House of Commons, "Library Closures," HC 587 (London: The Stationery Office, 2012), http://www.publications.parliament.uk/pa/cm201213/cmselect/cmcumeds/587/587.pdf.

20. CIPFA, "Public Library Statistics 2014-2015 Estimates, 2013-2014 Actuals," (London: Chartered Institute of Public Finance and Accountancy, 2015).

21. Ian Anstice, "The Perils of a Discretionary Service and Localism," *Public Libraries News* (blog), December 7, 2014, http://www.publiclibrariesnews.com/2014/12/the-perils-of-a-discretionary-service-and-localism.html.

22. Ibid.; CIPFA, "Public Library Statistics".

23. Anstice, "The Perils of a Discretionary Service and Localism"; CIPFA, "Public Library Statistics".

24. Stonewall has only recently begun to incorporate trans* issues into its remit (Ruth Hunt and Ayaz Manji, "Trans People and Stonewall: Campaigning Together for Lesbian, Gay, Bisexual and Trans Equality" (Stonewall, 2015), http://www.stonewall.org.uk/other/startdownload.asp?openType=forced&documentID=4608). Prior to this, it had been strongly criticized by trans* activists and allies for excluding trans* issues from its remit (see for example Kat Gupta, "S_onewall and the Missing T," *Mixosaurus* (blog), July 31, 2014, http://mixosaurus.co.uk/2014/07/s_onewall-and-the-missing-t/; Natacha Kennedy, "Stonewall Is Holding Back Transgender Equality," *The Guardian*, October 20, 2010, http://www.theguardian.com/commentisfree/2010/oct/20/stonewall-holding-back-transgender-equality).

25. April Guasp and Sam Dick, "Living Together: British Attitudes to Lesbian, Gay and Bisexual People in 2012," (London: Stonewall, 2012), http://www.stonewall.org.uk/documents/living_together_2012.pdf.

26. Martin Mitchell and Charlie Howarth, "Trans Research Review," report no. 27 (Manchester: Equality and Human Rights Commission, 2009), http://www.equalityhumanrights.com/sites/default/files/documents/research/trans_research_review_rep27.pdf.

27. EHRC, "Who Do You See? Living Together in Wales," (Cardiff: Equality and Human Rights Commission, 2008), http://www.equalityhumanrights.com/sites/default/files/documents/download_who_do_you_see_publication_english.pdf; Mitchell and Howarth, "Trans Research Review"; Rachel Ormston et al., "Scottish Social Attitudes Survey 2010: Attitudes to Discrimination and Positive Action," report no. 12/2011, (Edinburgh: Scottish Centre for Social Research, 2011), http://www.scotland.gov.uk/Resource/Doc/355763/0120175.pdf.

28. April Guasp, "The School Report: The Experiences of Gay Young People in Britain's Schools in 2012," (London: Stonewall, 2012), http://www.stonewall.org.uk/documents/school_report_2012%282%29.pdf.

29. METRO Youth Chances, "Youth Chances Summary of First Findings: The Experiences of LGBTQ Young People in England," (London: METRO, 2014), http://www.youthchances.org/wp-content/uploads/2014/01/YC_REPORT_FirstFindings_2014.pdf.

30. LGBT Youth Scotland, "Life in Scotland for LGBT Young People - Education Report," (LGBT Youth Scotland, 2012), https://www.lgbtyouth.org.uk/files/documents/Life_in_Scotland_for_LGBT_Young_People_-_Education_Report_NEW.pdf.

31. Chapman, "Provision of LGBT-Related Fiction to Children and Young People in English Public Libraries: A Mixed-Methods Study"; Judith Elkin, Briony Train, and Debbie Denham, *Reading and Reader Development: The Pleasure of Reading* (London: Facet Publishing, 2003); Jamie Campbell Naidoo, "The Importance of Diversity in Library Programs and Material Collections for Children," (Chicago, IL: Association for Library Service to Children, 2014), http://www.ala.org/alsc/sites/ala.org.alsc/files/content/ALSCwhitepaper_importance%20of%20diversity_with%20graphics_FINAL.pdf.

32. Vincent, *LGBT People and the UK Cultural Sector*, 16.

33. Rosemary Stones, "13 Other Years: The Other Award 1975-1987," *Books for Keeps* 53 (November 1988), http://booksforkeeps.co.uk/issue/53/childrens-books/articles/other-articles/awards; John Vincent, "Political Correctness," *Public Library Policy and Social Exclusion Working Papers 14* (Leeds: Leeds Metropolitan University, 2000), http://eprints.rclis.org/7126/1/vol3wp14.pdf; *LGBT People and the UK Cultural Sector*.

34. *LGBT People and the UK Cultural Sector*.

35. Ibid., 39.

36. Richard Ashby, "Library Services to Gay and Lesbian People," *Assistant Librarian* 80, no. 10 (1987): 153.

37. Vincent, "Political Correctness"; *LGBT People and the UK Cultural Sector*.

38. *LGBT People and the UK Cultural Sector*, 61.

39. "Lesbians, Bisexuals, Gay Men and Transgendered People," 77.

40. *LGBT People and the UK Cultural Sector*, 88-91.

41. Ibid., 87.

42. Ibid., 92-93.

43. GLBTRT, "Gay, Lesbian, Bisexual, and Transgender Round Table (GLBTRT)," Chicago, IL: American Library Association, http://www.ala.org/glbtrt/glbtrt.

44. CILIP, "Sexual Orientation," London: CILIP, http://www.cilip.org.uk/get-involved/policy/equalopps/pages/sexualorientation.aspx, accessed March 19, 2010. Although the guidance has been removed from the website, this particular page can be accessed using the Wayback Machine (http://archive.org/web/).

45 "Sexual Orientation and Libraries," London: CILIP, http://www.cilip.org.uk/get-involved/policy/equalopps/Pages/sexorientationlibraries.aspx, accessed March 19, 2010.

46. "Other Services for LGBT Library Users," London: CILIP, http://www.cilip.org.uk/get-involved/policy/equalopps/Pages/lgbtotherservices.aspx, accessed March 19, 2010.

47. Jessica Waite, "To What Extent Do Public Libraries in the UK Provide Adequate Resources for Trans People?" (MA, University of Sheffield, 2013), http://dagda.shef.ac.uk/dispub/dissertations/2012-13/External/Waite_J_Y74.pdf.

48. Jacqueline D. Goldthorp, "A Voice for the Invisible?," *Information Scotland* 5, no. 1 (2007), http://www.slainte.org.uk/publications/serials/infoscot/vol5%281%29/vol5%281%29article7.htm.

49. CILIP, "CILIP Accredited Qualifications," London: CILIP, http://www.cilip.org.uk/cilip/jobs-careers/starting-library-and-information-career/how-become-librarian-or-information, accessed June 8, 2015.

50. University of Northumbria, "Information and Library Management Postgraduate Diploma/MA/MSc," Newcastle: University of Northumbria, https://www.northumbria.ac.uk/study-at-northumbria/courses/information-and-library-management-dl-dtplim6/, accessed June 8, 2015.

51. UCL, "INSTG034 Services to Children and Young People," London: University College London, https://www.ucl.ac.uk/dis/taught/pg/INSTG034, accessed June 8, 2015.

52. Elizabeth L. Chapman, "No More Controversial Than a Gardening Display? Providing LGBT Fiction to Children and Young People in Libraries" (guest lecture, Department of Information Studies, University College London, London, November 28, 2011).

53. "Provision of LGBT-Related Fiction to Children and Young People in English Public Libraries: A Mixed-Methods Study."

54. CILIP, "My Professional Knowledge and Skills Base," London: CILIP, 8, http://www.cilip.org.uk/cilip/jobs-and-careers/professional-knowledge-and-skills-base/download-professional-knowledge-and.

55. QAA, "Subject Benchmark Statement: Librarianship, Information, Knowledge, Records and Archives Management," Gloucester: The Quality Assurance Agency for Higher Education, http://www.qaa.ac.uk/en/Publications/Documents/SBS-librarianship-15.pdf.

56. Michele Hilton Boon and Vivian Howard, "Recent Lesbian/Gay/Bisexual/Transgender Fiction for Teens: Are Canadian Public Libraries Providing Adequate Collections?," *Collection Building* 23, no. 3 (2004); Vivian Howard, "Out of the Closet...But Not on the Shelves?," *Progressive Librarian* 25 (2005); Jamie Campbell Naidoo, "Over the Rainbow and under the Radar: Library Services and Programs to LGBTQ Families," *Children and Libraries: The Journal of the Association for Library Service to Children* 11, no. 3 (2013); Paulette M. Rothbauer and Lynne E. F. McKechnie, "Gay and Lesbian Fiction for Young Adults: A Survey of Holdings in Canadian Public Libraries," *Collection Building* 18, no. 1 (1999); "The Treatment of Gay and Lesbian Fiction for Young Adults in Selected Prominent Reviewing Media," *Collection Building* 19, no. 1 (2000); Alex Spence, "Gay Young Adult Fiction in the Public Library: A Comparative Survey," *Public Libraries* 38, no. 4 (1999); "Controversial Books in the Public Library: A Comparative Survey of Holdings of Gay-Related Children's Picture Books," *Library Quarterly* 70, no. 3 (2000); Virginia Kay Williams and Nancy Deyoe, "Diverse Population, Diverse Collection? Youth Collections in the United States," *Technical Services Quarterly* 31, no. 2 (2014).

57. Sally Bridge, "No Place on the Shelves? Are Northern Ireland's School Libraries Addressing the Information Needs of Their Lesbian, Gay, Bisexual and Transgendered Students?" (MSc, Aberystwyth University, 2010), http://cadair.aber.ac.uk/dspace/handle/2160/5714; Elizabeth L. Chapman and Caroline Wright, "Provision of Lesbian, Gay, Bisexual, and Trans (LGBT) Materials for Young People in UK Public and Secondary School Libraries," in *Forbidden Fruit: The Censorship of Literature and Information for Young People*, ed. Sarah McNicol (Boca Raton, FL: BrownWalker Press, 2008); Janine Walker and Jo Bates, "Developments in LGBTQ Provision in Secondary School Library Services since the Abolition of Section 28," *Journal of Librarianship and Information Science* (2015), http://dx.doi.org/10.1177/0961000614566340.

58. Laura Armstrong, "Do Personal and Institutional Anxieties within Sheffield Central Library and Norwich Millennium Library Affect the Promotion of Particular Genres (Black British/Asian and Gay/Lesbian Fiction)?" (MA, University of Sheffield, 2006), http://dagda.shef.ac.uk/dissertations/2005-06/External/Armstrong_Laura_MALib.pdf; Phil Brett, "Politics and Public Library Provision for Lesbians and Gay Men in London," *International Journal of Information and Library Research* 4, no. 3 (1992); Sarah E. Currant, "In or Out? An Examination of Public Library Staff Attitudes Towards the Provision of Gay and Lesbian Materials in South Yorkshire" (Unpublished MSc, University of Sheffield, 2002); Jacqueline D. Goldthorp, "Can Scottish Public Library Services Claim They Are Socially Inclusive of All Minority Groups When Lesbian Fiction Is Still So Inaccessible?" *Journal of Librarianship and Information Science* 39, no. 4 (2007); Mark Norman, "OUT on Loan: A Survey of the Use and Information Needs of Users of the Lesbian, Gay and Bisexual Collection of Brighton and Hove Libraries," *Journal of Librarianship and Information Science* 31, no. 4 (1999); Megan O'Leary, "Pink Perceptions: The Information Needs of Lesbian, Gay, Bisexual and Transgender Library Users as Perceived by Public Librarians and by the LGBT Communities within Sheffield UK and Denver CO, USA" (MA, University of Sheffield, 2005), http://dagda.shef.ac.uk/dissertations/2004-05/External/Oleary_Meagan_MALib.pdf; Waite, "To What

Extent Do Public Libraries in the UK Provide Adequate Resources for Trans People?".

59. Elizabeth L. Chapman, "Provision of LGBT-Related Fiction to Children and Young People in Public Libraries," (MA, University of Sheffield, 2007), http://dagda.shef.ac.uk/dissertations/2006-07/External/Chapman_Elizabeth_MALib.pdf; "No More Controversial Than a Gardening Display? Provision of LGBT-Related Fiction to Children and Young People in U.K. Public Libraries," *Library Trends* 61, no. 3 (2013); Chapman and Wright, "Provision of Lesbian, Gay, Bisexual, and Trans (LGBT) Materials for Young People in UK Public and Secondary School Libraries."

60. "Provision of LGBT-Related Fiction to Children and Young People in English Public Libraries: A Mixed-Methods Study."

61. B. J. Epstein, *Are the Kids All Right? The Representation of LGBTQ Characters in Children's and Young Adult Literature* (Bristol: HammerOn Press, 2013).

62. RNIB, "Availability of Accessible Publications: 2011 Update," London: RNIB, http://www.rnib.org.uk/sites/default/files/2011_Accessibility_Update_final_report.pdf.

63. Hillias J. Martin and James R. Murdock, *Serving Lesbian, Gay, Bisexual, Transgender and Questioning Teens: A How-to-Do-It Manual for Librarians* (New York/London: Neal-Schuman Publishers, 2007).

64. Chapman, "Provision of LGBT-Related Fiction to Children and Young People in Public Libraries"; Anne Curry, "If I Ask, Will They Answer? Evaluating Public Library Reference Service to Gay and Lesbian Youth," *Reference & User Services Quarterly* 45, no. 1 (2005).

65. Chapman, "Provision of LGBT-Related Fiction to Children and Young People in Public Libraries," 105.

66. Boon and Howard, "Recent Lesbian/Gay/Bisexual/Transgender Fiction for Teens"; Howard, "Out of the Closet...But Not on the Shelves?"; Rothbauer and McKechnie, "Gay and Lesbian Fiction for Young Adults"; Williams and Deyoe, "Diverse Population, Diverse Collection?"

67. Bridge, "No Place on the Shelves?"; Chapman and Wright, "Provision of Lesbian, Gay, Bisexual, and Trans (LGBT) Materials for Young People in UK Public and Secondary School Libraries"; Janine Walker, "Secondary School Library Services for Lesbian, Gay, Bisexual and Trans (LGBT) Students" (MA, University of Sheffield, 2013), http://dagda.shef.ac.uk/dispub/dissertations/2012-13/External/Walker_J_Y83.pdf.

68. Elizabeth L. Chapman, "Provision of LGBT-Related Fiction to Children and Young People in English Public Libraries: A Mixed-Methods Study."

69. Briony K. Birdi, "'We Are Here Because You Were There': An Investigation of the Reading of, and Engagement with, Minority Ethnic Fiction in UK Public Libraries" (Unpublished doctoral thesis, University of Sheffield, 2014), 28.

70. Elizabeth L. Chapman, "Provision of LGBT-Related Fiction to Children and Young People in English Public Libraries: A Mixed-Methods Study."

71. Ibid.

72. Chapman, Elizabeth L., "'I've Never Really Thought About It': Librarians' Attitudes to the Provision of LGBT-Related Fiction to Children and Young People in English Public Libraries" (paper presented at *Addressing the Silence: How Libraries can Serve Their LGBTQ Users*, IFLA WLIC 2014, 16-22 August 2014, Lyon, France), http://library.ifla.org/1017/1/151-chapman-en.pdf.

73. Bridge, "No Place on the Shelves?"; Darla Linville, "Beyond Picket Fences: What Gay/Queer/LGBTQ Teens Want from the Library," *Voice of Youth Advocates* 27, no. 3 (2004); Paulette M. Rothbauer, "Finding and Creating Possibility: Reading in the Lives of Lesbian, Bisexual and Queer Young Women" (Ph.D. diss., University of Western Ontario, 2004); Waite, "To What Extent Do Public Libraries in the UK Provide Adequate Resources for Trans People?"; Walker and Bates, "Developments in LGBTQ Provision in Secondary School Library Services since the Abolition of Section 28."

74. METRO Youth Chances, "Youth Chances Summary of First Findings."

75. Bernard Reed et al., "Gender Variance in the UK: Prevalence, Incidence, Growth and Geographic Distribution," (Ashtead: Gender Identity Research and Education Society, 2009), 4, http://www.gires.org.uk/assets/Medpro-Assets/GenderVarianceUK-report.pdf.

76. ONS, "Families and Households, 2014," (London: Office for National Statistics, 2014). http://www.ons.gov.uk/ons/dcp171778_393133.pdf.

77. ONS, "Families and Households, 2013," (London: Office for National Statistics, 2013). http://www.ons.gov.uk/ons/dcp171778_332633.pdf.

78. Currant, "In or Out?"; Waite, "To What Extent Do Public Libraries in the UK Provide Adequate Resources for Trans People?"; Walker, "Secondary School Library Services for Lesbian, Gay, Bisexual and Trans (LGBT) Students."

79. Bridge, "No Place on the Shelves?", 69.

80. CILIP, "My Professional Knowledge and Skills Base".

81. Jennifer Downey, "Self-Censorship in Selection of LGBT-Themed Materials," *Reference & User Services Quarterly* 53, no. 2 (2013): 105.

82. Armstrong, "Do Personal and Institutional Anxieties within Sheffield Central Library and Norwich Millennium Library Affect the Promotion of Particular Genres?"; Currant, "In or Out?"; Goldthorp, "Can Scottish Public Library Services Claim They Are Socially Inclusive of All Minority Groups When Lesbian Fiction Is Still So Inaccessible?".

83. Kerry Wilson and Briony Birdi, "The Right 'Man' for the Job? The Role of Empathy in Community Librarianship," (Sheffield: University of Sheffield, 2008), https://www.shef.ac.uk/polopoly_fs/1.128131!/file/AHRC-2006-8-final-report-04.08.pdf.

Bibliography

Armstrong, Laura. "Do Personal and Institutional Anxieties within Sheffield Central Library and Norwich Millennium Library Affect the Promotion of Particular Genres (Black British/Asian and Gay/Lesbian Fiction)?", MA, University of Sheffield, 2006. http://dagda.shef.ac.uk/dissertations/2005-06/External/Armstrong_Laura_MALib.pdf.

Ashby, Richard. "Library Services to Gay and Lesbian People." *Assistant Librarian* 80, no. 10 (1987): 132-34.

Birdi, Briony K. "'We Are Here Because You Were There': An Investigation of the Reading of, and Engagement with, Minority Ethnic Fiction in UK Public Libraries." Unpublished doctoral thesis, University of Sheffield, 2014.

Boon, Michele Hilton, and Vivian Howard. "Recent Lesbian/Gay/Bisexual/Transgender Fiction for Teens: Are Canadian Public Libraries Providing Adequate Collections?". *Collection Building* 23, no. 3 (2004): 133-38.

Brett, Phil. "Politics and Public Library Provision for Lesbians and Gay Men in London." *International Journal of Information and Library Research* 4, no. 3 (1992): 195-211.

Bridge, Sally. "No Place on the Shelves? Are Northern Ireland's School Libraries Addressing the Information Needs of Their Lesbian, Gay, Bisexual and Transgendered Students?", MSc, Aberystwyth University, 2010. http://cadair.aber.ac.uk/dspace/handle/2160/5714.

Casselden, Biddy, Alison J. Pickard, and Julie McLeod. "The Challenges Facing Public Libraries in the Big Society: The Role of Volunteers, and the Issues That Surround Their Use In England," *Journal of Librarianship and Information Science* (2014). http://dx.doi.org/10.1177/0961000613518820.

Chapman, Elizabeth L. "'I've Never Really Thought About It': Librarians' Attitudes to the Provision of LGBT-Related

Fiction to Children and Young People in English Public Libraries." Paper presented at Addressing the Silence: How Libraries can Serve Their LGBTQ Users, IFLA WLIC 2014, 16-22 August 2014, Lyon, France. http://library.ifla.org/1017/1/151-chapman-en.pdf.

———. "No More Controversial Than a Gardening Display? Providing LGBT Fiction to Children and Young People in Libraries." Guest lecture, Department of Information Studies, University College London, London, November 28, 2011.

———. "No More Controversial Than a Gardening Display? Provision of LGBT-Related Fiction to Children and Young People in U.K. Public Libraries." *Library Trends* 61, no. 3 (2013): 542-68.

———. "Provision of LGBT-Related Fiction to Children and Young People in English Public Libraries: A Mixed-Methods Study." PhD, University of Sheffield, 2015.

———. "Provision of LGBT-Related Fiction to Children and Young People in Public Libraries." MA, University of Sheffield, 2007. http://dagda.shef.ac.uk/dissertations/2006-07/External/Chapman_Elizabeth_MALib.pdf.

Chapman, Elizabeth L., and Caroline Wright. "Provision of Lesbian, Gay, Bisexual, and Trans (LGBT) Materials for Young People in UK Public and Secondary School Libraries." In *Forbidden Fruit: The Censorship of Literature and Information for Young People*, edited by Sarah McNicol, 19-40. Boca Raton, FL: BrownWalker Press, 2008.

CILIP. "CILIP Accredited Qualifications." London: CILIP. http://www.cilip.org.uk/cilip/jobs-careers/starting-library-and-information-career/how-become-librarian-or-information, accessed June 8, 2015.

———. "My Professional Knowledge and Skills Base." London: CILIP. http://www.cilip.org.uk/cilip/jobs-and-careers/professional-knowledge-and-skills-base/download-professional-knowledge-and.

———. "Other Services for LGBT Library Users." London: CILIP. http://www.cilip.org.uk/get-involved/policy/equalopps/Pages/lgbtotherservices.aspx, accessed March 19, 2010.

———. "Sexual Orientation." London: CILIP. http://www.cilip.org.uk/get-involved/policy/equalopps/pages/sexualorientation.aspx, accessed March 19, 2010.

———. "Sexual Orientation and Libraries." London: CILIP. http://www.cilip.org.uk/get-involved/policy/equalopps/Pages/sex-orientationlibraries.aspx, accessed March 19, 2010.

CIPFA. "Public Library Statistics 2014-2015 Estimates, 2013-2014 Actuals." London: Chartered Institute of Public Finance and Accountancy, 2015.

Culture Media and Sport Committee, House of Commons. "Library Closures," HC 587. London: The Stationery Office, 2012. http://www.publications.parliament.uk/pa/cm201213/cmselect/cmcumeds/587/587.pdf.

Currant, Sarah E. "In or Out? An Examination of Public Library Staff Attitudes Towards the Provision of Gay and Lesbian Materials in South Yorkshire." Unpublished MSc, University of Sheffield, 2002.

Curry, Anne. "If I Ask, Will They Answer? Evaluating Public Library Reference Service to Gay and Lesbian Youth." *Reference & User Services Quarterly* 45, no. 1 (2005): 65-75.

———. *The Limits of Tolerance: Censorship and Intellectual Freedom in Public Libraries.* Lanham, Maryland: Scarecrow Press, 1997.

DCMS. "Libraries, Museums, Galleries and Archives for All." London: DCMS, 2001.

Department for Education. "Children Looked After in England, Including Adoption." London: Department for Education, 2013, https://www.gov.uk/government/statistics/children-looked-after-in-england-including-adoption

Downey, Jennifer. "Self-Censorship in Selection of LGBT-Themed Materials." *Reference & User Services Quarterly* 53, no. 2 (2013): 104-07.

EHRC. "Who Do You See? Living Together in Wales." Cardiff: Equality and Human Rights Commission, 2008. http://www.equalityhumanrights.com/sites/default/files/documents/download_who_do_you_see_publication_english.pdf.

Elkin, Judith, Briony Train, and Debbie Denham. *Reading and Reader Development: The Pleasure of Reading.* London: Facet Publishing, 2003.

Epstein, B. J. *Are the Kids All Right? The Representation of LGBTQ Characters in Children's and Young Adult Literature.* Bristol: HammerOn Press, 2013.

GLBTRT. "Gay, Lesbian, Bisexual, and Transgender Round Table (GLBTRT)." Chicago, IL: American Library Association. http://www.ala.org/glbtrt/glbtrt.

Goldthorp, Jacqueline D. "Can Scottish Public Library Services Claim They Are Socially Inclusive of All Minority Groups When Lesbian Fiction Is Still So Inaccessible?" *Journal of Librarianship and Information Science* 39, no. 4 (2007): 234-48.

———. "A Voice for the Invisible?". *Information Scotland* 5, no. 1 (2007): 13-14. http://www.slainte.org.uk/publications/serials/infoscot/vol5%281%29/vol5%281%29article7.htm.

Guasp, April. "The School Report: The Experiences of Gay Young People in Britain's Schools in 2012." London: Stonewall, 2012. http://www.stonewall.org.uk/documents/school_report_2012%282%29.pdf.

Guasp, April, and Sam Dick. "Living Together: British Attitudes to Lesbian, Gay and Bisexual People in 2012." London: Stonewall, 2012. http://www.stonewall.org.uk/documents/living_together_2012.pdf.

Howard, Vivian. "Out of the Closet...But Not on the Shelves?". *Progressive Librarian* 25 (Summer 2005): 62-75.

Hunt, Ruth, and Ayaz Manji. "Trans People and Stonewall: Campaigning Together for Lesbian, Gay, Bisexual and Trans Equality." London: Stonewall, 2015. http://www.stonewall.org.uk/other/startdownload.asp?openType=forced&documentID=4608.

IDeA. "Sexuality - the New Agenda: A Guide for Local Authorities on Engaging with Lesbian, Gay and Bisexual Communities." London: Improvement and Development Agency, 2007.

LGBT Youth Scotland. "Life in Scotland for LGBT Young People - Education Report." LGBT Youth Scotland, 2012. https://www.lgbtyouth.org.uk/files/documents/Life_in_Scotland_for_LGBT_Young_People_-_Education_Report_NEW.pdf.

Linville, Darla. "Beyond Picket Fences: What Gay/Queer/LGBTQ Teens Want from the Library." *Voice of Youth Advocates* 27, no. 3 (August 2004): 183-86.

Martin, Hillias J., and James R. Murdock. *Serving Lesbian, Gay, Bisexual, Transgender and Questioning Teens: A How-to-Do-It Manual for Librarians*. New York/London: Neal-Schuman Publishers, 2007.

METRO Youth Chances. "Youth Chances Summary of First Findings: The Experiences of LGBTQ Young People in England." London: METRO, 2014. http://www.youthchances.org/wp-content/uploads/2014/01/YC_REPORT_First-Findings_2014.pdf.

Mitchell, Martin, and Charlie Howarth. "Trans Research Review," report no. 27. Manchester: Equality and Human Rights Commission, 2009. http://www.equalityhumanrights.com/sites/default/files/documents/research/trans_research_review_rep27.pdf.

Naidoo, Jamie Campbell. "The Importance of Diversity in Library Programs and Material Collections for Children." Chicago, IL: Association for Library Service to Children, 2014. http://www.ala.org/alsc/sites/ala.org.alsc/files/content/ALSCwhitepaper_importance%20of%20diversity_with%20graphics_FINAL.pdf.

———. "Over the Rainbow and under the Radar: Library Services and Programs to LGBTQ Families." *Children and Libraries: The Journal of the Association for Library Service to Children* 11, no. 3 (2013): 34-40.

Norman, M. "OUT on Loan: A Survey of the Use and Information Needs of Users of the Lesbian, Gay and Bisexual Collection of Brighton and Hove Libraries." *Journal of Librarianship and Information Science* 31, no. 4 (1999): 188-96.

O'Leary, M. "Pink Perceptions: The Information Needs of Lesbian, Gay, Bisexual and Transgender Library Users as Perceived by Public Librarians and by the LGBT Communities within Sheffield UK and Denver CO, USA." MA, University of Sheffield, 2005. http://dagda.shef.ac.uk/dissertations/2004-05/External/Oleary_Meagan_MALib.pdf.

ONS. "Families and Households, 2013." London: Office for National Statistics, 2013. http://www.ons.gov.uk/ons/dcp171778_332633.pdf.

———. "Families and Households, 2014." London: Office for National Statistics, 2014. http://www.ons.gov.uk/ons/dcp171778_393133.pdf.

Ormston, Rachel, John Curtice, Susan McConville, and Susan Reid. "Scottish Social Attitudes Survey 2010: Attitudes to Discrimination and Positive Action," Report no. 12/2011. Edinburgh: Scottish Centre for Social Research, 2011. http://www.scotland.gov.uk/Resource/Doc/355763/0120175.pdf.

QAA. "Subject Benchmark Statement: Librarianship, Information, Knowledge, Records and Archives Management," Gloucester: The Quality Assurance Agency for Higher Education. http://www.qaa.ac.uk/en/Publications/Documents/SBS-librarianship-15.pdf.

Reed, Bernard, Stephenne Rhodes, Pietà Schofield, and Kevan Wylie. "Gender Variance in the UK: Prevalence, Incidence, Growth and Geographic Distribution." Ashtead: Gender Identity

Research and Education Society, 2009. http://www.gires.org.uk/assets/Medpro-Assets/GenderVarianceUK-report.pdf.

RNIB. "Availability of Accessible Publications: 2011 Update." London: RNIB. http://www.rnib.org.uk/sites/default/files/2011_Accessibility_Update_final_report.pdf.

Rothbauer, Paulette M. "Finding and Creating Possibility: Reading in the Lives of Lesbian, Bisexual and Queer Young Women." Ph.D. diss., University of Western Ontario, 2004.

Rothbauer, Paulette M., and Lynne E. F. McKechnie. "Gay and Lesbian Fiction for Young Adults: A Survey of Holdings in Canadian Public Libraries." *Collection Building* 18, no. 1 (1999): 32-39.

———. "The Treatment of Gay and Lesbian Fiction for Young Adults in Selected Prominent Reviewing Media." *Collection Building* 19, no. 1 (2000): 5-16.

Spence, Alex. "Controversial Books in the Public Library: A Comparative Survey of Holdings of Gay-Related Children's Picture Books." *Library Quarterly* 70, no. 3 (2000): 335-79.

———. "Gay Young Adult Fiction in the Public Library: A Comparative Survey." *Public Libraries* 38, no. 4 (1999): 224-43.

Stones, Rosemary. "13 Other Years: The Other Award 1975-1987." *Books for Keeps* 53 (November)(1988). http://booksforkeeps.co.uk/issue/53/childrens-books/articles/other-articles/awards.

Tompkins, Avery. "Asterisk." *Transgender Studies Quarterly* 1, no. 1-2 (2014): 26-27.

UCL. "INSTG034 Services to Children and Young People." London: University College London, https://www.ucl.ac.uk/dis/taught/pg/INSTG034, accessed June 8, 2015.

University of Northumbria. "Information and Library Management Postgraduate Diploma/MA/MSc." Newcastle: University of Northumbria, https://www.northumbria.ac.uk/study-at-northumbria/courses/information-and-library-management-dl-dtplim6/, accessed June 8, 2015.

Vincent, John. "Lesbians, Bisexuals, Gay Men and Transgendered People." *Public Library Policy and Social Exclusion Working Papers 5*. Leeds: School of Information Management, Leeds Metropolitan University, 2000. http://eprints.rclis.org/7121/1/vol3wp5.pdf.

———. "Political Correctness." *Public Library Policy and Social Exclusion Working Papers 14*. Leeds: Leeds Metropolitan University, 2000. http://eprints.rclis.org/7126/1/vol3wp14.pdf.

———. *LGBT People and the UK Cultural Sector: The Response of Libraries, Museums, Archives and Heritage since 1950*. Farnham, Surrey: Ashgate, 2014.

Waite, Jessica. "To What Extent Do Public Libraries in the UK Provide Adequate Resources for Trans People?" MA, University of Sheffield, 2013. http://dagda.shef.ac.uk/dispub/dissertations/2012-13/External/Waite_J_Y74.pdf.

Walker, Janine. "Secondary School Library Services for Lesbian, Gay, Bisexual and Trans (LGBT) Students." MA, University of Sheffield, 2013. http://dagda.shef.ac.uk/dispub/dissertations/2012-13/External/Walker_J_Y83.pdf.

Walker, Janine, and Jo Bates. "Developments in LGBTQ Provision in Secondary School Library Services since the Abolition of Section 28." *Journal of Librarianship and Information Science* (2015). http://dx.doi.org/10.1177/0961000614566340.

Williams, Virginia Kay, and Nancy Deyoe. "Diverse Population, Diverse Collection? Youth Collections in the United States." *Technical Services Quarterly* 31, no. 2 (2014): 97-121.

Wilson, Kerry, and Briony Birdi. "The Right 'Man' for the Job? The Role of Empathy in Community Librarianship." Sheffield: University of Sheffield, 2008. https://www.shef.ac.uk/polopoly_fs/1.128131!/file/AHRC-2006-8-final-report-04.08.

Appendix
List of LGBTQ* Fiction Aimed at Children and Young People Available from Publishers Domiciled in the UK

The checklist stage of the research was carried out in 2010-2011. Since then, I have done my best to maintain the currency of the list, but some items may be omitted. The list used for the purposes of the thesis did not include items that were then out of print in the UK, but some may have gone out of print subsequently; for further details of the eligibility criteria, see the original study.[84] It is also worth noting that, even among these titles published by UK publishers, many are written by US authors and were published in the US first. Where a title is marked with an asterisk, this indicates that only the ebook version was published by the UK arm of the company, with the print version being published by the US arm.

Picture books

Argent, Hedi, and Amanda Wood (ill.). *Josh and Jaz Have Three Mums*. London: British Association for Adoption and Fostering, 2007.

Carter, Vanda. *If I Had a Hundred Mummies*. London: Onlywomen Press, 2007.

Cole, Babette. *Mummy Never Told Me*. London: Red Fox, 2004.

Crawford, Georgina, and Emily McCann (ill.). *The Tales of Zebedy-Do-Dah*. London: Onlywomen Press, 2009.

Hoffman, Mary, and Ros Asquith (ill.). *The Great Big Book of Families*. London: Frances Lincoln Children's Books, 2010.

Hoffman, Mary, and Ros Asquith (ill.). *Welcome to the Family!* London: Frances Lincoln Children's Books, 2014.

Kilodavis, Cheryl, and Suzanne DeSimone (ill.). *My Princess Boy*. London: Simon & Schuster, 2011.

Lang, Suzanne, and Max Lang (ill.). *Families, Families, Families!* London: Corgi, 2015.

Merchant, Ed, and Rachel Fuller (ill.). *Dad David, Baba Chris and Me.* London: British Association for Adoption and Fostering, 2010.

Newman, Lesléa, and Laura Cornell (ill.). *Heather has Two Mummies* [Updated edition]. London: Walker Books, 2015.

Parr, Todd. *The Family Book.* London: Little, Brown Young Readers, 2010.

Parr, Todd. *It's Okay to be Different.* London: Little, Brown Young Readers, 2009.

Parr, Todd. *We Belong Together: A Book About Adoption and Families.* London: Little, Brown Young Readers, 2008.

*Richardson, Justin, Peter Parnell, and Henry Cole (ill.). *And Tango Makes Three.* London: Simon & Schuster, 2005.

*Scanlon, Liz Garton, and Marla Frazee (ill.). *All the World.* London: Simon & Schuster, 2011.

Walker, Tamsin. *Not Ready Yet!* London: Onlywomen Press, 2009.

Watson, Katy, and Vanda Carter (ill.). London: Onlywomen Press, 2006.

Wilson, Anna, and Vanda Carter (ill.). London: Onlywomen Press, 2010.

Books for junior school children (upper elementary)

Boyne, John. *The Terrible Thing That Happened to Barnaby Brocket.* London: Doubleday, 2012.

Coville, Bruce. *Charlie Eggleston's Talking Skull* [also published as *The Skull of Truth*]. London: Hodder Children's Books, 2003.

Day, Susie. *Pea's Book of Best Friends* [*Pea's Book* series book 1]. London: Red Fox, 2012.

Day, Susie. *Pea's Book of Big Dreams* [*Pea's Book* series book 2]. London: Red Fox, 2013.

Day, Susie. *Pea's Book of Birthdays* [*Pea's Book* series book 3]. London: Red Fox, 2013.

Day, Susie. *Pea's Book of Holidays* [*Pea's Book* series book 4]. London: Red Fox, 2014.

Day, Susie. *The Secrets of Sam and Sam.* London: Red Fox, 2015.

Federle, Tim. *Better Nate Than Ever.* London: Walker Books, 2015.

*Federle, Tim. *Five, Six, Seven, Nate!* London: Simon & Schuster, 2015.

Gino, Alex. *George.* London: Scholastic, 2015.

Gleitzman, Morris. *Two Weeks With the Queen.* London: Puffin Books, 1999.

Howe, James. *The Misfits.* London: Walker Books, 2002.

Ignatow, Amy. *The Popularity Papers, Book One: Research for the Social Improvement and General Betterment of Lydia Goldblatt and Julie Graham-Chang.* London: Amulet, 2010.

Ignatow, Amy. *The Popularity Papers, Book Two: The Long-Distance Dispatch between Lydia Goldblatt and Julie Graham-Chang.* London: Amulet, 2011.

Ignatow, Amy. *The Popularity Papers, Book Three: Words of (Questionable) Wisdom from Lydia Goldblatt and Julie Graham-Chang.* London: Amulet, 2011.

Ignatow, Amy. *The Popularity Papers, Book Four: The Rocky Road Trip of Lydia Goldblatt and Julie Graham-Chang.* London: Amulet, 2012.

Ignatow, Amy. *The Popularity Papers, Book Five: The Awesomely Awful Melodies of Lydia Goldblatt and Julie Graham-Chang.* London: Amulet, 2013.

Ignatow, Amy. *The Popularity Papers, Book Six: Love and Other Fiascos with Lydia Goldblatt and Julie Graham-Chang.* London: Amulet, 2013.

Naylor, Phyllis Reynolds. *Alice Alone.* London: Simon & Schuster, 2004.

Naylor, Phyllis Reynolds. *Alice on the Outside.* London: Simon & Schuster, 2004.

Rylant, Cynthia. *The Van Gogh Café*. Oxford: Pearson Education, 2007.

Walliams, David. *The Boy in the Dress*. London: HarperCollins, 2008.

Young adult

Albertalli, Becky. *Simon vs. the Homo Sapiens Agenda*. London: Penguin, 2015.

Amateau, Gigi. *Claiming Georgia Tate*. London: Walker Books, 2006.

Anderson, R. J. *Quicksilver*. London: Orchard Books, 2013.

Beam, Cris. *I Am J*. London: Little, Brown Young Readers, 2012.

Bell, Julia. *The Dark Light*. London: Macmillan, 2015.

Benway, Robin. *Emmy & Oliver*. London: Simon & Schuster, 2015.

Best, Rosie. *Skulk*. London: Watkins Media, 2013.

Black, Holly. *The Coldest Girl in Coldtown*. London: Indigo, 2013.

Black, Holly. *The Darkest Part of the Forest*. London: Indigo, 2015.

Black, Holly. *Ironside: A Modern Faery's Tale*. London: Simon & Schuster, 2008.

Black, Holly. *Tithe: A Modern Faerie Tale*. London: Simon & Schuster, 2008.

Blackman, Malorie. *Boys Don't Cry*. London: Doubleday, 2010.

Blackman, Malorie, ed. *Love Hurts*. London: Corgi, 2015.

Block, Francesca Lia. *Weetzie Bat* [*Weetzie Bat* book 1]. London: Atom Books, 2002.

Block, Francesca Lia. *Witch Baby* [*Weetzie* Bat book 2]. London: Atom Books, 2002.

Block, Francesca Lia. *Missing Angel Juan* [*Weetzie Bat* book 4].[85] London: Atom Books, 2002.

Block, Francesca Lia. *Baby Be-Bop* [*Weetzie Bat* book 5]. London: Atom Books, 2002.

Block, Francesca Lia. *Dangerous Angels* [bind-up of the first five *Weetzie Bat* books]. London: HarperCollins, 2010.

Block, Francesca Lia. *The Rose and the Beast*. London: HarperCollins, 2001.

Block, Francesca Lia. *Roses and Bones: Myths, Tales and Secrets* [bind-up of *Psyche in a Dress, Echo,* and *The Rose and the Beast*]. London: HarperCollins, 2010.

Boock, Paula. *Dare, Truth or Promise*. London: Livewire, 1998.

Bray, Libba. *Beauty Queens*. London: Scholastic, 2011.

Bray, Libba. *The Sweet Far Thing*. London: Simon & Schuster, 2008.

Brennan, Herbie. *Faerie Wars*. London: Bloomsbury, 2002.

Brennan, Herbie. *Ruler of the Realm*. London: Bloomsbury, 2006.

Brennan, Sarah Rees. *The Demon's Lexicon* [*Demon's Lexicon* book 1]. London: Simon & Schuster, 2009.

Brennan, Sarah Rees. *The Demon's Covenant* [*Demon's Lexicon* book 2]. London: Simon & Schuster, 2010.

Brennan, Sarah Rees. *The Demon's Surrender* [*Demon's Lexicon* book 3]. London: Simon & Schuster, 2011.

Brennan, Sarah Rees. *Unspoken* [*Lynburn Legacy* book 1]. London: Simon & Schuster, 2012.

Brennan, Sarah Rees. *Untold* [*Lynburn Legacy* book 2]. London: Simon & Schuster, 2013.

Brennan, Sarah Rees. *Unmade* [*Lynburn Legacy* book 3]. London: Simon & Schuster, 2014.

Brockenbrough, Martha. *The Game of Love and Death*. London: Scholastic, 2015.

Brooks, Kevin. *Black Rabbit Summer*. London: Penguin, 2008.

Brugman, Alyssa. *Alex As Well*. Oxford: Curious Fox, 2014.

Bujold, Lois McMaster. *Ethan of Athos*. London: Headline, 1989.

Bujold, Lois McMaster. *Memory*. London: Earthlight, 1998.

Burchill, Julie. *Sugar Rush*. London: Macmillan, 2004.

Burgess, Melvin. *Bloodsong*. London: Andersen Press, 2005.

Burnham, Niki. *Royally Crushed*. London: Simon & Schuster, 2004.

Bushnell, Candace. *The Carrie Diaries*. London: HarperCollins, 2010.

Cashore, Kristin. *Bitterblue*. London: Gollancz, 2012.

Cast, P. C., ed. *Immortal: Love Stories with Bite*. London: Atom Books, 2010.

Cast, P. C., and Kristin Cast. *Marked* [*House of Night* book 1]. London: Atom Books, 2007.

Cast, P. C., and Kristin Cast. *Betrayed* [*House of Night* book 2]. London: Atom Books, 2007.

Cast, P. C., and Kristin Cast. *Chosen* [*House of Night* book 3]. London: Atom Books, 2008.

Cast, P. C., and Kristin Cast. *Untamed* [*House of Night* book 4]. London: Atom Books, 2009.

Cast, P. C., and Kristin Cast. *Hunted* [*House of Night* book 5]. London: Atom Books, 2009.

Cast, P. C., and Kristin Cast. *Tempted* [*House of Night* book 6]. London: Atom Books, 2009.

Cast, P. C., and Kristin Cast. *Burned* [*House of Night* book 7]. London: Atom Books, 2010.

Cast, P. C., and Kristin Cast. *Awakened* [*House of Night* book 8]. London: Atom Books, 2010.

Cast, P. C., and Kristin Cast. *Destined* [*House of Night* book 9]. London: Atom Books, 2011.

Cast, P. C., and Kristin Cast. *Hidden* [*House of Night* book 10]. London: Atom Books, 2012.

Cast, P. C., and Kristin Cast. *Revealed* [*House of Night* book 11]. London: Atom Books, 2013.

Cast, P. C., and Kristin Cast. *Redeemed* [*House of Night* book 12]. London: Atom Books, 2014.

Chambers, Aidan. *Dance on my Grave*. London: Red Fox, 1982.

Chambers, Aidan. *Postcards from No Man's Land*. London: Red Fox, 1999.

Chbosky, Stephen. *The Perks of Being a Wallflower*. London: Pocket Books, 1999.

Clare, Cassandra. *City of Bones* [*The Mortal Instruments* book 1]. London: Walker Books, 2007.

Clare, Cassandra. *City of Ashes* [*The Mortal Instruments* book 2]. London: Walker Books, 2008.

Clare, Cassandra. *City of Glass* [*The Mortal Instruments* book 3]. London: Walker Books, 2009.

Clare, Cassandra. *City of Fallen Angels* [*The Mortal Instruments* book 4]. London: Walker Books, 2011.

Clare, Cassandra. *City of Lost Souls* [*The Mortal Instruments* book 5]. London: Walker Books, 2012.

Clare, Cassandra. *City of Heavenly Fire* [*The Mortal Instruments* book 6]. London: Walker Books, 2014.

Clare, Cassandra, Sarah Rees Brennan, and Maureen Johnson. *The Bane Chronicles* [*The Mortal Instruments* companion novel]. London: Walker Books, 2014.

Clarke, Cat. *A Kiss in the Dark*. London: Quercus, 2014.

Clarke, Cat. *Falling*. Edinburgh: Barrington Stoke, 2013.

Clarke, Cat. *The Lost and the Found*. London: Quercus, 2015.

Clarke, Cat. *Undone*. London: Quercus, 2013.

Clarke, Julia. *Between You and Me*. Oxford: Oxford University Press, 2002.

Cohn, Rachel. *Shrimp*. London: Simon & Schuster, 2005.

Collins, B. R. *The Traitor Game*. London: Bloomsbury, 2008.

Collins, B. R. *Love in Revolution*. London: Bloomsbury, 2013.

Cremer, Andrea. *Nightshade*. London: Atom Books, 2010.

Cremer, Andrea. *Wolfsbane* [*Nightshade* book 2]. London: Atom Books, 2011.

Cremer, Andrea. *Bloodrose* [*Nightshade* book 3]. London: Atom Books, 2012.

Cremer, Andrea. *Rift* [*Nightshade* prequel 1]. London: Atom Books, 2012

Cremer, Andrea. *Rise* [*Nightshade* prequel 2]. London: Atom Books, 2013.

Cremer, Andrea, and David Levithan. *Invisibility*. London: Penguin, 2013.

David, Keren. *This Is Not a Love Story*. London: Atom Books, 2015.

Davis, Will. *My Side of the Story*. London: Bloomsbury, 2007.

Dawson, James. *All of the Above*. London: Hot Key Books, 2015.

Dawson, James. *Cruel Summer*. London: Indigo, 2013.

Dawson, James. *Hollow Pike*. London: Indigo, 2012.

Day, Susie. *The Twice-Lived Summer of Bluebell Jones*. London: Marion Lloyd Books, 2012.

Dent, Grace. *Too Cool for School*. London: Hodder Children's Books, 2008.

Donoghue, Emma. *Kissing the Witch: Old Tales in New Skins*. London: Hamish Hamilton, 1997.

Donovan, John. *I'll Get There, It Better Be Worth the Trip*. London: Macdonald, 1970.

Downham, Jenny. *Unbecoming*. Oxford: David Fickling Books, 2015.

Durant, Alan. *A Short Stay in Purgatory*. London: Bodley Head, 1994.

Eagland, Jane. *Wildthorn*. London: Picador, 2009.

Earls, Nick. *48 Shades of Brown*. London: Walker Books, 2005.

Eve, Helen. *Siena*. London: Macmillan Children's Books, 2015.

*Felin, M. Sindy. *Touching Snow.* London: Simon & Schuster, 2011.

Fowey-Doyle, Moira. *The Accident Season.* London: Corgi, 2015.

Fox, John. *The Boys on the Rock.* London: Arrow Books, 1985.

Freymann-Weyr, Garret. *My Heartbeat.* London: Macmillan Children's Books, 2003.

Gantos, Jack. *Desire Lines.* London: Random House Children's, 1997.

Gardner, Sally. *Maggot Moon.* London: Hot Key Books, 2012.

Gibbons, Alan. *Hate.* London: Indigo, 2014.

Goodman, Alison. *Eon: Rise of the Dragoneye.* Oxford: David Fickling Books, 2009.

Goodman, Alison. *Eona: Return of the Dragoneye.* Oxford: David Fickling Books, 2011.

Goodman, Alison. *Singing the Dogstar Blues.* London: Collins Voyager, 2003.

Gould, Andre. *A Summer's Exile.* London: Gay Men's Press, 1996.

Grant, Michael. *Hunger* [*Gone* book 2].[86] London: Egmont, 2009.

Grant, Michael. *Lies* [*Gone* book 3]. London: Egmont, 2010.

Grant, Michael. *Plague* [*Gone* book 4]. London: Egmont, 2011.

Grant, Michael. *Fear* [*Gone* book 5]. London: Egmont, 2012.

Grant, Michael. *Light* [*Gone* book 6]. London: Egmont, 2013.

Gray, Keith, ed. *Losing It.* London: Andersen Press, 2010.

Green, John, and David Levithan. *Will Grayson, Will Grayson.* London: Penguin, 2012.

Green, Sally. *Half Bad.* London: Penguin, 2014.

Green, Sally. *Half Wild.* London: Penguin, 2015.

Guran, Paula, ed. *Brave New Love.* London: Little, Brown, 2012.

Guy, Rosa. *Ruby.* London: Gollancz, 1981.

Halpin, Brendan, and Emily Franklin. *Tessa Masterson Will Go To Prom*. London: Walker Books, 2013.

Hautzig, Deborah. *Hey Dollface*. London: Fontana Lions, 1978.

Hawkins, Rachel. *Hex Hall*. London: Simon & Schuster, 2010.

Hawkins, Rachel. *Raising Demons*. London: Simon & Schuster, 2011.

Healey, Karen. *Guardian of the Dead*. London: Little, Brown, 2010.

Heath, Jack. *Replica*. Oxford: Oxford University Press, 2014.

Hoffman, Alice. *The Foretelling*. London: Egmont, 2006.

Homes, A. M. *Jack*. London: Penguin, 1991.

*Hopkins, Ellen. *Perfect*. London: Simon & Schuster, 2011.

*Hopkins, Ellen. *Tilt*. London: Simon & Schuster, 2012.

Hopkins, Ellen. *Tricks*. London: Simon & Schuster, 2009.

Horniman, Joanne. *About a Girl*. London: Quarto Publishing, 2011.

Jinks, Catherine. *Pagan in Exile*. London: HarperCollins, 2004.

Johnson, Maureen. *The Bermudez Triangle*. London: Puffin Books, 2004.

Johnson, Maureen. *The Shadow Cabinet [Shades of London* book 3].[87] London: Hot Key Books, 2015.

Kerr, M. E. *Night Kites*. London: Pan, 1987.

Kessler, Liz. *Read Me Like a Book*. London: Indigo, 2015.

King, A. S. *Ask the Passengers*. London: Little, Brown, 2012.

Knowles, Jo. *See You At Harry's*. London: Walker Books, 2013.

Koertge, Ronald. *The Arizona Kid*. London: Pan, 1990.

Koertge, Ronald. *The Brimstone Journals*. London: Walker Books, 2001.

Krol, S. Joseph. *Northridge High Football Camp*. London: Gay Men's Press, 1996.

Lackey, Mercedes. *Magic's Promise*. London: Penguin, 1990.

Lam, Laura. *Pantomime*. London: Watkins Media, 2013.

Lam, Laura. *Shadowplay*. London: Watkins Media, 2014.

Larder, Helen. *Anarchy*. London: Onlywomen Press, 2008.

Levithan, David. *Every Day*. London: Electric Monkey, 2013.

Levithan, David. *Another Day* [sequel to *Every Day*]. London: Electric Monkey, 2015.

Levithan, David. *Hold Me Closer: The Tiny Cooper Story*. London: Penguin, 2015.

Levithan, David. *Two Boys Kissing*. London: Electric Monkey, 2014.

Limb, Sue. *Girl, Nearly 16: Absolute Torture*. London: Bloomsbury, 2005.

Link, Kelly, and Gavin J. Grant, eds. *Steampunk!* London: Walker Books, 2012.

Lloyd, Saci. *The Carbon Diaries 2015*. London: Hodder Children's Books, 2008.

Lo, Malinda. *Adaptation*. London: Hodder Children's Books, 2014.

Lo, Malinda. *Ash*. London: Hodder Children's Books, 2010.

Lo, Malinda. *Huntress*. London: Atom Books, 2011.

Lo, Malinda. *Inheritance* [sequel to *Adaptation*]. London: Hodder Children's Books, 2014.

Long, Hayley. *What's Up With Jody Barton?* London: Macmillan Children's Books, 2012.

Lowell, Sophia. *Glee: The Beginning*. London: Headline, 2010.

Lowell, Sophia. *Glee: Foreign Exchange*. London: Headline, 2011.

Lowell, Sophia. *Glee: Summer Break*. London: Headline, 2011.

Magrs, Paul. *Strange Boy*. London: Simon & Schuster, 2002.

Magrs, Paul. *The Diary of a Dr. Who Addict*. London: Simon & Schuster, 2009.

Manning, Sarra. *Guitar Girl*. London: Hodder Children's Books, 2003.

Manning, Sarra. *Pretty Things*. London: Hodder Children's Books, 2005.

Marriott, Zoë. *FrostFire*. London: Walker Books, 2012.

Marriott, Zoë. *The Night Itself* [*The Name of the Blade* book 1]. London: Walker Books, 2013.

Marriott, Zoë. *Darkness Hidden* [*The Name of the Blade* book 2]. London: Walker Books, 2014.

Marriott, Zoë. *Frail Human Heart* [*The Name of the Blade* book 3]. London: Walker Books, 2015.

Marriott, Zoë. *Shadows on the Moon*. London: Walker Books, 2011.

Mayhew, Julie. *The Big Lie*. London: Hot Key Books, 2015.

*Medina, Nico. *The Straight Road to Kylie*. London: Simon & Schuster, 2012.

Miles, Liz, ed. *Truth & Dare*. London: Little, Brown, 2011.

Moore, Perry. *Hero*. London: Corgi, 2007.

*Moskowitz, Hannah. *Gone, Gone, Gone*. London: Simon & Schuster, 2012.

*Moskowitz, Hannah. *Not Otherwise Specified*. London: Simon & Schuster, 2015.

*Moskowitz, Hannah. *Teeth*. London: Simon & Schuster, 2013.

Muchamore, Robert. *Class A* [*Cherub* book 2].[88] London: Hodder Children's Books, 2004.

Muchamore, Robert. *Man Vs. Beast* [*Cherub* book 6]. London: Hodder Children's Books, 2006.

Muchamore, Robert. *Shadow Wave* [*Cherub* book 12]. London: Hodder Children's Books, 2010.

Nelson, Blake. *Girl*. London: Pocket Books, 1999.

Nelson, Jandy. *I'll Give You the Sun*. London: Walker Books, 2015.

Ness, Patrick. *More Than This*. London: Walker Books, 2013.

Ness, Patrick. *The Rest of Us Just Live Here*. London: Walker Books, 2015.

Newbery, Linda. *The Shell House*. Oxford: David Fickling Books, 2002.

Newbery, Linda. *Sisterland*. Oxford: David Fickling Books, 2003.

Nielsen, Susin. *We Are All Made of Molecules*. London: Andersen Press, 2015.

Noël, Alyson. *Evermore*. London: Macmillan Children's Books, 2009.

Packham, Simon. *Only We Know*. London: Piccadilly Press, 2015.

Paulsen, Gary. *The Car*. London: Macmillan Children's Books, 1995.

Pearce, Jackson. *As You Wish*. London: HarperCollins, 2010.

Peck, Dale. *Sprout*. London: Bloomsbury, 2009.

Perkins, Stephanie. *Lola and the Boy Next Door*. London: Usborne, 2014.

Perrotta, Tom. *Election*. London: Harper Perennial, 2009.

Peters, Julie Anne. *Between Mom and Jo*. London: Little, Brown, 2009.

Peters, Julie Anne. *grl2grl*. London: Little, Brown, 2007.

Peters, Julie Anne. *Keeping You a Secret*. London: Little, Brown, 2005.

Peters, Julie Anne. *Lies My Girlfriend Told Me*. London: Little, Brown, 2014.

Peters, Julie Anne. *Luna*. London: Little, Brown, 2007.

Peters, Julie Anne. *Pretend You Love Me* [previously published as *Far From Xanadu*]. London: Little, Brown, 2011.

Pollock, Tom. *The Glass Republic* [*Skyscraper Throne* book 2].[89] London: Quercus, 2013.

Pollock, Tom. *Our Lady of the Streets* [*Skyscraper Throne* book 3]. London: Quercus, 2014.

Reed, Amy. *Clean*. London: Simon & Schuster, 2011.

*Reed, Amy. *Crazy*. London: Simon & Schuster, 2012.

*Reed, Amy. *Over You*. London: Simon & Schuster, 2013.

Rees, David. *In the Tent*. London: Dobson, 1979.

Reeve, Philip. *Scrivener's Moon*. London: Scholastic, 2011.

Riordan, James. *The Cello*. Oxford: Oxford University Press, 2003.

Ruditis, Paul. *The Four Dorothys*. London: Simon & Schuster, 2007.

Ryan, Sara. *Empress of the World*. London: Penguin, 2006.

Rushton, Abbie. *Unspeakable*. London: Atom Books, 2015.

Sáenz, Benjamin Alire. *Aristotle and Dante Discover the Secrets of the Universe*. London: Simon & Schuster, 2012.

Sanchez, Alex. *Bait*. London: Simon & Schuster, 2009.

*Sanchez, Alex. *Rainbow Road*. London: Simon & Schuster, 2010.

Scott, Elizabeth. *Between Here and Forever*. London: Simon & Schuster, 2011.

Sharpe, Tess. *Far From You*. London: Indigo, 2015.

Sheldon, Dyan. *Planet Janet*. London: Walker Books, 2002.

Sheldon, Dyan. *Planet Janet in Orbit*. London: Walker Books, 2004.

Shepard, Sara. *Pretty Little Liars* [*Pretty Little Liars* book 1]. London: Little, Brown, 2007.

Shepard, Sara. *Flawless* [*Pretty Little Liars* book 2]. London: Little, Brown, 2007.

Shepard, Sara. *Perfect* [*Pretty Little Liars* book 3]. London: Little, Brown, 2008.

Shepard, Sara. *Unbelievable* [*Pretty Little Liars* book 4]. London: Little, Brown, 2009.

Shepard, Sara. *Wicked* [*Pretty Little Liars* book 5]. London: Atom Books, 2011.

Shepard, Sara. *Killer* [*Pretty Little Liars* book 6]. London: Atom Books, 2011.

Shepard, Sara. *Heartless* [*Pretty Little Liars* book 7]. London: Atom Books, 2011.

Shepard, Sara. *Wanted* [*Pretty Little Liars* book 8]. London: Atom Books, 2011.

Shepard, Sara. *Twisted* [*Pretty Little Liars* book 9]. London: Atom Books, 2012.

Shepard, Sara. *Ruthless* [*Pretty Little Liars* book 10]. London: Atom Books, 2012.

Shepard, Sara. *Stunning* [*Pretty Little Liars* book 11]. London: Atom Books, 2012.

Shepard, Sara. *Burned* [*Pretty Little Liars* book 12]. London: Atom Books, 2012.

Shepard, Sara. *Pretty Little Secrets* [*Pretty Little Liars* companion novel]. London: Atom Books, 2012.[90]

Smith, Andrew. *Grasshopper Jungle*. London: Egmont, 2014.

Smith, Andrew. *Winger*. London: Penguin, 2014.

Stainton, Keris. *Starring Kitty*. London: Catnip Publishing, 2014.

Steinhöfel, Andreas. *The Centre Of My World*, trans. Alisa Jaffa. London: Andersen Press, 2006.

Stiefvater, Maggie. *The Dream Thieves* [*The Raven Cycle* book 2].[91] London: Scholastic, 2013.

Stiefvater, Maggie. *Blue Lily, Lily Blue* [*The Raven Cycle* book 3]. London: Scholastic, 2014.

Storr, Catherine. *Two's Company*. Cambridge: The Lutterworth Press, 1984.

Talley, Robin. *Lies We Tell Ourselves*. London: Mira, 2014.

Tiernan, Cate. *Changeling* [*Wicca* book 2].[92] London: Puffin Books, 2002.

Tiernan, Cate. *Dark Magick* [*Wicca* book 4]. London: Puffin Books, 2002.

Tiernan, Cate. *Awakening* [*Wicca* book 5]. London: Puffin Books, 2002.

Tiernan, Cate. *The Calling* [*Wicca* book 7]. London: Puffin Books, 2002.

Tiernan, Cate. *Strife* [*Wicca* book 9]. London: Puffin Books, 2002.

Tiernan, Cate. *Reckoning* [*Wicca* book 13]. London: Puffin Books, 2003.

Tiernan, Cate. *Night's Child* [*Wicca* book 15]. London: Puffin Books, 2003.

Vilmure, Daniel. *Toby's Lie*. London: Bloomsbury, 1995.

Von Ziegesar, Cecily. *Because I'm Worth It* [*Gossip Girl* book 4].[93] London: Bloomsbury, 2004.

Von Ziegesar, Cecily. *I Like It Like That* [*Gossip Girl* book 5]. London: Bloomsbury, 2004

Von Ziegesar, Cecily. *Only In Your Dreams* [*Gossip Girl* book 9]. London: Bloomsbury, 2008.

Von Ziegesar, Cecily. *Would I Lie To You?* [*Gossip Girl* book 10]. London: Bloomsbury, 2008.

Von Ziegesar, Cecily. *Don't You Forget About Me* [*Gossip Girl* book 11]. London: Bloomsbury, 2008.

Von Ziegesar, Cecily. *I Will Always Love You* [*Gossip Girl* book 12]. London: Headline, 2009.

Von Ziegesar, Cecily. *It Had To Be You* [*Gossip Girl* prequel]. London: Headline, 2007.

Wallach, Tommy. *We All Looked Up*. London: Simon & Schuster, 2015.

Wasserman, Robin. *Skinned*. London: Simon & Schuster, 2009.

Weingarten, Lynn. *Suicide Notes from Beautiful Girls*. London: Electric Monkey, 2015.

Westerfeld, Scott. *Afterworlds*. London: Simon & Schuster, 2014.

Wild, Margaret. *Jinx*. London: Quarto Publishing, 2002.

Wilkinson, Lili. *Pink*. London: Quarto Publishing, 2010.

Williamson, Lisa. *The Art of Being Normal*. Oxford: David Fickling Books, 2015.

Wilson, Jacqueline. *Kiss*. London: Random House, 2007.

Wittlinger, Ellen. *Hard Love*. London: Simon & Schuster, 2004.

Wittlinger, Ellen. *Heart on my Sleeve*. London: Simon & Schuster, 2005.

Wolff, Virginia Euwer. *True Believer*. London: Faber & Faber, 2003.

Wood, Eleanor. *My Secret Rock Star Boyfriend*. London: Macmillan Children's Books, 2015.

Woodson, Jacqueline. *If You Come Softly*. London: Puffin Books, 2002.

Wright, Bil. *Putting Makeup on the Fat Boy*. London: Simon & Schuster, 2011.

Wynne-Jones, Tim. *The Uninvited*. London: Walker Books, 2010.

Appendix Endnotes

84. Elizabeth L. Chapman, "Provision of LGBT-Related Fiction to Children and Young People in English Public Libraries: A Mixed-Methods Study."

85. Book 3 in the series, *Cherokee Bat and the Goat Guys,* contains minimal LGBT content.

86. The first book in the series, *Gone*, also includes the lesbian character, but her sexuality is not mentioned until the second book.

87. Previous books in the series do not include the queer character.

88. Series titles omitted here contain no or only very brief mention of the gay character.

89. The first book in the series, *The City's Son*, also includes the lesbian character, but her sexuality is not mentioned until the second book.

90. Subsequent books in the series have not yet been published in the UK.

91. The first book in the series, *The Raven Boys*, also includes the queer character, but his sexuality is not made clear until the second book.

92. Series titles omitted here contain no or only very brief mention of LGBTQ* characters.

93. Series titles omitted here contain no or only very brief mention of LGBTQ* characters.

Chapter 3

IN THE DEMOCRATIC REPUBLIC OF THE CONGO, A DEFIANT LGBTQ COMMUNITY FLOURISHES: COLLABORATING TO PRESERVE THEIR MEMORY DESPITE THE DRC'S ARCHIVES ACT

Louis Kamwina Nsapo

Translated from French to English by Heather Moulaison Sandy

Introduction

When homosexuality is mentioned in the Democratic Republic of the Congo (DRC), negative ideas quickly surface. Having been exposed to incomplete and fragmented information, Congolese communities automatically think that homosexual relations are not *politically correct*. Homosexuality, to them, is not a legitimate lifestyle. In this context, the law is mute on the work that archives, as state agencies, should be doing, despite the renewed historical interest in LGBTQ activities. An absence of instructions regarding the conditions for opening private archives (i.e., non-governmental archives such as personal papers or institutional records), selecting, processing, classifying and preserving material, means that private archives in the DRC remain homogeneous, effectively excluding LGBTQ materials. Given the legislative silence concerning LGBTQ identity in the Democratic Republic of the Congo, how can LGBTQ collections be preserved? LGBTQ community members were sampled as part of a study of the preservation of their personal collections.

Situating Archives

Archival content is preserved in order to be used by present and future generations.[1] Archives are much more than a bunch of "old papers" produced through the daily work of people and institutions; rather—they constitute part of our collective documentary history from the moment they are signed or completed. Archival materials can include correspondence, invoices, reports, registers and forms, event documentation, publicity materials, health pamphlets, calendars, date books, and computer databases. Furthermore, they can also include ephemera that might otherwise be thrown away: tickets, t-shirts, stickers, bottles, packaging, signs, pins, bags, etc. These documents have the potential to support the archival model put forth by Bruno Delmas.[2] The International Council on Archives (ICA) confirms that «Open access to archives enriches our knowledge of human society, promotes democracy, protects citizens' rights and enhances the quality of life" [our translation].[3] At the same time, Yvon Lemay reminds us that memory is the "ability to retain and recall past states of consciousness and that which is associated: our soul, in the way it preserves the past" [our translation]. Serving the collective memory, archival documents keep track of the past and help us to remember it «and that which is associated" [our translation].[4] Thus, archives allow the story of a community or organization to be written.

Legislation on Archives and on their Administrative Management before the Act of 1978

Between 1482 and 1960, all written documents produced in this territory had the same legal status: records of colonial exploits in the indigenous brush.[5] Historian Bogumil Jewsiewicki confirms that, in the early days of the Congo Free State (1885), nothing had been done to preserve these records and papers.⁶ Circular no. 59 of December 1, 1888 from the General Administration of the Interior included measures for the preservation of archives in the different departments of the public administration, and required the creation of an office charged with caring for the archives of the State.⁷ Additionally, the Governor General's circular of May 27, 1902 introduced the notion of administrative public archives and gave State services the prerogative to keep their archives. Having the archives organized in that way put a relational dynamic into play. The silence was damning. King Leopold II declared: "The Congo and its archives belong to me [...], they can take my Congo, but they will not take what has happened there" [our translation].⁸ Gustave Stinglhamber, aide de camp to the King, was involved with the archives.

> [...] left the royal palace to go see a friend in the Congo Free State's offices, which were close by. The two men approached an open window so they could talk; Stinglhamber down sat on a radiator and immediately jumped to his feet: it was burning hot. While they called the concierge to ask for an explanation, he responded: "Apologies; we are burning the archives of the State." [...] As the boiler filled the sky of Brussels with smoke, the palace also ordered the destruction of the archives kept in the Congo. Colonel Maximilian Strauch, counselor of the King for Congolese affairs for many years, declared: "The voices that could have spoken in the place of the destroyed archives have been systematically condemned to silence" [our translation].⁹

Following that silencing were the Circulars of January 21, 1912, January 6, 1920, February 3, 1921, and January 6, 1928; the Regent's Decree of July 1, 1947 created an office under the Governor General's General Secretary to oversee archives and libraries. That being done, the Circular of February 11, 1950 required the State's services to deposit their materials in the Archives. According to Antoine Lumenganeso Kiobe, curator of the National Archives of the Congo, the service began to function in 1953; the circular of January 24, 1958 required a classification plan to guide the public administration services in the arrangement and description of documents.¹⁰ The decree of March 26, 1957 created relay stations in the towns and capitals of the provinces, districts, and territories, with the goal of transferring the records to Belgium via a large depot in Kinshasa.[11]

LGBT Archives and the Public Administration Documents of the Belgian Colony

During colonization, who would dare to speak openly about sexual orientation or gender identity without extremes of discomfort or audacity? Even the most tenacious search for documents related to homosexual identities during colonialization would not be rewarded, since homosexuality was a topic that invited polemics and thus engendered secrecy. A more pragmatic approach would examine the extent of the relevant legislation. From this we see instructions for public archives, but little to guide the creation of private archives so that individuals and corporate bodies could fulfill their liberties[12] and define their activities in a way that would be both free and autonomous. The decree of December 1, 1888 narrowly defines archives as being composed of records pertaining to the affairs of a particular department. Private archives were not officially defined; nonetheless, essential papers were kept in Belgium. Our country's under-studied homosexual subculture is not represented in the archives, yet at the moment when the Congolese came into contact with the colonizers, homosexuals were included in the teams sent. Even during colonization, it might have been legitimate to talk about LGBTQ papers. Summarizing a conference on "Sir Roger Casement: The Creation of a Gay Icon," which was held on Friday, March 19, 2004, McGill University professor of history, Brian Lewis, stated the following:

> Roger Casement, an Irishman engaged in the British consular service in the early twentieth century was known for three things: his humanitarian work (his investigations into the atrocities committed in the rubber-growing industry in the Congo and in the Amazon earned him the title "Sir Roger"); [...] and his diaries relating his homosexual cruising activities (that made him a gay icon several decades after his death) [our translation].[13]

Undoubtedly, it is for this reason that a number of homosexuals view Sir Casement as epitomizing the hidden homosexual life. Today, many of the philanthropist's papers have been lost. Efforts to ignore homosexuality might be one reason why private papers in the Congo were not collected and many archival documents were sent to Belgium to be destroyed. In the DRC, a serious and honest discussion can and should be opened on this subject.

Law No 89-927 of January 26, 1989 on the Construction of the National Archives[14]

A building was ceded in 1958 by the Administration of the Interior. It was an old printing house of the General Government[15] and archival materials began to be processed and filed there in 1959. Mobutu Sese Seko Kuku Ngbendu Wa Za Banga, president of the Mouvement Populaire de la Révolution (MPR)[16] reopened its doors with a new law, No. 89-027 of 26 January 1989, which established a national service called the "National Archives of the Congo" (ARNACO). In this way, ARNACO became a specialized service of the Ministry of Culture and Arts, created to maintain and enhance all documents produced by State services, and represented the highest interest in the history of the DRC.[17]

Law No 78-013 of July 11, 1978 on the General System of Archives in DRC[18]

Summary of the Laws on Archives in DRC

Table 1 presents 6 chapters and 31 articles. To make the chart more readable, however, chapter 2 and article 5 were retained.

Date	Chapter	Article	Principle	Application or Origin	Effect	Observations
July 11, 1978	I	1	Definition of archives and types of archives	Institutions, individuals or corporate bodies	Preservation: State archives	
		2		Archival services	Archival Services	Decision of the competent state service
		3 & 4	Public archives	State archives / Public archives	Anachronous	
	II	5	Private archives	Private archives, personal papers		Private property
	III	6	Constitution and preservation of national archives	Public services (State heritage)		
				Private archives: Individuals and corporate bodies		Audits
		7		Public services: Individuals and corporate bodies		
		8			State archives	
		9 & 10				Exemption from the president of the MPR
		11 to 14		Legal deposit, optional deposit, purchases, gifts, and bequests	Public services repository	
		15 to 17		Accession of documents (over 30 years old)	State archives	
		18		Accession of documents (under 30 years old)	Fuzzy	
January 26, 1989	IV	19 & 20			Destruction of documents	The departmental decree was never implemented
		21	Management of the national archives	Individuals: purchases, gifts, deposits, expropriation		Who assessed the relevance of an historical document?

	22		State archives		No departmental decrees were created
	23 & 24		Public institution, Law 89-027 of January 26, 1989		
V	25 to 27	Access to archives	High Council on archives, state archives		Creation of the president of the MPR. The High Council on Archives was never created
	28				
	29				
VI	30 to 31	Sanctions	State archives: Unrestricted access.	Without a fine	
			Secret or criminal archives, or papers on an individual's private life: access in 50+ years		Authorization of the president of the MPR or notice of the Minister of Culture and the Arts
			Personal papers: free access		
			Penal Code		Rights payments; Criminal provision

Table 1: Laws on DRC Archives

Reflection on Chapter II of the Act of 1978

Table 1 reveals that, in Chapter 2, the law addresses both public and private archives in three articles. Only Article 5 defines private archives: "Private archives are those archives belonging to individuals or corporate bodies, who remain owners of those archives." Behind these words, which no doubt have tricked archivists and ordinary persons alike, hides the real kicker —the law does not enumerate its constituents and there is no notification for the opening of classings of historical private archives, in determining preservation conditions. The letter of the law does not supply any kind of instructions about how to accession private archives, nor does it provide a framework or even conditions for the filings. The law artificially groups all kinds of archives as a way of restricting the creation of private archives.

The Processing of Private Papers in the Act of 1978

1	Nonexistent rules
2	Lack of scientific and technical oversight of archives
3	Absence of delineation between public archives, private archives, and specific archives
4	The refusal by Parliament to include private papers in the National Archives
5	Owners' rights are not established

Table 2. Principles of arrangement and classification of private records missing or lacking in the Act of 1978

Practically speaking, the Act of 11 July 1978 does not provide enough security for private archives. There are no practical or regulatory initiatives that address paper-based private archives or, *a fortiori*, electronic ones. Guidelines for personal data have not yet been formulated. The law sought to solve the problem of the preservation of public archives, but in doing so, created problems for private archives, because they were not adequately addressed. Since 1978, the DRC has not enacted any new laws covering archival materials, allowing the silence on private archives there to remain.

"Fag"[19] Archives: Fitting Heteronormative Standards in the DRC?

"Paradoxically, homosexuals, are controversial but also influential" [our translation].[20] In fact, the debate surrounding archives of members of the homosexual community is always tumultuous, due to their cultural practices and *modus operandi*.[21] The 1978 Act is partly at fault, since it did not address the need.[22] Thanks to the parliamentarians,[23] the people, and their constellation of churches continue to discuss it even now. Almost across the board, the churches cling to their assumptions and stereotypes, presenting only the doctrinal positions that they support.[24] They feel the gays are disquieting; they rouse our consciences and challenge our mental structures and our knowledge base. With that said, how could their papers be best preserved? Difficult questions emerge regarding ownership, custody, access and professional liability. Today, the writings, texts, and events that had been secret, now thrill and amuse the public at large.

Making Strides: The Growth of LGBTQ Archives

Many Homosexuals; Many Archives

Philippe Gouillou said that "The most common mistake about homosexuals is to consider that they form a united group with objectives and common approaches" [our translation].[25] Françoise Mukuku says there is no data on the situation of LGBTQ people in the Congo.[26] The percentage of homosexuals in the DRC is not known, and there are no official figures for the number and types of homosexuals. This suggests that there are multiple types of homosexual with different identities, based on what is known of their movements, the places they frequent, and their experiences. Benoit Migneaux claimed that the list of types of homosexuals has grown over time. Muriel Schmid is a good indicator of this change. She prefers the long and difficult to pronounce acronym LGBTTQQI2SA: lesbian, gay, bisexual, transgender, transsexual, questioning, queer, intersex, two-spirited, and allies.[27] The present community here can provide context. Any number of terminologies, customs, and traditions may soon encounter a new anti-subculture. In terms of archives, the result is that there are a number of prejudices against LGBTQ archival collections, which makes it difficult to address this part of history openly. Maintaining homosexual collections and promoting them is not easy for either the Congolese archivists or the homosexuals themselves.

The Rebirth of LGBTQ Archives

The law of 1978, instead of promoting equality and encouraging public memory projects to grow, was instead subverted by organizational inequalities. In other words, the National Archives, which purports to support equal rights for all individuals, actually is an instrument that legitimizes the hegemony of public records over private papers. Not only is access to various preservation services and their conditions of use sanctioned by the "authorization of the MPR President, or the opinion of the Minister of Culture and Arts," they mostly remained subordinate to and dependent on an ideology that claims «authenticity» is based on good morals and African traditions.[28] The «others»[29] who are both victims of their gender expression and unhappy with the way that others look upon them (those, in short, who find themselves rejected and despised because they revolted against heterosexual norms)[30] are not incentivized to take part in the debate. For them, using the existing rules is not the preferred way to express their expectations, because they represent an imposition of forces supporting a machismo conception of archives. They instead resort to less conventional and institutionalized methods, potentially leading to a break with the so-called classical forms. Yet it remains possible, without denying the importance of state law in organizing the archives, to undertake the work of maintaining memory from another point of view, and to ultimately provide another paradigm for preserving tomorrow's archival materials and collections.

LGBTQ Archives: The State of Our Memories

Samuel Zralos[31] reflects on the starting point of archives: a correlation between history, forgetting, and memory. This triptych should be constantly linked to the ability to acquire LGBT archives and the places where their memories can be retained. For Zralos, as for archivists, homosexuals leave traces, memories and objects, which provide evidence of their existence through time. They also reflect and compose places where memory resides, despite the trials and tribulations that imposed by censorship. This reflection does not invalidate premises, but rather allows us to contextualize and specify them. How do LGBTQ people in the DRC find novel ways to preserve their memory, despite the current legislation?

LGBT Archives without Place: Fanzines for All

In terms of politics, economics, and culture, homosexuals in the DRC remain well hidden. Nonetheless, they do organize meetings and produce documents. This hidden but active culture becomes increasingly important when considering issues of preserving archives. According to Munor Kabondo, homosexuals struggle to organize and defend their rights within the current structures, which forces them to stay hidden and do nothing.[32] Corroborating these statements, Junior Kimbouga explains that coming together as a group of self-identified homosexuals and assembling documentation for archiving can be risky. Members of this community therefore silently keep their own documents, which makes sense, but is limiting. This is further reinforced by Hai-siatu's story. After discovering that she had AIDS in 2008, she gave all her personal papers documenting her life to a group supporting HIV/AIDS patients. Her intention was that after she passed away, the papers would explain to her family what had happened to her. Hopefully, these papers will survive any prudishness of the part of her heirs. In recent months, I have had the honor to work with the theatre actor Jean-Brettant Ngole, to collect homosexual papers from among notebooks and old syllabi which had been kept in an orange envelope in an attic. Such a method of housing archival records runs counter to good conservation and preservation practices because it deteriorates the paper and degrades the media. In such worst-case scenarios as presented here, the digital medium provides a solution for recording the historical events of tomorrow today by promoting easier exchange of materials and defeating some of the obstacles as soon as LGBTQ subjects are identified.

LGBTQ Archives and Digital Repositories

According to Kodjo Ndukuma Adjayi, "Online activities are not regulated by legal provisions in the DRC" [our translation].[33] Interviews with LGBTQ citizens reveal that homosexuals are regularly using Dailymotion, YouTube, and Facebook. Unintended effects of the law allowed for the publication of records that, to this point, had remained secret and private, by using a public space: the Internet. This, may have encouraged new habits among LGBTQ people who had started using websites as archival repositories. This confluence of unplanned and organic networks[34] allows anyone to put themselves at the center of preservation and to participate in access. This liberating echo cannot exist without considering neutrality, universality, immateriality, interactivity, and internationality of the "Net,"[35] which is what increases visibility and communication. As a result, regardless of how they are being measured, LGBTQ people respond dynamically to the silence that has always enveloped them and helps them to be forgotten. Homosexuals in the DRC adopt different social media networks to handle their archival materials; Twitter, WhatsApp, Inbox, Viber, email, and Facebook are some of the tools that enable them to share archives and information among their members. A number of documents are stored on websites. Kiswahili Mamboka, a 27-year-old gay man says that "we tend to adopt a heterosexual identity on social networks and we often change our photos by adding a rainbow sky or wearing sunglasses." According to Olga Sunduku, a 32-year-olf seamstress, "when we participate in cultural activities and festivals, we post and are archiving photos, reports, press releases and other documents relating to ourselves in private websites that are secure, maintained by white women or lesbian groups" [our translation]. Among the many platforms of this type, we noted the "Kinshasa lesbian groups of the Lemba and Limete neighborhoods" and "sexy girls in Lubumbashi."

Conclusion

Maintaining LGBTQ archives requires not only following established rules, but also having a passion and an indefatigable involvement. Such a path can be adhered to and validated in the context of what is at the core of the Kasai animism, and seems to require neither long nor scholarly communication. This idea can also be used to perpetuate and mobilize the virtues of a group of people or a community of the «other» to serve as archetypes of new social behaviors and integrate it as a social and cultural element that gives meaning to one's being by connecting it through the past, present, and future. Luba traditions tell of an old man planting oaks as a memorial of his life passage. The proverb states: "Kashawuke kuna Nsanga-, Nsanga- ishaale tshimuenenu ne: ke muaa kashawuke muamua," which means, "Lowly humans plant oaks so that over time, these oaks bear witness to their existence." The lesson is that, whoever you are, you have an obligation to leave behind traces of your passage on this earth.

Endnotes

1. International Council on Archives, Principes relatifs à l'accès aux archives adoptés par l'AGM le 24 aout 2012, 6, accessed January 2, 2016, http://www.ica.org/sites/default/files/ICA_Access-principles_FR.pdf.

2. Delmas's model is the following: *Prove*: legal usefulness; *Remember*: administrative utility; *Understand*: scientific utility; *Log*: social utility. See Bruno Delmas, *La société sans mémoire: propos dissidents sur la politique des archives en France*, (Paris : Burin, 2006), 15.

3. International Council on Archives, *Déclaration universelle sur les archives*, accessed February 8, http://www.archives49.fr/fileadmin/ad49/actus/2015/Declaration_universelle_des_archives.pdf. [English-language Universal Declaration on Archives: http://www.ica.org/en/universal-declaration-archives]. N.B. In the context of this paper, *Private*

archives refer to papers from persons (relating to their private lives as well as to their professional and association-related activities) or families, but also to records of professional groups, companies, associations, or even political parties and unions.

4. Yvon Lemay, "Livres d'artistes et documents d'archives," *Revue de Bibliothèque et Archives nationales du Québec*, 2 (2010): 72, http://www.banq.qc.ca/documents/a_propos_banq/nos_publications/revue_banq/revue2_2010-p_70-81.pdf.

5. In 1512, the Portuguese drafted the *Regimento*, which is a kind of a colonial charter stipulating that "in any affairs in which the king should appeal to the Portuguese ambassador, the ambassador should obey him as he would the King of Portugal." This provision [at the same time] required King Nzinga kuwu (known as Ndofunsu I or Alfonso I) to obey the authority of the Pope, King of the Catholic Church.

6. Bogumil Jewsiewicki, "Les Archives administratives zaïroises de l'époque coloniale," *Anale Aequatoriat : Recueil d'études,* tome 1, Vol. 1, (1980): 169.

7. Louis Kamwina Nsapo, *Inventaire analytique des documents d'archives des foyers sociaux du Congo Belge, 1946-1960,* (ISS, Kinshasa, Thesis, 1997-1998), f. 12.

8. Antoine Lumenganeso Kiobe, *Congo guide des Archives Nationales*, (Kinshasa, [S.E], 2001), p. 22.

9. Adam Hochschild, *Les fantômes du Roi Léopold II : un holocauste oublié*, trans. Marie-Claude Elsen and Frank Straschits (Paris: Belfond, 1998), 346-347.

10. Lumenganeso Kiobe, *Congo guide des Archives Nationales* p. 23.

11. The administrators of the territories, the commissioners of the districts, the governors of the provinces, along with the Governor General, wrote a roughly 100-page report at the end of each calendar year on the business of each jurisdiction as part of his duties. Several of these archival resources which could function as research instruments are located in Belgium and in other archives worldwide, making them completely inaccessible to the Congolese people. Munayi Muntu-Monji, in his thesis entitled *Le mouvement Kimbanguiste dans le haut Kasaï : 1921-1960*

(The Kimbanguiste Movement in Upper Kasai: 1921-1960), (University of Province, Aix-Marseille, 1974), notes that even the reports of the Governor General are not in the National Archives of the Congo.

12. Flwine Sarr, "L'Afrique a besoin d'une utopie [Entretien avec Jacque Nguimbous et Jean Merckaert, Paris, 26 févier 2016.]," in *Congo-Afrique, 56ᵉ année*, 504 (April 2016): 308.

13. Sir Roger Casement: La création d'une icône gaie, *L'Archigai. Mémoire de notre communauté. Bulletin des archives gaies du Québec*, no. 13, (December 2003), 8, accessed March 5, 2016, http://www.agq.qc.ca/archigai/Archigai_2003.pdf; Roger Casement [1864-1916] poses with young men and boys in the photograph published by Cahir O'Oherty, *What to make of a 1916 gay icon? Roger Casement's heroic status was denied*, accessed May 10, 2016, http://www.irishcentral.com/roots/history/What-to-make-of-a-gay-1916-icon--Roger-Casements-heroic-status-was-denied.html. No information is available on the history of Congolese homosexuals.

14. République du Zaïre, *Journal officiel*, no. 4, February 15, 1989, p. 18; See also: République Démocratique du Congo, *Les Codes larcier de la République Démocratique du Congo*, Tome 6., B- Droit administratif (Bruxelles: De Boeck, 2010), pp. 661-662.

15. Bob, Bobutaka Bateko, *RD Congo-Belgique : Archives, Bibliothèque et Bibliologie*, Paris, Editions Universitaires Européennes, 2015, p. 99.

16. The *Movement populaire de la révolution* (MPR) (Popular Movement of the Revolution) was the only party in which the people were politically organized under the dictatorship of Mobutu. See Emery Mukendi Wafwana et al., *Les Constitutions de la République Démocratique du Congo. De 1908 à 2011* (Kinshasa: Juricongo, 2011); Ambrose Kamukuny Mukinay, *Droit constitutionnel congolais* (Kinshasa: Edition Universitaires Africaines, 2011).

17. Kamwina Nsapo Louis, *Inventaire analytique des documents d'archives des foyers sociaux du Congo Belge, 1946-1960* (ISS, Kinshasa, undergraduate thesis, 1997-1998), f. 16-17.

18. République du Zaïre, *Journal officiel*, No. 14, (July 15, 1978), p. 7. Read also, République Démocratique du Congo, *Les Codes larcier de la*

République Démocratique du Congo, Tome 6., B- Droit administratif (Brussels : De Boeck, 2010), pp. 648-649. This law needs to be revisited. There are no clauses repealing previous archival laws to the Law of 11 July 1978, which is regrettable.

19. Some homosexuals already accept the term "pédé" or "*fag.*" See Mr. Q. " Je me dis 'pédé,'" *Yagg,* accessed April 3 2016, http://yagg.com/2016/04/20/mr-q-je-me-dis-pede/.

20. In October 2010, bishop and MP Evariste Ejiba Yamapia initiated a draft law concerning unnatural sexual practices. As well, December 13, 2013, the MP Stive Mbikayi filed a proposed law criminalizing homosexuality. Both intentions are not disclosed by the office of the National Assembly.

21. On the topic of hhomosexuality in Africa, the host of the page (https://www.facebook.com/African-history-Histoire-africaine-170981123072691/) in correspondence on April 9, 2016, summarized it thusly: «It must be recognized that this practice has existed everywhere on earth in all civilizations [...] but Africa as a whole, rejects such practices. That's why you still see today in Africa, how African populations get very nasty or very severe, when cases of homosexuality are found in African cities and countries (our translation).» In the case that homosexual archives existed, they could potentially attenuate these or other concerns. Is the archivist a knowledge seeker or a simple collector? Is the archivist an owner, an association, an historian, a volunteer, a genealogist, etc.? In 2009, Iain Blair acknowledged that «Gay Archives require archivists, librarians, technicians and technicians in museology, and documentation of all sorts of people from the education sector, all people interested in preserving LGBT heritage (our translation)." See Iain Blair, "La relève," *L'Archigai: Mémoire de notre communauté: Bulletin des archives gaies du Québec,* 19 (2009): 3, accessed April 24, 2016, http://www.agq.qc.ca/archigai/Archigai_2009.pdf.

22. The legislature has given this organic institution of the DRC four main missions: 1) preserving all documents received from government and para-statals; 2) developing rescues archival master plans attendants deposits in the management of documents, sorting and grading

operations; 3) communicating the historical archives to the public and to researchers as prescribed by the law governing the archives – i.e., designing a framework of regulations in the archival field, checking deposits, and initiating short-term training, awareness seminars, workshops, visits and conferences; and 4) preparing and publishing inventories, guides and directories. South Africa is the only country on the African continent that, as of May 8, 1996, respects sexual orientation in its constitution. See Sarah Jean-Jacques, *L'Afrique du Sud et la dépénalisation universelle de l'homosexualité: Echec d'un acteur phare des droits humains?*, Masters thesis, (2013-2014), 16, accessed April 3, 2016, http://www.iris-france.org/docs/kfm_docs/memoire-sarah-jj-article-iris.pdf

23. Steves Mbikayi, op. cit., confronted Parliament on its website in an attempt to transmit his homophobic position and to parlay it into a ban on homosexuality and as a way to cover up the history of the gay movement in the DRC. His legislation was not supported at the National Assembly, and his reaction was immediately made clear in his tweet of March 21, 2016: «[...] It is true that in this room, there are some men and women who must be homosexuals. They constantly fight to obstruct my bill» STEVE Mbikayi @ Cartesien243. See also, "RD Congo : le député Steve Mbikayi décidé à interdire l'homosexualité," accessed February 2, 2016, http://www.medias-presse.info/rd-congo-le-depute-steve-mbikayi-decide-a-interdire-lhomosexualite/52097

24. Kamwina Nsapo, Louis, "Quand l'arc-en-ciel pénètre dans nos bibliothèques. Le vade-mecum de la bibliothèque de l'université protestante au Congo et de l'université catholique au Congo, à la lumière de la Déclaration de Lyon" (paper presented at the World Library and Information Congress, Cape Town, South Africa, August 15-21, 2015), accessed June 26, 2016, http://library.ifla.org/1291/1/128-kamwina-fr.pdf.

25. Phillippe Gouillou, *Pourquoi les femmes des riches sont belles: programmation génétique et compétition sexuelle*, (Bruxelles: De Boeck, 2003), p. 156.

26. Françoise Mukuku who heads the non-governmental organization (NGO) *Si jeunesse savait* (*If the youth knew*) and who is an activist for human rights in the DRC, is pleased that the country has not had laws that

prohibit or permit homosexuality or transgender identities. See http://www.norvege.no/News_and_events/policy/Droits-humains-pour-toute-s---rencontre-internationale-sur-des-differents-sujets-concernant-les-droits-humains-des-LGBT/#.VzMXJ0P8iIU, Maëlle Le Corre. "Vers la création d'un réseau militant LGBT francophone" *Yagg*, December 12, 2014, accessed March 22, 2016, http://yagg.com/2014/12/12/vers-la-creation-dun-reseau-militant-lgbt-francophone.

27. Michel Danthe, "Dix théologiens protestants croient à une Eglise qui accepte toutes les minorités sexuelles,» *Le Temps*, October 26, 2015, accessed March 11, 2016, http://www.letemps.ch/societe/2015/10/26/dix-theologiens-protestants-croient-une-eglise-accepte-toutes-minorites.

28. In speaking about *authenticity* to the UN tribune on October 4, 1973, Mobutu highlights: Authenticity is an awareness on the part of the Zairian people to use their own sources and to seek the values of their ancestors, in order to appreciate the values that contribute to their harmonious and natural development [...] To be authentic is to be yourself, that is to say, to be natural or to be close to nature. One can only be true to oneself through contact with nature [...] Authenticity is the philosophy that binds us to nature, which reconciles us with the past, which enforces its origins and perpetuates the glory of our ancestors. Authenticity is not only a thorough knowledge of one's own culture, but also a respect of the cultural heritage of others. For readings on authenticity, see: Union des écrivains zaïrois, "Authenticité et développement," In *Actes du colloque national sur l'authenticité organisé par l'Union des écrivains zaïrois*, Kinshasa 14-21 septembre 1981 (Paris, Presence Africaine 1982). The institutionalization of the MPR and the affirmation of «Authentic Zairian nationalism» as am indicated path of development in cultural matters were the basis of authenticity. See also Bureau du President de la République (ed.), *Panorama des 20 ans du mouvement populaire de la révolution*, (Kinshasa, Bureau du président-fondateur, 1987). The legal value of Authenticity is demonstrated by professors Kalongo Mbikayi and Ndeshyo Rurihose, "Le recours à l'authenticité et le droit zaïrois, Dans Revue Juridique du Zaïre : droit écrit et droit coutumier, Kinshasa," *Société d'Etudes Juridiques du Zaïre*, 52, no. 3 (1976): 39-44 and Kalongo Mbikayi and Ndeshyo Rurihose, "Le recours à l'authenticité et le droit zaïrois

(suite et fin), *Revue Juridique du Zaïre : droit écrit et droit coutumier, Kinshasa, Société d'Etudes Juridiques du Zaïre,* 53, no. 1-3 (1977) : 24-40. The word of the Founding President of the MPR, Mobutu Sese Seko, had the force of law.

29. Majority groups classified homosexuals with the "others" as a minority. Read Marcel F. Raymond, "La mémoire des autres," *Archigai: Mémoire de Notre Communauté: Bulletin des Archives Gaies du Québec,* No. 16, November 2006, 2, accessed March 5, 2016, http://www.agq.qc.ca/archigai/Archigai_2006.

30. Drucker, "La fragmentation des identités LGBT à l'ère du néolibéralisme."

31. Samuel Zralos, "Archives LGBT: où sont nos mémoires?" *Yagg,* accessed April 22, 2016, http://yagg.com/2013/07/10/lgbt-ou-sont-nos-memoires/.

32. *Munor Kabondo, La* guerre contre l'homosexualité en République Démocratique du Congo, *Speak,* March 21, 2014, accessed March 14, 2016, http://speakjhr.com/2014/03/la-guerre-contre-lhomosexualite-en-republique-democratique-du-congo/.

33. Kodjo Ndukuma Adjayi, *Cyberdroit* : télécoms, internet, contrats de e-commerce : une contribution au droit Congolais, (Kinshasa: PUC, 2009).pp. 35-36.

34. Andrew Tannebaum and David Wetherall, *Réseaux,* 5th ed., (Paris, Nouveaux Horizons, 2011), p. 60.

35. Jérôme Huet and Emmanuel Dreyer, *Droit de la communication numérique,* (Paris, LGDJ, 2011), p. 16-24.

Bibliography

African history – histoire africaine [Facebook community]. https://www.facebook.com/African-history-Histoire-africaine-170981123072691/

Blair, Iain. "La relève." *Archigai: Mémoire de Notre Communauté: Bulletin des Archives Gaies du Québec* 19, (2009): 3. Accessed April 24, 2016. http://www.agq.qc.ca/archigai/Archigai_2009.pdf.

Bobutaka, Bateko Bob. *RD Congo-Belgique : archives, bibliothèque et bibliologie*. Paris: Éditions universitaires européennes, 2015.

Bureau du Président de la République (ed). *Panorama des 20 ans du Mouvement Populaire de la Révolution*. Kinshasa, 1987.

Danthe, Michel. "Dix théologiens protestants croient à une église qui accepte toutes les minorités sexuelles." *Le Temps*. October 26, 2015. Accessed March 11, 2016. http://www.letemps.ch/societe/2015/10/26/dix-theologiens-protestants-croient-une-eglise-accepte-toutes-minorites.

Delmas, Bruno. *La société sans mémoire: propos dissidents sur la politique des archives en France*. Paris: Burin, 2006.

"'Droits humains pour tou-te-s' - rencontre sur des sujets concernant les droits humains des LGBT," December 19, 2014, http://www.norvege.no/News_and_events/policy/Droits-humains-pour-tou-te-s---rencontre-internationale-sur-des-differents-sujets-concernant-les-droits-humains-des-LGBT/#.VzMXJ0P8iIU.

Drucker, Peter. "La Fragmentation des identités LGBT à l'ère du néolibéralisme." *Période*. Trans. Olivier Surel. Originally published in English in *Historical Materialism*, vol. 19, no. 4, pp. 3-32. (2014, October 16). Accessed http://revueperiode.net/la-fragmentation-des-identites-lgbt-a-lere-du-neoliberalisme.

Gouillou, Phillippe. *Pourquoi les femmes des riches sont belles: programmation génétique et compétition sexuelle*. Bruxelles: De Boeck, 2003.

Hochschild, Adam. *Les Fantômes du Roi Léopold II: un holocauste oublié*. Paris: Belfond, 1998.

Huet, Jerome and Emmanuel Dreyer. *Droit de la communication numérique*. Paris: LGDJ, 2011.

International Council on Archives. "Principes relatifs à l'accès aux archive : adoptés par l'AGM le 24 aout 2012." Accessed January 2, 2016. http://icarchives.webbler.co.uk/13619/toolkits-guides-manuals-and-guidelines/draft-principles-of-access-to-archives.html.

International Council on Archives. "Déclaration universelle sur les archives." Accessed February, 2016. http://www.ica.org/en/universal-declaration-archives.

Jean-Jacques, Sarah. "L'Afrique du Sud et la dépénalisation universelle de l'homosexualité: échec d'un acteur phare des droits humains?" *Masters thesis, 2013-2014. Printed October 15, 2014.* Accessed April 3, 2016. http://www.iris-france.org/docs/kfm_docs/memoire-sarah-jj-article-iris.pdf.

Jewsiewicki, Bogumil. "Les archives administratives Zaïroises de l'époque coloniale." *Anale Aequatoriat*, vol. 1, no. 1 (1980): 169-184.

Kabondo, Munor. "La Guerre contre l'homosexualité en République Démocratique du Congo." *Speak*. March 21, 2014. Accessed March 14, 2016. http://speakjhr.com/2014/03/la-guerre-contre-lhomosexualite-en-republique-democratique-du-congo.

Kalongo, Mbikayi and Rurihose Ndeshyo. "Le recours à l'authenticité et le droit zaïrois" *Revue Juridique du Zaïre: Droit Écrit et Droit Coutumier* 52, no. 3 (1976): 39-44.

Kalongo, Mbikayi and Rurihose Ndeshyo. "Le recours à l'authenticité et le droit zaïrois (part II)" *Revue Juridique du Zaïre : Droit Écrit tt Droit Coutumier* 53, no. 1-3 (1977): 24-40.

Kamukuny Mukinay, Ambroise. *Droit Constitutionnel Congolais.* Kinshasa: Edition Universitaires Africaines, 2011.

Kamwina Nsapo, Louis. *Inventaire analytique des documents d'archives des foyers sociaux du Congo Belge, 1946-1960.* Kinshasa: Undergraduate Thesis, 1997-1998.

Kamwina Nsapo, Louis. *La force des conventions de L'UNESCO sur la protection du patrimoine culturel dans la législation congolaise.* Post-Masters thesis. UNIKIN: Inédit, 2009.

Kamwina Nsapo, Louis. Quand l'arc-en-ciel pénètre dans nos bibliothèques: le vade-mecum de la bibliothèque de l'université protestante au Congo et de l'université catholique au Congo, à la lumière de la déclaration de Lyon" [conf]. Accessed January 2, 2016. http://library.ifla.org/1291/1/128-kamwina-fr.pdf.

Le Corre, Maëlle. "Vers la création d'un réseau militant LGBT francophone" *Yagg*. December 12, 2014, http://yagg.com/2014/12/12/vers-la-creation-dun-reseau-militant-lgbt-francophone/.

Lemay, Yvon. "Livres d'artistes et documents d'archives." *Revue de Bibliothèque et Archives Nationales du Québec*, no 2 (2010): 70-81.

Lumenganeso Kiobe, Antoine. *Congo guide des archives nationales*. Kinshasa, 2001.

Mukendi Wafwana, Emery. *Les constitutions de la République Démocratique du Congo de 1908 à 2011*. Kinshasa: Juricongo, 2011.

Muya Kalamba, Albert. *Mes proverbes Tshiluba favoris (interprétés en français)*. Kinshasa: Médiaspaul, 2013.

Ndukuma Adjayi, Kodjo. *Cyberdroit* : télécoms, internet, contrats de e-commerce : une contribution au droit Congolais. Kinshasa: PUC, 2009.

Raymond, Marcel. "La mémoire des autres.". *L'Archigai: Mémoire De Notre Communauté::Bulletin des Archives Gaies du Québec* (2006): 2. Accessed March 5, 2016. http://www.agq.qc.ca/archigai/Archigai_2006.

République Démocratique du Congo. *Les Codes Larcier de la République Démocratique du Congo*. Bruxelles: De Boeck, 2010.

République du Zaïre. *Journal Officiel* no 14 (1978): 7.

République du Zaïre. *Journal Officiel* no 4 (1989): 18.

Sarr, Felwine. "L'Afrique a besoin d'une utopie [Entretien avec Jacque Nguimbous et Jean Merckaert, Paris, 26 févier 2016.], " *Congo-Afrique* 56, no 504 (2016): 308-312.

"Sir Roger Casement: La création d'une icône gaie." *Archigai* : *Mémoire de Notre Communauté: Bulletin des Archives Gaies du Québec* 13 (2003): 8. Accessed March 5, 2016. http://www.agq.qc.ca/archigai/Archigai_2003.pdf.

Tanenbaum, Andrew and David Wetherall. *Réseaux,* 5ᵉ éd. Paris: Nouveaux Horizons, 2011.

Tsimba, Fresnel Bongol. "RD Congo : le député Steve Mbikayi décidé à interdire l'homosexualité. " Medias-Presse-Info. April 1, 2016. http://www.medias-presse.info/rd-congo-le-depute-steve-mbikayi-decide-a-interdire-lhomosexualite/52097.

Union des Écrivains Zaïrois. *Authenticité et développement. Actes du colloque national sur l'authenticité organisé par l'union des écrivains Zaïrois.* Paris: Présence Africaine, 1982.

Zralos, Samuel. "Archives LGBT: où sont nos mémoires?" July 10, 2013. Accessed April 22, 2016. http://yagg.com/2013/07/10/lgbt-ou-sont-nos-memoires.

Chapter 4

UNIVERSAL DECIMAL CLASSIFICATION: A UNIVERSAL DISCRIMINATIVE CLASSIFICATION?

Gregory Toth

In the Library

In the autobiographical comic book *Fun Home*, the young Alison Bechdel joyfully discovers that she can look up the term homosexuality by herself in the library card catalog.[1] Through the printed word, consumed privately and anonymously, she discovers her identity and eventually finds a community. Weston says that looking up the term homosexuality in a library catalogue is a "stock episode" in coming-out narratives.[2] This classic image represents a transition from the "only one in the world" syndrome to the realization that there "must be not only someone like me, but also someone out there somewhere."[3] Bechdel's drawing allows us to behold this wonderful revelation; we see over the shoulder of the young girl who opens the catalog drawer. Witnessing this speaks to every librarian's sense of triumph. Our catalogue users must indeed be able to locate desired subjects, related to their interest, on their first attempt—without being confused, mislead, prejudiced against, or offended by the very terminology that discovery platforms use.

However, everyday life shows a darker reality than the optimism expressed above. There is a well-documented history in grassroots archives of lesbian, gay, bisexual, trans, queer, and other (hereafter referred to as LGBTQ+) people going to the library as part of the soul-searching preceding their coming-out process, and leaving disappointed. This is due to the fact that many classification systems are based on out-of-date vocabularies that do not follow direct, contemporary language; they are full of sex, ethnic, age, and other biases in terms related to people, and suffer from a lack of comprehensive indexes. For example, in the subject headings devised by the Library of Congress (hereafter referred to as LC) the terms HOMOSEXUALITY and LESBIANISM had a "see also from" reference to SEXUAL PERVERSION up until 1972. It was not until 1976 that the same institution recognized LESBIANS and HOMOSEXUALS, MALE as classes of people. The term GAYS, even though in widespread use since the 1920s, was not approved as a subject descriptor in Washington, DC until sixty years later. It took LC thirteen years to eliminate JEWISH QUESTION and eighteen years to dismiss YELLOW PERIL. GOD (CHRISTIANITY) finally entered the Library of Congress Subject Headings (hereafter referred to as LCSH) some thirty-five years after it was first suggested.

Subject headings carry a lot of weight: The right ones help readers to find what they want; the wrong ones, or none at all, cut off access. The terms SECOND-WAVE FEMINISM and QUEER THEORY were introduced to LCSH less than a decade ago. Those who wish to quickly locate DRAG QUEEN RACE or TRANS PEOPLE IN PRISON in the index of the Dewey Decimal Classification (hereafter referred to as DDC), will have great difficulties. There are clearly time lags when it comes to responding to political developments. Since Cutter's seminal work, all librarians have been taught to recognize that their catalog is necessary in order to enable their reader to find a book when either the author, the title, or the subject (emphasis my own) is known. But when our library catalogs continuously misidentify the subject of our resources, we might as well mark them missing. *Fun Home* straddles the line between fiction and autobiography. It thus raises interesting questions; I fear that stepping out of it, Bechdel might have a very different reader experience when identity-searching in many of our libraries.

Radical Librarians

Haykin's Subject Headings set out the guiding principles for the establishment of taxonomy in LC, stating that "the reader is the focus in all cataloging principles and practice."[4] His guideline dictates that catalogers abandon logic in favor of an unknown reader's psychological approach to the library catalog. Subject headings are thus determined by what the cataloger believes the majority of readers will think. This intuitively sounds like it would allow for flexibility, however, for many decades this hypothetical reader was explicitly described in the following terms: American/Western European, white, Christian (usually Protestant), heterosexual and male.[5] As LCSH is the chief source for subject cataloging in most American and other libraries, LC principles have not been questioned for many years.

In 1969, forty years before *Fun Home* was published, a letter written by a local librarian from the University of Zambia was sent to *Library Journal*. The writer, Sanford Berman, called the existing major cataloging and classification schemes "white, imperialist and Christian oriented" and their subject headings "chauvinistic."[6] Berman sparked a movement to correct prejudiced nomenclature and promote activist librarianship in which speaking up for social justice and campaigning for catalogs that serve real library users (not ones designed for other catalogers) are parts of professional work. Radical librarians place librarianship within a critical theorist framework that is epistemological, self-reflective, and activist in nature. Their actions seek to transform and empower, to challenge power and privilege, and to engage with concerns related to diversity, information ethics, access to information, academic freedom, and human rights, among others.[7] When one meets radical librarians, it is immediately clear that they are passionate about their mission and they want no "archaic, foolish, clumsy, inauthentic and biased" subject terms.[8]

The critical cataloging movement addresses the problem of bias chiefly as a functional problem: materials are catalogued incorrectly.

A research study conducted last year revealed that many librarians were already concerned with social justice but needed to be more fully versed in critical theory.[9] The findings recommended that librarians move beyond addressing the micro-issue of biased taxonomies and that critical theory should be incorporated into library and information science courses. This is where a new group of radical librarians take up their position, notably around Drabinski.[10] They argue that once critical theory becomes part of LIS education, the next generation of librarians will be able to apply it in their classrooms. The implication is that these new professionals will treat existing taxonomies as tools to be critically engaged with rather than simply accepted.[11] Regardless what approach librarians choose, what we see is that the wider information profession is prepared for classification languages to be changed. Yet DDC and LC do not seem to provide room for such transformation.

Berman essayed a long time ago the notion that libraries are the foundation of a free society because they have an obligation to provide the widest possible access to alternative information. He understood that "culturally sensitive catalog headings are not a quirky, unnecessary luxury but proof of our commitment to the truth and accuracy".[12]

The Solution: UDC?

Due to their geographical location, most radical librarians' chief interests have always been LC and DDC. It cannot be denied that, especially in North America, other classification languages such as the Universal Decimal Classification (hereafter referred to as UDC), do not enjoy the same popularity as their competitors. In the English-speaking world UDC (a multilingual and highly flexible classification scheme for all fields of knowledge in any medium), has always been, and continues to be, used mainly in special libraries. However, in many non-English language areas it has had, and maintains, a greater hold in public, national, and academic libraries. At one point it was estimated that UDC has been used throughout the world by some five thousand organizations.[13] UDC is truly international in a sense that none of the other major systems are: it is used in over one hundred countries worldwide, with editions of various lengths in almost every single language.[14] A comparison of the size of UDC to the size of DDC revealed that the full edition of the former contained ten times more entries than the latter. Even the popular English edition was three times larger than DDC some twenty years ago.[15] Due to its vast size and popularity, it is no wonder that some believe that it is the most widely used of all classification systems.[16]

Early works on UDC are full of discussions regarding the advantages and disadvantages of the facet approach and issues concerning citation order. Theorists have spent decades debating about these issues because they assumed that UDC subject headings themselves were without bias. They presumed that all key concepts would be recognized and cited even if they were not named in the title.[17] Indeed, when trawling through the last sixteen years of literature written on the scheme (and a selected bibliography on earlier works) no mention of prejudiced terminology can be found.[18] Expressing all facets in the best possible citation order is certainly very appealing and is exactly what every radical librarian dreams of. However, it can only be achievable if there is a subject descriptor for everything that needs to be expressed. We demonstrated earlier that both LC and DDC fail to deliver this. UDC on the other hand has the potential to offer user-friendly and unbiased headings due to its scope and the way numbers are built. To appreciate how UDC fulfills this promise, we first need to understand its heritage.

History of UDC

The history of UDC begins at the end of the nineteenth century when two young Belgians, Paul Otlet (1869-1944) and Henri La Fontaine (1854-1943), were working on a universal bibliographic directory intended to become a comprehensive classified index to all published information. After examining the existing classification systems, Otlet and La Fontaine concluded that DDC—then in its fifth edition—offered the most promising basis. They wrote to Dewey and sought his permission to translate his scheme into French, as well as to modify and expand upon the scheme. Permission was given to extend the schedules on the condition that the order of the main classes and divisions be maintained and that new developments strive for the maximum amount of comparability. The two Belgians proceeded to enlarge the schedules of DDC by adding extensively to its enumerative classes and, more significantly, providing a much more extensive apparatus for synthesis, or number-building. By 1895 Otlet, La Fontaine and their fellow workers, chiefly women, had classified some four hundred thousand cards for their *Répertoire Bibliographique Universel*. They presented this to the world at the first International Conference on Bibliography held in Brussels. The attendees of the conference immediately proposed to found the Institut International de Bibliographie (hereafter referred to as IIB), an organization meant to develop and maintain the new taxonomy. In 1937, the IIB became Federation Internationale de Documentation (hereafter referred to as FID).

Otlet and La Fontaine's idea soon outgrew the plan of merely translating and expanding upon Dewey, and a number of radical innovations were made. First, they adopted a purely enumerative classification in which all subjects are listed and coded into one classification, which allowed for synthesis (i.e., the construction of compound numbers to denote interrelated subjects that could never be exhausted). They also realized that characteristics common to many subjects could be assembled as a separate list—detaching the terminal digits and listing them as tables of auxiliary numbers that could be added as required by the user. This synthetic principle meant that a level of detail could be obtained that was much greater than what was actually displayed in the published scheme. This allowed for greater precision, combined with an economy of presentation. The first international edition of their modified DDC was published in 1899 as the *Manuel du Répertoire Bibliographique Universel*. It is estimated that this first edition consisted of some thirty thousand subdivisions in the schedules, with an alphabetical index of some thirty-eight thousand entries.

The scheme continued to expand, though interrupted by the First World War, and work progressed on a second edition. The second edition was published from 1927 to 1933; by that time it contained over fifty thousand subdivisions. This edition was offered independently under the title *Classification Decimale Universelle*, the name by which, in various translations, it is still known. A third edition, the first in German, was begun next and published from 1934 to 1951. It was approximately double the size of the second edition, with about a hundred thousand subdivisions.[19] Today the official content of UDC is a database with seventy thousand entries known as the Master Reference File.[20] The reference file is maintained by the UDC Consortium, which includes the FID and five other publishers as members.

Number Building

The arrangement of UDC is based on DDC: every number is thought of as a decimal fraction with the initial point omitted, and this determines the filing order. Both DDC and UDC claim that the advantage of this system is that it is infinitely extendable, and when new subdivisions are introduced, they need not disturb the existing allocation of numbers. This is an important aspect that we will re-visit later. Just like DDC, UDC is also a hierarchical classification: knowledge is divided into ten main classes, called "schedules;" each class is then subdivided; each subdivision is further subdivided, and so on. The more detailed the subdivision, the longer the number that represents it. The most innovative feature of UDC is its auxiliary signs and subdivisions. They not only contain more detail, but they are better organized than those in the scheme's competitors. They allow for the construction of a synthesis of compound numbers with the help of devices provided in the schedule. The ten main classes are accompanied by auxiliaries; these are signs and subdivisions which can be used throughout the classes, allowing for the construction of compound numbers. The most commonly used signs are the plus, the stroke and the colon; they are used to link two numbers, thereby expressing relations of various kinds between two subjects.[21] The following examples demonstrate how two dissimilar subjects can be linked; one subject is extended to a second one, and any topic can be related to any other.

Addition (+) is when two dissimilar subjects are linked:
316.837+737
Gay and lesbian relations AND Numismatics

Extension (/) is when one subject is extended to a second:
78.071(43)-055.36"1933/1945"
Bisexual German musician BETWEEN 1933 and 1945

Relation (:) is when one subject is related to another:
347.96-055.2:364.633
Female lawyers RELATION TO sexual abuse

Auxiliary subdivisions, on the other hand, consist of tables that represent notions such as place, time, language, general characteristics, and physical form of the document. These numbers are simply added at the end of the number for the subject in order to express a more detailed classification. Below are some individual examples.

Place is added using brackets (_):
343.541(417)
Sexual offences in the Republic of Ireland

Time is added using inverted comas ("_"):
726.84"2015"
Mass burial features in 2015

Language is added using equal signs (=):
342.724=112.2
Racial equality in German

Characteristic, persons is added with a dash zero five (-05):
656.61.071.22**-05**5.2
Women marine engineers

Form is added with bracket zero (0:
94(41)**(0**58)
History of the British Isles, Yearbooks

When a class number is created by the synthesis of these elements taken from different places in the schedule, the resulting number is truly a complex, and thus highly descriptive, taxonomical number:

656.61.071.22(058)(417)=112.2"2015"-055.2
Yearbook on women marine engineers of 2015 in the Republic of Ireland in German

Everyday Usage

The main and auxiliary tables have an official filing order as given in every edition. With numerals this is self explanatory, especially to DDC users, but in the case of auxiliary symbols, filing guidelines need to be provided. As was illustrated above with the last example, classification numbers with several auxiliary subdivisions added to them do become lengthy, and as a result, filing and retrieval become more challenging. Difficulty arises because, unlike most classification schemes well-known to library users, UDC was not principally intended as an apparatus for ordering books on shelves but rather in a card catalogue based on the Manuel du Repertoire. Because filing and locating items are burdensome when class marks are so long, many librarians would justify simple and short numbers for ease of use. Of course it means that one of the greatest advantages of UDC is lost during the classification process. Long and thus expressive UDC class marks carry as much responsibility as the appropriate LC and DDC numbers: the right ones help readers to find what they want and short ones tend to limit access.

In an online environment where records are most likely downloaded via WorldCat or Copac, it is disappointing to see that neither of these two suppliers provides their bibliographic records with UDC numbers.[22] This is another reason why shorter class marks are more common; in everyday life it forces catalogers to create subject numbers locally for every single document. Would they really have time to create truly expressive classification? Or would the situation once again justify the ease of using simple numbers? We have seen that one of the advantages of UDC is the possibility of creating complex compound classification numbers that are enhanced with various common auxiliary subdivisions. However, complex compounds are not applied in practice as often as they should be. Catalogers either do not have the necessary time to create them or they do not build them simply because complex numbers are too specialized and difficult to use.

Bias in UDC

Let us suppose that the cataloger does have the time to create complex compounds such as the one given above on women marine engineers of 2015 in the Republic of Ireland. It was possible to build this multifaceted descriptive taxonomical heading because every class number and auxiliary subdivision that we needed existed. UDC's colossal scope indicates that it is a viable option for avoiding sex, ethnic, age, and other biases in people-related terms. The presence of the "general characteristics" auxiliary subdivision itself indicates that UDC is a tool with which catalogers can escape building prejudiced headings. A good example of such is the introduction of the -05 auxiliary. This denotes the person's concern or their characteristics, and was possibly influenced by the great Indian mathematician and librarian Ranganathan's (1892-1972) idea of the "personality" facet of classification.[23] It was first widely applicable in the Class 3 (Social Sciences), although its use was restricted chiefly to 616 in 6 (Pathology in Applied Science).[24] By the 1970s it was transferred to common auxiliaries and since then it may be used at any point whenever it is necessary. The -05 auxiliary expresses various person-related facets that DDC will never be able to. For example it can be used to describe variety of people's age or age-groups, ethnic characteristics or nationality, gender and kinship, occupation, education, etc. When classifying in UDC, it is convenient for creating non-biased subject headings such as for items that are about female sailors (656.61.071.22-055.2), lesbian writers (341.462.2-055.34-055.2), or unmarried gardeners living together with their partners (647.3-058.837).

Building these numbers is easy because the relevant auxiliaries can be looked up in the schedule. When UDC, as with DDC, claims that new subdivisions do not disturb the existing allocation of numbers, one might say that it must have an available number for a variety of people-related auxiliaries. Or at least if they did not, it would take no time to introduce them. Sadly, the opposite can be seen throughout the scheme. Although a number exists for heterosexuals (-055.32), homosexuals/gays (-055.34), and bisexuals (-055.36), it is surprising that it is not currently possible to express two further sexual orientations: asexuality or pansexuality.[25] There is also real limitation with UDC's two gender categories: man (-055.1) and woman (-055.2). How would one express transgender police officers or androgynous scientists when no numbers are available? When social network sites list more than seventy gender options to their users in the United Kingdom, in a desire to better reflect the country's diversity, UDC feels anything but universal and flexible.[26]

Similar trends can be observed with sex categories. While class numbers for male (-055.1) and female persons (-055.2) are part of the auxiliary subdivisions, and thus give the opportunity to allocate them to every class, intersexuality is under 612.6 (Reproduction. Growth. Development under Medial science). Its number, 612.6.058 Hermaphroditism (intersexuality), is not suitable for easy expression because it is not an auxiliary subdivision. Additionally, it is listed under medical science which has always had a negative connotation. It might make more sense to create a third sex category, e.g. Intersexual persons (-055.3), since this would not disturb the existing numbers.

In addition to the lack of available numbers, there is also the problem of getting UDC to appeal impartially to all cultures and schools of thoughts. Class 2 (Religion. Theology) is one such topic of difficulty. Back in the early 1980s the Indian Institute of Islamic Studies continuously expressed their disappointment with the scheme's limited treatment of Islamic culture. For the purpose of classifying Islam and related subjects, UDC schedules were found absolutely inadequate and an eighty-four page amendment was proposed for incorporation into UDC.[27] The proposal was rejected by FID on the ground that revisions should preferably be done by amendment in situ with the minimum disturbance compatible with the requirements.[28] The UDC scheme has a great deal to offer, if only it could live up to its claim of universality.[29]

The real question is why these biases have not been corrected already. A classification language that claims to be universal and flexible should respond to these challenges instantly. Is the problem perhaps related to the way the schedule is developed and revised? In order to answer this question, we need to understand how UDC is maintained and reviewed today.

Problem of Revision

On-going development and revision of the schedules in order to keep them up-to-date is the responsibility of FID through its network of the UDC Revision Committees and individual experts. Revision proposals can originate from UDC Revision Committees, National UDC bodies, individuals, or even independent groups. Sadly, the pace of revision has been somewhat slow and the work has fallen behind. This might be due to financial insecurity and the fact that population of UDC users is not increasing.[30]

Revision does not happen as fast as many would expect because deep connections have survived between UDC and DDC. For example, many of the earlier mentioned biases in UDC originate from DDC itself. In 1960 Lloyd (editor of the English UDC editions and head of the UDC department of FID for decades) presented a comparative study of both systems on the basis of the first three digits, which showed the high degree of conformity existing between the two systems.[31] Since the creation of DDC, however, many new areas have achieved disciplinary status. At the same time, new focuses and combinations have created further ones. UDC relied heavily on DDC when it was being developed, and has carried the same heritage and issues with it.

In order to move beyond these problems, FID made the important decision to sever connections with DDC, except those for those regarding information exchange.[32] Following the recommendation of its Central Classification Committee, the two systems finally diverged: Class 1 (Philosophy. Psychology) was completely revised in accordance with the present state of knowledge. Class 4 (Language) was set free and relocated to Class 8 (Literature). With these decisions, UDC has started its own dynamic journey that hopefully will help create the missing categories that catalogers need to express unbiased subjects. There is really no excuse not to continue the journey and further enhance the schedule with more up-to-date and additional subdivisions and auxiliaries.

Conclusion

Berman once famously quipped that "if someone's name is Jane and yet she's persistently called Henrietta, that doesn't make her Henrietta. She is still Jane."[33] If Jane happens to be a writer or a topic and a reader is looking for books written by or about her, the catalog must be able to lead the reader to Jane without confusing, misleading, prejudicing, or offending either Jane or the reader. After all, the overall purpose of any classification system is to allow each and every library user to locate any item within the collection; they make documents retrievable. Classification headings, whether they are based on human languages or codes, ought to satisfy readers' expectations by providing access to documents. However, the process of using set categories creates a fundamental issue: librarians are left without the flexibility for easy modification. These rigid systems claim to provide full access to human knowledge but in fact favor white, Christian and heteronormative world-views.

They evolve too slowly, become too firmly set, and deal with diversity in slow motion. What subject classification indeed achieves is quite often the blocking of access to human knowledge, especially for some vulnerable reader groups.

At first glance, UDC seems to offer a solution. Its auxiliary numbers denote recurrent characteristics applicable over a range of subjects. Its flexibility provides an opportunity to insert new subdivisions that do not disturb the existing numbers. Its complex compounds, created by synthesis of various elements taken from different places in the schedule, are truly evocative. The revision procedure has recently responded to current challenges much better than the scheme's competitors. UDC could thus be the taxonomy that does not accommodate prejudiced subject headings. However, close reading reveals that, just like its competitors, it discriminates against many readers. The special and unique auxiliary numbers are not able to fully cover some of the people-related characteristics. It has biases in sex, sexual orientation, and gender identity, all topics of particular importance for LGBTQ+ communities. It lacks real flexibility when new class numbers are proposed.

This chapter has brought attention to some issues that UDC must consider in order to ease the problem of prejudice in its classification. Diane Choquette once said that "subject cataloguing is a responsible activity. The librarian must always be willing to change."[34] We believe that information professionals, regardless if they are radical or not, are happy to change. It is time now for our classification systems, including UDC, to accommodate this willingness.

Postface

The author has used UDC for two years at a university library and another two years in a research library. Later he worked with the scheme for seven years in a museum library. This article represents his experience of the taxonomy—not the UDC community's. Today he classifies with DDC and LCSH. UDC examples in this article were created by using the Standard English edition.[35]

Endnotes

1. Alison Bechdel, *Fun Home: A Family Tragicomic* (London: Jonathan Cape, 2006), 75.

2. Kath Weston, "Get Thee to a Big City: Sexual Imaginary and the Great Gay Migration," *GLQ: A Journal of Lesbian and Gay Studies* 2, no. 3 (1995): 257.

3. Weston, "Get Thee to a Big City," 281.

4. David J. Haykin, *Subject Headings: A Practical Guide* (Washington, DC.: Library of Congress, 1951), 7.

5. Joan K. Marshall, *On Equal Terms* (New York: Neal-Schuman, 1977), 6.

6. Sanford Berman, *The Joy of Cataloguing* (Phoenix: Oryx, 1981), 65.

7. Kenny Garcia, "Keeping Up With... Critical Librarianship", accessed 4 August 2015, http://www.ala.org/acrl/publications/keeping_up_with/critlib.

8. Berman, *The Joy of Cataloguing*, 4.

9. Robert Schroeder and Christopher V. Hollister, "Librarians' Views on Critical Theories and Critical Practices," *Behavioral and Social Sciences Librarian* 33, no. 2 (2014).

10. Two good examples of this position are Emily Drabinski, "Teaching About Class in the Library," *Radical Teacher* Winter 2009 and Emily Drabinski, "Queering the Catalog: Queer Theory and the Politics of Correction," *Library Quarterly* 83, no. 2 (2013).

11. Drabinski, "Teaching About Class in the Library," 15.

12. Chris Dodge and Jan DeSirey, eds., *Everything You Always Wanted to Know About Sandy Berman But Were Afraid to Ask* (Jefferson: McFarland, 1995), 31.

13. Jack Mills, *The Universal Decimal Classification* (New Brunswick, N.J.: Graduate School of Library Service, 1964), 11.

14. Aida Slavic-Overfield, "Classification Management and Use in a Networked Environment: The Case of the Universal Decimal Classification" (PhD diss., University of London, 2005), 211 and 213.

15. Alan Gilchrist and David Strachan, *The UDC: Essays for a New Decade* (London: ASLIB, 1990), v.

16. H. Bose, *Universal Decimal Classification: Theory and Practice* (New Delhi: Sterling, 1987), 4.

17. British Standards Institution, *Guide to the Universal Decimal Classification (UDC)* (London: BSI, 1963), 29.

18. Bibliography sections investigated from *Extensions & Corrections to the UDC 17* (1995) to 33 (2011) and David C. Weeks, Mildred Benton and Mary L. Thomas, *Universal Decimal Classification* (Washington, D.C.: The George Washington University, 1971).

19. The numbers of subdivisions are taken from Bjorn L. Hegseth and Knut Thalberg, eds., *UDC and EDP Lectures from a Seminar in Oslo November 1-3 1976* (Oslo: Riksbibliotektjenesten, 1977), 37. Robinson gives slightly different numbers: first edition thirty-three thousand; second edition seventy thousand; third edition hundred and forty thousand subdivisions. See Geoffrey Robinson, *UDC a Brief Introduction* (The Hague : FID, 1979), 7-8.

20. UDCC, "About UDC MRF," accessed 12 March 2015, http://www.udcc.org/index.php/site/page?view=mrf.

21. Perreault devised one hundred twenty various codes of colon to express different logical relations. Although not accepted, the proposal clearly demonstrates the possibility that UDC has over DDC when it comes to express relations. See Jean M. Perreault, *Towards a Theory for UDC* (London: Clive Bingley, 1969).

22. This is no surprise because WorldCat is provided by OCLC who owns all copyright rights of DDC.

23. Eric de Grolier, *A Study of General Categories Applicable to Classification and Coding in Documentation* (Paris: UNESCO, 1962), 34.

24. H. Bose, "Universal Decimal Classification in Transition," *Library Herald* 9, no. 4 (1967): 300.

25. Not to mention further categories such proposed in the 90s by Fausto-Sterling who came up with five different sex categories. See Anne Fausto-Sterling, "The Five Sexes: Why Male and Female Are Not

Enough," *The Sciences* March/April 1993: 20-24. Accessed 03 April 2015. http://www.uta.edu/english/timothyr/Fausto-Sterling.pdf.

26. James Vincent, "Facebook Introduces More Than 70 New Gender Options to the UK," *Independent,* 27 June 2014, accessed 01 June 2015, http://www.independent.co.uk/life-style/gadgets-and-tech/facebook-introduces-more-than-70-new-gender-options-to-the-uk-we-want-to-reflect-society-9567261.html.

27. Indian Institute of Islamic Studies. *Library Classification Schedule on Islam and Related Subjects* (New Delhi: Indian Institute of Islamic Studies, 1981).

28. Federation Internationale de Documentation. *Principles of the Universal Decimal Classification (UDC) and Rules for its Revision and Publication.* 5th edition. (The Hague: FID, 1981): 16. In the last couple of years finally Class 2 was completely revised.

29. Gilchrist and Strachan, The UDC, 21.

30. Gilchrist and Strachan, The UDC, 30.

31. Geoffrey A. Lloyd, "Comparison of Dewey DC and UDC at a Minimum Three Figure Level," *Revue de la Documentation* 27, no. 2 (1960).

32. Ingetraut Dahlberg. "Possibilities for a New Universal Decimal Classification. *Journal of Documentation* 27, no. 1 (1971): 18.

33. Berman, The Joy of Cataloguing, 83.

34. Sanford Berman. Subject Cataloguing: Special Issue of *Technical Services Quarterly* 2, no. 1/2 (1984), 29.

35. British Standards Institution. *UDC: Universal Decimal Classification.* Standard ed. (London: British Standards Institution, 2005).

Bibliography

Bechdel, Alison. *Fun Home: A Family Tragicomic.* London: Jonathan Cape, 2006.

Berman, Sanford. *Subject Cataloguing: Special Issue of The Technical Services Quarterly* 2, no. 1/2 (1984).

Berman, Sanford. *The Joy of Cataloguing.* Phoenix: Oryx, 1981.

Bose, H. "Universal Decimal Classification in Transition." *Herald of Library Science* 9, no. 4 (1967): 300.

Bose, H. *Universal Decimal Classification Theory and Practice*. New Delhi: Sterling, 1987.

British Standards Institution. *Guide to the Universal Decimal Classification (UDC)*. London: BSI, 1963.

British Standards Institution. *UDC: Universal Decimal Classification*. Standard ed. London: British Standards Institution, 2005.

Dahlberg, Ingetraut. "Possibilities for a New Universal Decimal Classification. *Journal of Documentation* 27, no. 1 (1971): 18-36.

de Grolier, Eric. *A Study of General Categories Applicable to Classification and Coding in Documentation*. Paris: UNESCO, 1962.

Dodge, Chris and Jan DeSirey. eds., *Everything You Always Wanted to Know About Sandy Berman But Were Afraid to Ask*. Jefferson: McFarland, 1995.

Drabinski, Emily. "Queering the Catalog: Queer Theory and the Politics of Correction." *Library Quarterly* 83, no. 2 (2013): 94-111.

Drabinski, Emily. "Teaching About Class in the Library." *Radical Teacher*. Winter 2009: 15-16.

Extensions & Corrections to the UDC 17 (1995) to 33 (2011). Accessed between 01 and 31 January 2015. http://www.udcc.org/index.php/site/page?view=ec.

Fausto-Sterling, Anne. "The Five Sexes: Why Male and Female Are Not Enough." *The Sciences* March/April 1993: 20-24. Accessed 03 April 2015. http://www.uta.edu/english/timothyr/Fausto-Sterling.pdf.

Federation Internationale de Documentation. *Principles of the Universal Decimal Classification (UDC) and rules for its revision and publication*. 5th edition. The Hague: FID, 1981.

Federation Internationale de Documentation. *Bibliographical Survey of UDC Editions*. The Hague: FID, 1982.

Garcia, Kenny. "Keeping Up With... Critical Librarianship." Accessed 4 August 2015. http://www.ala.org/acrl/publications/keeping_up_with/critlib.

Gilchrist, Alan and David Strachan. *The UDC: Essays for a New Decade.* London: ASLIB, 1990.

Haykin, David J. *Subject Headings: A Practical Guide.* Washington, DC.: Library of Congress, 1951.

Hegseth, Bjorn L. and Knut Thalberg. eds. *UDC and EDP Lectures from a Seminar in Oslo November 1-3 1976.* Oslo: Riksbibliotektjenesten, 1977.

Indian Institute of Islamic Studies. *Library Classification Schedule on Islam and Related Subjects* (New Delhi: Indian Institute of Islamic Studies, 1981).

Lloyd, Geoffrey. A. "Comparison of Dewey DC and UDC at a Minimum Three Figure Level," *Revue de la Documentation* 27, no. 2 (1960). 45-80.

Marshall, Joan K. *On Equal Terms.* New York: Neal-Schuman, 1977.

Mills, Jack. *The Universal Decimal Classification.* New Brunswick, NJ: Graduate School of Library Service, 1964.

Perreault, Jean M. *Towards a Theory for UDC.* London: Clive Bingley, 1969.

Robinson, Geoffrey. *UDC a Brief Introduction.* The Hague : FID, 1979.

Schroeder, Robert and Christopher V. Hollister. "Librarians' Views on Critical Theories and Critical Practices." *Behavioral and Social Sciences Librarians* 33, no. 2 (2014): 91-119.

Slavic-Overfield, Aida. "Classification Management and Use in a Networked Environment: The case of the Universal Decimal Classification." PhD diss., University of London, 2005.

UDCC. "About UDC MRF." Accessed 12 March 2015. http://www.udcc.org/index.php/site/page?view=mrf.

Vincent, James. "Facebook Introduces More Than 70 New Gender Options to the UK." *Independent*, 27 June 2014. Accessed 01 June 2015. http://www.independent.co.uk/life-style/gadgets-and-tech/facebook-introduces-more-than-70-new-gender-options-to-the-uk-we-want-to-reflect-society-9567261.html.

Weeks, David C., Mildred Benton and Mary L. Thomas. *Universal Decimal Classification*. Washington, D.C.: The George Washington University, 1971.

Weston, Kath. "Get Thee to a Big City: Sexual Imaginary and the Greet Gay Migration." *GLQ: A Journal of Lesbian and Gay Studies* 2, no. 3 (1995): 253-277.

PART TWO:
IMAGININGS - QUEERING PROFESSIONAL PRACTICE

Chapter 5

RURAL AND URBAN QUEERING ALLIANCES OUT OF THE LIBRARY TOWARDS LEGAL PROTECTION OF LESBIAN, GAY, BISEXUAL, TRANSGENDER, AND QUESTIONING PEOPLE IN INDIA

Bharat Mehra and Lisette Hernandez

Introduction

The denial of human rights of lesbian, gay, bisexual, transgender, and questioning (LGBTQ) people is a globally widespread phenomenon.[1] In many countries, there is no legal protection for sexual minorities who experience daily fear for their security and wellbeing, as well as hate-driven crimes and verbal, physical, and emotional abuse. Cultural ostracism is widespread as a result of socially-imposed values of heterosexism[2], patriarchal taboos, and homophobia.[3] This chapter examines the types of "queering alliances of support" that libraries can develop in India—a place where as recently as December 11, 2013, the Supreme Court re-established a ban on gay sex. This followed a four-year period of decriminalization that had succeeded in bringing homosexuality out of the closet in this communally conservative country.[4] The legal re-authorizing of Section 377 of the Indian Penal Code, which dates back to 1860, criminalizes sexual activities that are "against the order of nature," arguably including homosexual acts.[5] It is important to note that the reinstated ban does not distinguish between same-sex acts involving men or women, nor does it provide a social response to behaviors unique to lesbians, gay men, bisexuals, or transgender individuals.

Content analysis of online news items published between November 14, 2013 and January 14, 2014 in The Times of India (http://timesofindia.indiatimes.com/india), one of India's most widely-read English-language newspapers, forms the basis of this research on developing strategic queering alliances through the library. This chapter proposes alliances at the economic, educational, legal, political, and social levels to promote lawful protection of sexual minorities in India. We intentionally use the terms "sexual minorities" and "queering alliances" to name these groups, largely unrepresented due to complex cultural murkiness and differences in perceptions regarding sexuality, identity, behavior, and terminology associated with the population in India.[6]

The findings are especially relevant in the world's largest democracy where, in 2013, sixty-eight percent of its 1.252 billion population was rural[7] and of that group, sixty percent earned less than thirty-five rupees (fifty-five cents) a day, while the average per capita daily expenditure of the urban population was sixty-six rupees ($1.04).[8] Due to a lack of resources and a large diverse population (among other factors), information poverty is foremost among India's many social and economic challenges for realizing its timely goal of building healthy and sustainable communities in both rural and urban settings.[9] Despite the country's broadcasted proclamations about its information and communication technology (ICT) revolutions,[10] information poverty (including lack of information access and use) is especially significant for LGBTQ people in India. They are considered culturally "invisible"[11] and have faced recent legal prosecution which was sanctioned and approved by political representatives, government authorities, pundits dictating cultural norms, and others from nearly every sector of society.[12]

The perspective and opinions of librarians has been missing on the matter, an absence that can be attributed to their limited role, neglect,[13] and uniformed public opinion about their potential to impact and promote progressive, community-wide changes.[14] Can libraries counter their poor reputations and lack of influence in India and become effective advocates of social justice for LGBTQ people (and others) and re-establish vigor and vitality in the conceptualization, ranks, and practices of the profession?

The authors believe that libraries and their professional associations/organizations in India are at a potentially monumental crossroad.[15] They can either decide to be forward-looking or remain passive agencies that continue to adopt a "neutral" stance, similar to bygone libraries in the United States that have drawn much contemporary criticism.[16] In response to the dismal plight of LGTBQ people, who lack legal protection in a hostile cultural climate, this chapter explores different types of library partnerships that could be established with various external stakeholder communities to further social justice agendas in support of this marginalized population. The purpose is to identify an active role for Indian libraries as progressive institutions. The research includes libraries and associated information organizations in a broad sense, including academic, public, and school libraries, as well as museums, archives, and others groups that work with processes of information creation, organization, management, and dissemination.[17]

The Role of Libraries in India

Libraries in India have their roots in ancient times when they served as storehouses of knowledge in princely kingdoms, temples, and centers of learning. This role has been documented in several sources, such as Panini, Patanjali, and other Indian works, as well as in travelogues of the great Chinese explorers who visited from the fourth to fifth centuries AD onwards.[18] In a modern sense, however, the origin of Indian libraries can be traced to 1835, when the first public library was established in Calcutta through the philanthropic support of private individuals.[19] Library development during India's long colonial history[20] was cemented during the post–independence era in the Madras Public Library Act of 1948, which became the first legislation specific to public library services in sovereign India.[21]

Any mention of Indian library history would be remiss without a reference to the pioneering work of S. R. Ranganathan and his immense contributions to the library and information science (LIS) professions worldwide.[22] These include his Colon Classification system, his Five Laws of Library Science, his public library vision, his role as the director of the first Indian school of librarianship to offer higher degrees, and his leadership as the president of the Indian Library Association.[23] Other influences on Indian library development include the country's rich cultural history of print, imprint, and publishing, the recent growth of the software industry, and the extensive use of ICTs in select regions.[24]

It is not this chapter's purpose to provide a detailed account of library history in India, since there are already extensive works on the subject.[25] Recent accounts also describe Indian LIS-related advancements in specific domains, such as in LIS education,[26] LIS research,[27] public library development,[28] database development and management,[29] regional language search engines,[30] and digital libraries.[31] There have also been analyses of the regional and geographical distribution of libraries in India, including rural and urban comparisons.[32]

Here, it is important to identify current directions that could be taken regarding the future of libraries in India and their potential to impact changes in the marginalizing conditions experienced by sexual minorities. Ranganathan's advocacy and his vision for promoting public library service to the rural masses has remained an unfulfilled dream owing to a state of disrepair.[33] In order to address the uneven distribution of economic and technological growth in India, and to invest in an improved public infrastructure that includes education, information, and library services, a working group of the National Knowledge Commission developed ten recommendations to improve India's neglected library system in a report titled, *Libraries: Gateways to Knowledge*.[34] This report describes the role and benefits of libraries in these terms: "Libraries have a recognized social function in making knowledge publicly available to all. They serve as local gateways to national and global knowledge." A highlight of these recommendations is to mobilize public (as well as other type) libraries in India to serve as community information centers to actualize their potential as "local centers of information and learning for the deprived masses."[35] It represents a strategy for effectively addressing the challenges that lie ahead in implementing a new vision for public library revitalization via a critical invitation for concerted action, reflection, and dialog.

In 2012, the first author of this chapter proposed a similar direction for LIS in his keynote address at the 57th Indian Library Association Annual Conference. He outlined the urgent need for the country's library professions to articulate connections between the following three components: 1) a vision of where they plan to go; 2) key milestones/goals they need to establish; and 3) strategies to implement such a plan.[36] An important aspect of this plan was to establish a consensus about the profession's identity by focusing on "helping our users in meeting and representing their information needs, wants, values, expectations, practices, and goals of all people, irrespective of their differences, and especially of those people on the margins of society. We have to draw explicit social justice and social equity conceptualization and outcomes in the services, programs, events, and organization systems we develop for our users."[37] Further, rural public libraries have remained highly under-developed in India.[38] This chapter recognizes alliance opportunities that libraries in rural and urban India can develop on behalf of sexual minorities, a disenfranchised population that has been denied legal, political, cultural, social, and individual rights by the highest court in the country.

Sexual Minorities in India

Classical and contemporary writings on human rights have explored its underlying philosophy in relation to genocide, ethnic cleansing, minority cultures, women's rights, gay and lesbian rights, the environment, and other topics.[39] Navi Pillay, the United Nations High Commissioner for Human Rights, described the Supreme Court's move to re-criminalize gay sex in 2013 as a "significant step backwards for India" that violates international law.[40] Soutik Biswas of the *BBC News* quoted

G. Ananthapadmanabhan of Amnesty International India as saying: "This decision is a body-blow to people's rights to equality, privacy and dignity."[41]

The Supreme Court's move to ban gay sex has drawn criticism from those in liberal quarters who question the validity and relevance of an outdated judicial institution in the modern age,[42] especially one that evokes a late nineteenth-century law from the Victorian colonial period of Indian history with its twisted cultural value system.[43] *NDTV*, recognized as a broadcasting news leader of impartial and wide-ranging coverage in India and abroad, questioned whether "by passing the buck to Parliament, has the top court let down India on a basic question of fundamental rights?"[44] In the segment, a panelist stated: "The whole purpose of having a court—and a Supreme Court at that—is to protect the rights of minorities no matter how "miniscule" they may be… Supreme Courts are expected to decide if, on the basis of fundamental understanding of the right to life regardless whether or not that concerns a miniscule minority—or for that matter one person…And I would say that if the law violates the rights of even one person if it does, it has to be declared unconstitutional." Unfortunately, libraries are conspicuous for their lack of participation in collective public discourse regarding this issue.[45]

With the re-installment of Section 377 in 2013, India re-joined seventy-five other countries that have laws on their books that punish gay sex through imprisonment—more than half of them are former colonies of the British Empire. India became the forty-second of fifty-two British Commonwealth countries in this regard.[46] Firm adherence to Victorian-era mores gave governments of newly-created states a strategy to develop a national identity around shared values and a convenient means to strengthen state control.[47] However, Section 377 is in violation of the twenty-nine "Principles on the Application of International Human Rights Law in relation to Sexual Orientation and Gender Identity" (the Yogyakarta Principles), which describe a series of international human rights standards for all countries to comply with, as well as providing actions and directions for nations and other agencies to promote compliance.[48]

Others have focused on the problematic consequences of changes in the political situation after the16th Lok Sabha (Lower House of Parliament) general elections held in India between April and May of 2014, which significantly raised the level of fear and insecurity among LGBTQ people in regard to state-sponsored terrorism.[49] The sweeping win in the national elections by the conservative Bharatiya Janata Party (BJP) led by Prime Minister Narendra Modi, and public statements by some of the party's highest officials, has only intensified the fears faced by LGBTQ people. Rajnath Singh, who was president of the BJP and became a cabinet minister, told journalists after the December ruling that "Gay sex is not natural and we cannot support something which is unnatural."[50] The BJP is the largest party in the world based on primary membership and has majority representation in the Indian National Parliament and state assemblies.[51] It is a right-wing party[52] with close ideological and organizational links to the Hindu nationalist Rashtriya Swayamsevak Sangh.[53] Gay rights activists have publicly stated that they did not vote for Modi's party because of the BJP's social conservatism.[54] On the topic of homosexuality, BJP spokesman M. J. Akbar stated that it "is a matter for the courts, not the government," adding "I don't have any sense of Modi's view on homosexuality."[55] The Prime Minister's silence on the topic is seen as perpetuating the status quo—a matter of serious concern considering that, according to Union Ministry statistics, 587 people were arrested under Section 377 in 2014.[56] Union Minster Dr. Harsh Vardhan's public announcement supporting the need to protect human rights for everyone, including those in the LGBTQ community, has not alleviated the fear and uncertainty.[57]

Recently, the *NDTV* news channel reported that the LGBTQ community in India was outraged with a proposal by Ramesh Tawadkarover, a state-level minister of Goa's BJP government holding the sports and youth affairs portfolio, for government-planned re-education centers. Tawadkarover stated that "we will make LGBTQ youth normal" during an event to launch a policy document on youth, at the state capital of

Panaji.[58] Harish Iyer, a gay rights activist, believes that the silence of national BJP leaders after the irresponsible statement actually admits their unspoken support. In an attempt at damage control, an embarrassed Chief Minister of Goa, Lakshmikant Parsekar, stated that his minister's comments were made in ignorance. He explained that "homosexuality is a natural gift" and "LGBTQs (Lesbians, Gay, Bisexual and Transgender) are not suffering from any disease. There is no government policy on 'normalizing' them."[59]

Ignorant remarks by Indian politicians in the wake of the legal ban and denial of human rights for LGBTQ people has drawn negative international attention and damaged the country's humanistic credibility, spiritual heritage, and rich traditions of democracy, argumentative discourse, and acceptance of diverse viewpoints and lifestyles.[60] The head of the UN, Ban Ki-moon, who was visiting Delhi at the time, stated that he "staunchly opposed the criminalization of homosexuality" in India. "I am proud to stand for the equality of all people—including those who are lesbian, gay, bisexual and transgender," the UN chief said in a public statement, adding that "I speak out because laws criminalizing consensual, adult same-sex relationships violate basic rights to privacy and to freedom from discrimination. Even if they are not enforced, these laws breed intolerance."[61] The judicial, political, and religious stakeholders have to take responsibility for the damage they have caused in their support of human rights violations against LGBTQ people and for having tarnished the international reputation of India. The first step in this regard has to be the unconditional scrapping of Section 377, despite the hedging that Indian politicians have recently engaged in about the matter.[62]

Methodological Approach

The Dataset and Search Process

The research dataset consisted of 114 unique online news articles published between November 14, 2013 and January 14, 2014, retrieved from the website of *The Times of India* newspaper using a variety of keywords associated with sexual minorities in India. The selection of this time range was relevant: it ran from one month and three days prior to the date of the reinstatement of the law banning gay sex until one month and three days after that date. The selection of the newspaper was made based on its wide readership and circulation. *The Times of India* is the third-largest newspaper in India by circulation and the best-selling English-language daily in the world,[63] with a readership of 7.643 million[64] and is ranked 174th in 2014 among India's most trusted brands.[65]

The search vocabulary used in this research included: gay, lesbian, bisexual, hijra, intersexual, queer, trans, sexual minority, LGBTQ, MSM, and variations. The term "hijra," India's third gender includes eunuchs and people who are transgender or intersex and have historically been "ignored by the mainstream, often rejected by [their] own family, reduced to a joke in popular entertainment."[66] It has recently been legally recognized as the "third sex."[67] In 2005, Indian passport application forms were updated with three gender options: M, F, and E (for male, female, and eunuch, respectively).[68] In November 2009, voting rolls and voter identity cards in India began to include an "other" category for eunuchs and transgender people.[69] On April 15, 2014, the Indian Supreme Court passed a landmark judgment by recognizing a third gender that was neither male nor female, and that was entitled to consideration in education and jobs, stating: "Recognition of transgenders as a third gender is not a social or medical issue but a human rights issue."[70] In spite of these positive victories for the hijra community, it is debatable if any real changes in acceptance of them have occurred in the population at large, due to a long history of abuse and violence against them.

The term "MSM" stands for "men who have sex with men."[71] It is used in the context of India and other low-and-middle income nations,[72] where homosexuality is hidden due to cultural prejudice and poor or nonexistent legal protection, and where same-sex behavior may be more common than previously documented, even though identity terms (e.g., gay, lesbian, etc.) are not adopted in self-identification nomenclature.[73] Searches using variations of the term "sexual minority" retrieved several irrelevant results that included content related to "sex" and "minority," so the term was discarded. Searches using variations of the term "homosexuality" retrieved results that included nearly all the online news articles in the dataset, so this term was also discarded. The relevant results from the different searches were compiled and duplications were removed. The "Advanced Search" feature was used on the website with the results sorted by "Relevance." Each of the different keyword search terms were entered into the search box for results appearing "Anywhere," in "All Sections" of the online news articles published within the date range.

There were 414 occurrences of the keywords in 114 unique online news articles, since eighty of them had more than one keyword present. The largest number of relevant occurrences were retrieved using the keyword "gay" (n=187) and the smallest number of relevant occurrences were retrieved using the keyword "MSM" (n=2). The keyword "gay" occurred the most number of times in conjunction with other keywords (n=73) while the keyword "MSM" occurred the least number of times in conjunction with other keywords (n=2). In forty-five unique online news articles, the various keywords occurred irrelevantly fifty-one times; these records were removed from the dataset for the analysis reported.

Data Analysis and Findings

Once the final dataset was compiled, researchers conducted a content analysis of each online news article to identify and code which items had the following five kinds of information: economic, educational, legal, political, and social. These categories were used to analyze, evaluate, and categorize the information found in the articles and were defined as follows:

- economic: included information pertaining to finance, banks, funding, businesses, private sector, corporations, and related descriptions
- educational: included information pertaining to programs of study, colleges, universities, schools, vocational schooling, primary

and secondary education, graduates, curriculum, and related descriptions
- legal: included information pertaining to (legal) articles, bills, legislation, constitution, laws, petitions, cases, jury, and related descriptions
- political: included information pertaining to politicians, candidates, elections, religious leaders backing government/politicians/policies, government, and related descriptions
- social: included information pertaining to norms, values, beliefs, practices, how people relate to each other, social media, and related descriptions

The process used in coding and the detailed findings of the study are reported elsewhere.[74] An important note to make here is that the categorization of the online news articles was based on the occurrence of representative quotations related to the particular information category. Also, the coding was based on the occurrence of information in that category when it was described as having primary importance in the news article. The researchers identified a total of 234 representative occurrences of the five information categories in the 114 online news articles, with the social information category assigned to the largest number of relevant unique articles (n=90) and the economic information category assigned to the smallest number (n=7). There were 25 unique articles categorized as educational, 53 as legal, and 59 as political. There were 85 online news articles that were categorized as having more than one information category.

For this research, the next step involved identifying all the proper nouns and geographic locations mentioned in each news article in the five information categories. Analysis of the proper nouns revealed the instrumental AGENTS for each information category that were mentioned in the news coverage. These included individuals (e.g., religious figures, politicians, judges, lawyers, gay activists, authors, celebrities, educators, LGBTQ people, health providers, economists, bankers, anonymous people, etc.), state/central government agencies, non-governmental

Information Category	Economic		Educational		Legal		Political		Social		Total
AGENT Type	S	NS	S	NS	S	NS	S	NS	S	NS	
Anonymous people (or name changed)	1				8	3	2		56		70
Authors/Celebrities			6		1		2	1	42	1	53
Campaigns	3		1						17		21
Companies/Brands	8								9		17
Doctors/Health Providers			14	2					4		20
Economists/Merchants/Bankers	4	2		1	2		2		8		19
Educational institutions/Teachers					2				4		6
Gay activists	1		2		1				11		15
Judges/Lawyers			1		29	7	6	8	7		58
LGBTQ people	1		2		2				19		24
Media types (e.g., TV, newspapers)			1					1	6		8
Non-governmental organizations			18		3		3	1	54	1	80
Online social media tools									24	1	25
Political parties/Organizations					3	1	2	16	6		25
Religious figures/Politicians	1		2		3	1	29	27	5	2	70
State/Central government agencies					11	3	4	1	1		20
Total	19	2	47	3	62	15	50	55	273	5	531
	21		50		77		105		278		

Key: S = Supportive; NS = Non-supportive.

Table 1: Number of supportive and non-supportive types of agents for each of the five information categories (i.e., economic, educational, legal, political, and social) based on occurrences in the online news articles published in *The Times of India* during 11/14/2013–01/14/2014.

organizations (NGOs), educational institutions, political parties, online social media tools, media types (e.g., TV, newspapers), specific campaigns, companies/brands, and others. Content analysis of the news articles helped determine whether these AGENTS were supportive or non-supportive in their stance towards LGBTQ people.

Table 1 summarizes the number of supportive and non-supportive AGENTS for each of the five information categories. The largest number of supportive AGENTS (n=273) occurred in social news (90 articles, mean=3.03) while the smallest number (n=19) occurred in economic news (7 articles, mean=2.71). However, the lowest mean (.85) [i.e., number of supportive AGENTS per news article] was for the political information category with 50 supportive AGENTS identified in 59 news articles, followed by legal information (mean=1.17) with 62 supportive AGENTS in 53 news articles, and educational information (mean=1.88) with 47 supportive AGENTS in 25 news articles. The largest number of non-supportive AGENTS (n=55) occurred in political news information (59 articles, mean=.93), while the smallest number (n=2) occurred in economic news (7 articles, mean=.29). However, the lowest mean (.06) [i.e., number of non-supportive AGENTS per news article] was for the social information category with five non-supportive AGENTS identified in 90 news articles. Three non-supportive AGENTS were identified in 25 educational news articles (mean=.12) and 15 non-supportive AGENTS were identified in 53 legal news articles (mean=.28). Overall, there were 451 supportive AGENTS (84.93%) and 80 non-supportive AGENTS (15.07%) identified from a total of 531.

Further, an overwhelming proportion of the different AGENT types were supportive of LGBTQ people and/or critical of the legally-sanctioned gay ban. These included: 68/70 anonymous people (or those who were identified by changed names) (97.14%); 51/53 authors/celebrities (96.23%); 21/21 campaigns (100%); 17/17 companies/brands (100%); 18/20 doctors/health providers (90%); 16/19 economists/merchants/bankers (84.21%); 6/6 educational institutions/teachers (100%); 15/15 gay activists (100%); 43/58 judges/lawyers (74.14%); 7/8 specific media types (87.5%); 24/24 LGBTQ people (100%); 78/80 non-governmental

Sr. No.	Information Category	Examples of Supportive AGENTS	Examples of Non-Supportive AGENTS
1.	Economic	PEHCHAN (campaign), Indyapink (company/brand), Sanjay Malhotra (economist/merchant/banker), Manish Sharma (gay activist), Dipoti Dutta (LGBTQ person), Menaka Kinnar (religious figure/politician).	S. Gurumurthy (economist).
2.	Educational	Kokil Jaida (author/celebrity), Aman Ki Asha (campaign), Abhinav Singh (gay activist), National Institute of Mental Health & Neurosciences in Bangalore (heath service provider), Senior Advocate I. M. Ahmad (judge/lawyer), Pratap Sahu (LGBTQ person), The Times of India (media type), LESBIT (non-governmental organization), Menaka Kinnar (politician).	Dr. Indira Sharma (doctor), Dr. Jagdish Bhagwati (economist/merchant/banker).
3.	Legal	filmmaker Chitra Palekar (author/celebrity), John Connolly (economist/merchant/banker), Pakistani Peace Activist Saeeda Diep (gay activist), Mrunalini Deshmukh (judge/lawyer), Desmond Hope (LGBTQ person), Humsafar Trust (non-governmental organization), Union Home Minister Shusilkumar Shinde (politician), Tamil Nadu (state government), Dean Asha Bajpai (teacher).	Ramesh Desai (pseudonym of a gay lawyer from Valsad District), G. S. Singhvi (judge/lawyer), BJP (political party), Thomas Babington Macaulay (religious figure/politician), National Crime Records Bureau (NCRB) (state/central government agency).
4.	Political	A Catholic Church archbishop (anonymous), Prince Mavendra Singh Gohil (author/celebrity), Amartya Sen (economist), Attorney General G. E. Vahanvati (judge/lawyer), Samapathik Trust President Bindumadhav Khire (non-governmental organization), Congress President Sonia Gandhi (politician), Congress and the Samajwadi Party (political parties).	Justice G. S. Singhvi (judge/lawyer), Qari MM Mazhari editor of Secular Qayadat (media type), Kamaraj Foundation (non-governmental organization), Jamaat-e-Islami Hind (political party), Jamaat President Maulaha Syed Umari and Baba Ramdev (religious figures/politicians), Khap Panchayat (state government agency).
5.	Social	Jules (anonymous citizen), Supha Moti Bhavnani (author/celebrity), Global Day of Rage (campaign), Allen Solly (company/brand), Tanmay Sahay (economist/merchant/banker), Harish Iyer (gay activist), Department of AIDS Control (health service provider), Justice A P Shah (judge), Shazad Syed Hai (LGBTQ person), Humsafar Trust Founder Ashok Row Kavi (gay activist and non-governmental organization representative), The Times of India, (media type), Planet Romeo (online social media tool), Vadodara BJP MP Balkrishna Shukla (politician), Aam Aadmi Party (political party), Tamil Nadu (state government), Samira (teacher).	Facebook (online social media tool), Kamaraj Foundation (non-governmental organization), BJP President Rajnath Singh and Baba Ramdev (religious figures/politicians).

Table 2: Examples of supportive and non-supportive AGENTS for each of the five information categories (i.e., economic, educational, legal, political, and social) based on occurrences in the online news articles published in *The Times of India* during 11/14/2013-01/14/2014.

organizations (87.5%); 24/25 online social media tools (96%); and 16/20 state/central government agencies (80%). AGENT types that were not supportive of LGBTQ people and/or that approved the legally-sanctioned gay ban included: 17/25 (68%) political parties/political organizations and 30/70 religious figures/politicians (42.86%). **Table 2** provides specific examples of supportive and non-supportive AGENTS for each of the five information categories.

Discussion

The analysis of online news articles in this study showed the importance of the economic, educational, legal, political, and social information categories. Since there were a significantly greater number of supporters compared to non-supporters, libraries in India should take a multipronged approach to tap into the supportive AGENTS in each domain, as well as find strategies to convince non-supporter AGENTS to change their resistance towards LGBTQ concerns.

A large number of the non-supportive AGENT types included political parties and religious figures. The intertwining nature of religious and political news information is revealing. It shows the nexus between religious and political leaders in India where they wear interchangeable hats to influence the public, secure their voter base, occupy public positions, and create unfair laws to serve their agendas. Librarians have to educate the public about the self-serving agenda of politicians and religious leaders in India who misuse their power to create and manipulate archaic laws that marginalize the LGBTQ population (and others) by maintaining the status quo[75]. Librarians should also address how these stakeholders appeal to so-called "mainstream" points of view and perspectives about culture, tradition, identity, behavior, and acceptable or unacceptable social norms and beliefs[76].

Identifying the geographic locations as rural or urban for each article in the five information categories provided a situational context for the reported news. **Table 3** summarizes the number of rural and urban references based on associated words (e.g., village, city) found in the articles. Some contained both rural and urban references. Even if the news article contained multiple references to either rural or urban categories, it was counted only once for that category. Overall, there were fewer rural references in the news articles under study. Out of 234 total references, only 40 were in rural settings (17.09%) while 194 were in urban settings (82.91%). To highlight potential library alliances in both the environments, the authors selected specific quotations of supportive and non-supportive AGENTS identified in the news from rural and urban contexts in the economic, educational, legal, political, and social categories. The themes of nearly all issues that emerged in the analysis and the potential library alliances were relevant across both geographical settings. Also, there was often an intertwining of news presented in the five categories (e.g., political related to legal in a particular narrative, etc.).

Sr. No.	Information Category	No. of References	Rural References	Urban References	Total Rural and Urban References
1.	Economic	7	1 (12.5%)	7 (87.5%)	8
2.	Educational	25	6 (21.43%)	22 (78.57%)	28
3.	Legal	53	8 (14.82%)	46 (85.18%)	54
4.	Political	59	10 (16.95%)	49 (83.05%)	59
5.	Social	90	15 (17.65%)	70 (82.35%)	85
	Total	234	40 (17.09%)	194 (82.91%)	234

Table 3: Rural and urban references for each of the five information categories (i.e., economic, educational, legal, political, and social) based on occurrences in the online news articles published in *The Times of India* during 11/14/2013-01/14/2014.

Library Queering Alliances in Rural Areas

Table 4 presents select news quotations in rural environments representative of supportive and non-supportive AGENTS for each of the five information categories and potential library alliances to further LGBTQ equality. At the economic level, libraries can partner with LGBTQ (or LGBTQ-friendly) political candidates and the LGBTQ ally community in rural areas to develop a stronger financial infrastructure and resources to help these candidates raise money that they lack because of who they are and/or because of their support of LGBTQ causes. Libraries can develop cost-effective training workshops for campaigning and fundraising to teach LGBTQ candidates how to gain the support of the rural population. These may be considered controversial since the library profession is politically divided about promoting certain candidates over others. Poverty is a major problem in India in general, and in particular for LGBTQ people in the villages. Lack of financial independence and fear of being disowned by their families after being "outed" keeps LGBTQ individuals in the closet. Many experience poor and impoverished life conditions in rural environments. Rural libraries can develop alliances with financial planners and businesses that are seeking a skilled labor force to train LGBTQ people to further their career growth, job opportunities, and financial security.

The educational mission of libraries is of primary importance in rural settings to further partnering efforts (e.g., awareness training and developing materials) with institutions, government agencies, community organizations, and others, to remove ignorance, stigma, and cultural taboo surrounding the topic of homosexuality in India. This is of utmost urgency especially for health information support services in the context of HIV/AIDS and outreach to vulnerable communities (including LGBTQ people) in rural settings where such information and understanding may be lacking.

Partnering with progressive lawyers, judges, and other legal representatives to provide access to correct legal information and offering programs, forums, workshops, seminars, etc. for dialogue, discussion, and exchange of information with legal specialists on LGBTQ issues is another area of work for rural libraries in India. It is also important to provide legal options to resist and punish bullying, harassment, and intimidation by the police and others, in order to protect LGBTQ people in rural environments. Rural libraries can also partner with politicians, religious leaders, progressive psychologists, lawyers, health professionals, and others, to create greater awareness and respect for transgender/

Information Category Listed Alphabetically Supportive or Non-Supportive	Select Quotation Example(s) from an Online News Article and AGENT Identified
ECONOMIC Non-Supportive	"Swadeshi economics guru S Gurumurthy said there was a need to "preserve the Indian way of life", which involves a family and a miserly housewife at the core of it." [SJM delegates praise SC ruling, by TNN, 12/14/13 11:18 AM IST]. AGENT: Economist S Gurumurthy.
Potential Library Partners(s): LGBTQ patron community; Financial planners.	
Potential Library Alliance(s): 1) Provide career prospect opportunities and job openings for LGBTQ patron community that struggle for financial stability owing to family disownment; 2) Offer financial planning workshops for impoverished LGBTQ people, couples, and their families to improve life conditions.	
EDUCATIONAL Supportive	"Sitting in his two bedroom apartment, Anis recounts at length his growing up as a person with a different sexual orientation in the small provincial town of Chandernagore. "There was an unspoken 'blanket ban' on anything related to sex or sexuality; discussing same sex orientation was out of the question," he told TOI. He realized that he was different from his peers during his early teens. Unable to voice his concerns or ask for help, he turned to books." [Elderly parents knock on SC door for gay son's rights, by Sinjini Chanda, TNN, 12/18/13 04:59 AM IST] AGENT: LGBTQ people.
Potential Library Partners(s): LGBTQ and ally community; Educational institutions.	
Potential Library Alliance(s): 1) Partner with educational institutions to develop materials that address ignorance and internalized homophobia in LBGT people who are experiencing socio-psychological harm; 2) Provide "safe" space programs to foster communication and interactions between LGBTQ people to overcome fear of social and cultural persecution.	
LEGAL Supportive	"The couple's lawyer Durkesh Bopan, said, "The judge in the Gurgaon court had asked them to declare that they wanted to live together by choice and were not being coerced into doing so. They signed the affidavit and even their families didn't object to it. I met the couple as recently as April this year and they are living happily." [Kin's acceptance above SC verdict, by Maria Akram, TNN, 12/18/13 03:28 AM IST]. AGENT: Lawyer Durkesh Bopan.
Potential Library Partner(s): Progressive lawyers, judges, and other representatives in the legal community.	

	Potential Library Alliance(s): 1) Host progressive-minded lawyers and judges to provide access to correct legal information and support (e.g., on coming out implications, human rights research, etc.); 2) Programming of forums, workshops, seminars, etc. for dialogue, discussion, and exchange of information by legal specialists.
POLITICAL Non-Supportive	"An MLA from Sohna assembly constituency, Dharamvir is the first Congress leader to oppose the idea of protecting homosexuals." [Review Section 377 move, Hooda aide to Sonia Gandhi, 12/17/13 06:45 AM IST, by Manveer Saini, TNN, 12/17/13 06:45 AM IST]. AGENT: Chief Parliamentary Secretary Dharamvir Singh.
	Potential Library Partner(s): Progressive politicians and religious leaders.
	Potential Library Alliance: 1) Challenge politicians and religious leaders who blame the "advent" of homosexuality on outside influences rather than a natural occurrence within India ("not part of our culture"); 2) Create awareness of accurate and authoritative information sources that homosexuality is not an aberration but a reality in all cultures; 3) Make ancient texts and mythologies replete with homosexuality references available for everyone to read; 4) Make access to religious resources so LGBTQ patrons can have a platform for debate; 5) Host workshops for LGBTQ activists and religious/political leaders to dialogue and debate.
SOCIAL Supportive	"The duo was among 19 parents of members of the LGBTQ community from across the country who were petitioners in favour of upholding the 2009 Delhi High Court order scrapping Article 377 that criminalizes homosexuality." [Elderly parents knock on SC door for gay son's rights, by Sinjini Chanda, TNN, 12/18/13 04:59 AM IST]. AGENT: Parents Pramatha Nath & Vijaylakshmi Ray Chaudhuri.
	Potential Library Partner(s): Progressive parents of LGBTQ people.
	Potential Library Alliance(s): 1) Host forums for parents and families of LGBTQ people to share their stories of support via multi-media and in multiple regional languages.

Table 4: Select representative quotations from rural environments indicating the supportive and non-supportive agents for each of the five information categories (i.e., economic, educational, legal, political, and social; and potential library alliances to further LGBTQ equality.

transsexual people. Hosting helplines, offering workshops, creating authoritative resources, and serving as facilitators to bring various stakeholders together and improve the conditions experienced by trans people in India's villages is much needed.

Libraries should also challenge homophobic politicians/religious leaders who blame the "advent" of homosexuality on outside influences, rather than recognizing it as a natural occurrence within India. Rural libraries can make accurate and authoritative information sources available to provide evidence showing homosexuality is a reality rather than an aberration in all cultures, while collecting resources that document its occurrence in India's rich culture, myths, and history.

At the social level, providing a platform (virtual and non-virtual) for LGBTQ people, progressive-minded individuals (e.g., accepting parents of LGBTQ people), groups, and others to share their stories of support to LBGTQ people in multiple languages, is a relevant direction for libraries to pursue in India's rural environment. The need to establish multi-language platforms is especially relevant in India with its twenty-two major languages (listed in the Eighth Schedule of the Indian Constitution), written in thirteen different scripts with over 720 dialects.

Library Queering Alliances in Urban Areas

Table 5 presents select news quotations in urban environments representative of supportive and non-supportive AGENTS for each of the five information categories and potential library alliances to further LGBTQ causes. Most LGBTQ issues and library efforts in rural settings are applicable in urban India as well. Further, libraries can promote LGBTQ tourism in urban areas to support economic growth. They can develop information on "safe" travel destinations, help LGBTQ-friendly businesses distribute marketing materials via social media and print resources, and teach LGBTQ users information literacy skills to research LGBTQ-friendly companies. Libraries have to also create awareness in the public that the image of India as a homophobic culture is bad for the country at a cultural level, as well as for economic reasons.

As in India's rural areas, urban libraries have to partner with educational institutions, health care service providers, progressive psychologists, local, state, and central government welfare programs, and others, in support of LGBTQ people. These alliances can: 1) make accurate and authoritative LGBTQ-related information accessible (through online and print resources); 2) develop the library as a safe physical and online space for LGBTQ patrons to meet and discuss their concerns with each other and with experts (e.g., legal specialists, health care practitioners, etc.); 3) sponsor LGBTQ-supportive programming and events (workshops, seminars, classes, impromptu clinics, counseling centers); 4) mobilize librarians as community engagement activists who venture outside of the physical library domains, proactively bringing awareness of LGBTQ concerns to schools, colleges, and universities.

Urban libraries can also provide a forum for lawyers and judges to speak on behalf of LGBTQ rights and clarify the confusion brought about by the decriminalization of gay sex followed by the re-instatement of the gay sex ban. They can provide access to accurate and authoritative legal information and support, collect LGBTQ stories and legal grievances, and explore options to pursue legal actions (e.g., ordinances and petitions to challenge the law).

At the political level, urban libraries can create greater positive visibility for LGBTQ issues by partnering with progressive politicians and religious leaders, news media, prominent public figures, and others to: 1) develop forums for debate between supportive and non-supportive leaders on LGBTQ issues; 2) provide platforms where LGBTQ people can hear speeches delivered by prominent political figures in their support; 3) serve as online and offline archives for access to appropriate information resources that counter regressive politics and homophobic responses at various levels (e.g., workplace discrimination).

Urban libraries can play a pivotal role by partnering with like-minded agencies to develop socialization opportunities that make families and friends of LGBTQ people and others aware of accurate LGBTQ-related information and experiences; create social forums that help the general

Information Category Listed Alphabetically Supportive or Non-Supportive	Select Quotation Example(s) from an Online News Article and AGENT Identified
ECONOMIC Supportive	"Describing the judgment as "appalling", Indyapink — India's first travel company providing customized packages for the LGBTQ community director Sanjay Malhotra said, "This is going to be disastrous for the tourism sector. We would have become one of the top most destinations in the world with so much to offer. But now we cannot assure our customers acceptability, security and the freedom to travel as they want." [SC verdict may sound a death knell for fledgling LGBTQ tourism sector, by Himanshi Dhawan, TNN, 12/14/13 10:14 AM IST]. AGENT: Company/brand Indyapink founder Sanjay Malhotra.
Potential Library Partners(s): LGBTQ-friendly businesses, LGBTQ patron community.	
Potential Library Alliance(s): 1) Promote LGBTQ tourism by developing information on "safe" destinations; 2) Enable LGBTQ-friendly businesses to develop marketing materials via social media and print; 3) Provide user information literacy training on LGBTQ-friendly companies.	
EDUCATIONAL Non-Supportive	"A city-based activist fighting against AIDS has filed a police complaint, demanding the registration of an FIR (First Information Report) against Bollywood celebrities and NGOs vouching for the rights of homosexuals after the Supreme Court reinstated the ban on gay sex." [Book actors for backing gays: Activist, by TNN, 12/13/13 06:34 AM IST]. AGENT: HIV-AIDS awareness advocate Harit Kumar.
Potential Library Partner(s): Educational institutions; Health care service providers; Progressive psychologists; Local, state, and central government welfare programs.	
Potential Library Alliance: 1) Create educational delivery programs and accurate and authoritative brochure materials to address ignorance and fear about HIV/AIDS; 2) Act as health clinics where patients can get information and talk to physicians anonymously; 3) Act as community information referral agents to LGBTQ-friendly qualified physicians.	
LEGAL Non-Supportive	"Two months before the Supreme Court ruling that re-criminalized gay sex, the home ministry for the first time had asked the National Crime Records Bureau (NCRB) to collect data on offences registered under the Section 377 (unnatural sex) of the Indian Penal Code (IPC), people arrested and prosecuted." [NCRB to collect data on gay sex crimes from Jan, by Deeptiman Tiwary, TNN, 12/14/13 10:14 AM IST]. AGENT: National Crime Records Bureau (NCRB).

Potential Library Partner(s): LGBTQ people; Legal specialists.	
Potential Library Alliance(s): 1) Provide access to accurate and authoritative legal information and support; 2) Collect LGBTQ stories and grievances; 4) Explore options to pursue legal actions (e.g., ordinances and petitions to challenge the law).	
POLITICAL Supportive	"Manvendra Singh Go'nil, founder of the Lakshya Trust and known as the first Indian royal to come out as gay, said the huge turnout was heartening. "There is great solidarity within the LGBTQ movement," he said. "We may have differences of opinion on many things but at times like these, I'm very proud of how united we are. All we're asking is our right to live equally like other citizens." [Mumbai joins the global wave, rallies around its LGBTQ citizens, by Mithila Phadke, TNN, 12/16/13 02:27 AM IST]. AGENT: Manvendra Singh Gohil, founder of the Lakshya Trust and known as the first Indian royal to come out as gay.
Potential Library Partner(s): Religious leaders and politicians; LGBTQ celebrities.	
Potential Library Alliance(s): 1) Provide a forum for religious leaders and politicians to debate LGBTQ issues; 2) Provide platforms where sexual minorities can hear moving speeches delivered by prominent political figures. 3) Serve as an online and offline archive providing access to appropriate information resources that counter regressive politics and homophobic responses; 4) Promote political advocacy and mobilization of support from LGBTQ people and allies; 5) Become a safe political space with services that help tear the cloak of invisibility; 6) Provide information support assistance to LGBTQ candidates.	
SOCIAL Non-Supportive	"The Supreme Court had given the right verdict…There is a festival going on here. All the cinemas go against the moral culture of India," he said." [SJM delegates praise SC ruling, by TNN, 12/14/13 11:18 AM IST]. AGENT: P Gopinathan, Gandhi Smaraka Nidhi Chairman.
Potential Library Partner(s): Progressive celebrities; Educational institutions.	
Potential Library Alliance: 1) Use social media and print resources on the coming out process; 2) Host programs with well-known artists and politicians discussing their support of LGBTQ people; 3) Tap into film as medium to educate the masses; 4) Provide access to classes on use of social media to make international connections	

Table 5: Select representative quotations from urban environments indicating the supportive and non-supportive agents for each of the five information categories (i.e., economic, educational, legal, political, and social) and potential library alliances to further LGBTQ equality.

public recognize LGBTQ experiences (especially young people); and, promote ties with the global LGBTQ community.

Conclusion

It is pertinent for libraries to engage in coalition building with key stakeholders at the economic, educational, legal, political, and social levels that leads towards open advocacy based on the reality of being located in a country in which homosexuality is outlawed. Public libraries are vulnerable to constraint and control by the government because they are dependent on it for financial support. Strategic alliances with newspapers and news agencies are essential to see that they cover stories of governmental interference that curtail civil liberties of LGBTQ people (or libraries that support them) and of arm-twisting by political and religious leaders. Alliances with news companies can also further lobbying efforts to resist governmental threats of reduction in funding or their pressure tactics to force libraries to "out" their LGBTQ patrons or recipients of information as criminals.

The various cultural, economic, political, linguistic, and social influences, among others, have uniquely shaped and determined which aspects of library work are considered traditionally important in different geographic regions in India and other parts of the world.[77] We also need to consider the diversity of libraries in India in terms of the type of library (e.g., public library, college library, etc.), the functional aspect of information-related work (e.g., electronic resources, HIV/AIDS information services, information literacy skills, etc.), regional distribution (e.g., libraries in rural vs. urban areas), and other aspects. It would be a disservice to the 21st century library movement in India if the vastly different and uniquely historical set of socio-technological circumstances, regionally-shaped opportunities and challenges, and their complex interactions in the contemporary context were ignored, overlooked, or minimized.[78] Libraries in India have to establish their own trajectory in their varied manifestations and not necessarily replicate the limitations and successes of library growth and development in the Western world (particularly the United States), or blindly adopt their program conceptualizations, policies, and strategies.[79] The same is true regarding the limited role of libraries as passive bystanders (as opposed to active agents) in the United States[80] and their reliance on the argument of taking a "neutral" stance against a fuller engagement in social justice work.[81] Many scholars and practitioners have been critical of libraries in the United States because of this curtailed passive role[82] which has furthered the disenfranchisement of populations during their long history,[83] controlled as they were by an "internally-and-externally restrictive socio-cultural context."[84]

In India, the limited role of libraries in the nation's history and in the public's perception about them can significantly be altered if they chose to adopt a more progressive, unified, and user-centered focus in their social justice efforts and in the provision of services for communities on the margins of society.[85] This includes LGBTQ people, and this chapter advocates moving forward in this regard by identifying alliances and partnerships that libraries can develop to help them carve out a unique niche for the LIS professions in India. The authors believe that getting involved in social justice work on behalf of sexual minorities (and disenfranchised others) in India will provide a potential impetus that will help get libraries out of the rut that they are in. Representing sexual minorities and others in the civic realm may positively change the public's opinion about them in a positive manner. It may also further opportunities of community building, community development, funding and resource allocations, outcome-based assessment and evaluation, and others, that will help the LIS professions move forward and grow towards a greater impact and role in Indian society.

Acknowledgements

The authors thank Kathryn Brooks for her work on the endnotes developed in this chapter.

Endnotes

1. Mark S. Bonham, *Champions: Biographies of Global LGBTQ Pioneers* (Toronto: Bonham & Co. Inc, 2014); Bharat Mehra and LaVerne Gray, *'Don't Say Gay' in the State of Tennessee: Libraries as Transgender, and Queer (LGBTQ) People* (Lyon, France: Proceedings of the World Library and Information Congress, 2014).

2. In their seminal work entitled *Heterosexism: An Ethical Challenge* (New York: SUNY Press,1993) Patricia Beattie Jung and Ralph F. Smith define heterosexism as a system of attitudes, biases, and discrimination that privileges and considers superior opposite-sex sexuality and relationships.

3. Bharat Mehra, Eric Haley and Dylan Lane, "Culturally Appropriate Information Support Services for Lesbian, Gay, Bisexual and Transgender (LGBTQ) South Asians: Representing Multiple Shades of Identity Based on Sexual Orientation and Ethnicity," in *Expanding the Circle: Creating an Inclusive Environment in Higher Education for LGBTQ Students and Studies*, ed. John C. Hawley (New York: SUNY Press, 2015); UN News Center, "UN Issues First Report on Human Rights of Gay and Lesbian People" (2011).

4. Nirnimesh Kumar, "Delhi High Court Strikes Down Section 377 of IPC," *The Hindu: Online Edition of India's National Newspaper* (July 3, 2009).

5. Gardiner Harris, "India's Supreme Court Restores an 1861 Law Banning Gay Sex," *New York Times*, December 11, 2013.

6. Shivananda Khan, "Culture, Sexualities, and Identities: Men Who Have Sex with Men in India," *Journal of Homosexuality* 40, no. 3/4 (2001).

7. The World Bank Group, *Data: Rural Population (% of Total Population)* (June 1, 2015).

8. PTI, "60% of India's Rural Population Lives on Less Than Rs. 35 a Day," *Firstpost: India News* (May 3, 2012).

9. Knowledge@Wharton, "Public Policy: Why Housing Isn't Enough to Create Sustainable Communities" (Philidelphia, PA: The Wharton School, August 23, 2007).

10. Govindan Parayil, *Political Economy and Information Capitalism in India: Digital Divide, Development and Equity* (New York: Palgrave Macmillan,

2006); Jean Dreze and Sen Amartya Kumar, I*ndia: Development and Participation* (Oxford, Oxford University Press, 2002).

11. Sebastien Lifshitz, *The Invisibles: Vintage Portraits of Love and Pride. Gay Couples in the Early Twentieth Centruy* (New York: Rizzoli International Publications, 2014).

12. T.S. Sathyanarayana Rao and K.S. Jacob, "The Reversal on Gay Rights in India," *Indian Journal of Psychiatry* 56, no. 1 (2014): 1-2.

13. Maitrayee Ghosh, "The Public Library System in India: Challenges and Opportunities," *Library Review* 54, no. 3 (2005): 180-191; National Knowledge Commission, 2008. *Report to the Nation 2007* (New Delhi: Government of India).

14. Bharat Mehra and Ramesh Srinivasan, "The Library-Community Convergence Framework for Community Action: Libraries as Catalysts of Social Change," *Libri: International Journal of Libraries and Information Services* 57, no. 3 (2007): 123-139.

15. Rakesh K. Bhatt and S. Majumdar, "Libraries Through the Ages in India: Sojourn from Palm Leaf to Palmtop," in *Libraries in the Early 21st Century: An International Perspective* (Volume 2), ed. Ravindra N. Sharma (Berlin: Walter de Gruyter, 2012).

16. Paul T. Jaeger, Ursula Gorham, John Carlo Bertot, and Lindsay C. Sarin, *Public Libraries, Public Policies, and Political Processes* (Plymouth: Rowman & Littlefield, 2014).

17. Bharat Mehra and Donna Braquet, "Marriage between Participatory Leadership and Action Research to Advocate Benefits Equality for Lesbian, Gay, Bisexual, and Transgender People: An Extended Human Rights Role in Library and Information Science," in *Leadership in Academic Libraries Today: Connecting Theory to Practice*, ed. Bradford Lee Eden and Jody Condit Fagan (Toronto: Scarecrow Press, 2014).

18. Bimal Kumar Dutta, *Libraries and Librarianship of Ancient and Medieval India* (Delhi: Atma Ram, 1970);

Jashu Patel and Krishan Kumar, *Libraries and Librarianship in India* (Westport, CT: Greenwood Press, 2001).

19. Rakesh K. Bhatt, *History and Development of Libraries in India* (New Delhi: Mittal Publications, 1995).

20. M.P. Satija, "Doctoral Research in Library and Information Science in India: Some Observations and Comments," *Libri: International Journal of Libraries and Information Services* 49, no. 4 (1999).

21. R. Bhattacharjee, "Public Services in India: Systems and Deficiencies," *Public Libraries Section – Country Report: India* (IFLA, 2002).

22. Eugene Garfield, "Current Comments: A Tribute to S.R. Ranganathan, the Father of Indian Library Science. Part 1. Life and Works," *Essays of an Information Scientist* 7, no. 6 (1984): 37-44.

23. Abulfazal Kabir, "Ranganathan: A Universal Librarian," *Journal of Educational Media & Library Sciences* 40 (2003); Anand P. Srivastava, *Ranganathan: A Pattern Maker* (New Delhi: Metropolitan Book Co., 1977); Shiyali R Ranganathan, *The Five Laws of Library Science* (Bombay: Asia Publishing House, 1963).

24. Krishan Kumar and Jaideep Sharma, "Library and Information Science Education in India: A Historical Perspective," *DESIDOC Journal of Library and Information Technology* 30, no. 5 (2010).

25. Bijoy P. Barua, "Raja Ram Mohan Roy Library Foundation and Library movement in India" (Delhi: Indian Library Association, 1994); M. Jagdish, *Histories of Libraries and Librarianship in Modern India Since 1850* (Delhi: Atma Ram, 1979); R. Bhattacharjee, "Role of Raja Rammohan Roy Library Foundation in the Promotion of Public Library Movement in India," *Herald of Library Science* 30 (1999).

26. Bharat Mehra, Devendra Potnis and Jennifer Morden, "An Exploratory Study of the Nature and Composition of Current Library and Information Science Programs in Indian State Universities," *Perspectives in International Librarianship* 2012, no. 1; S.P. Singh, "Library and Information Science Education in India: Issues and Trends," *Malaysian Journal of Library & Information Science* 8, no. 2 (2003).

27. Swapan Kumar Patra, and Prakash Chand, "Library and Information Science Research in India: A Bibliometric Study," *Annuals of Library and Information Studies* 53, no. 4 (2006).

28. Zahid Ashraf Wani, "Development of Public Libraries in India," *Library Philosophy and Practice* (2008).

29. Shiva Kanaujia Sukula, "Indigenous Database Development in Indian Research and Development Library and Information Centres," *Online Information Review* 29, no. 2 (2005).

30. Anandh Jayaraman, Srinivas Sangani, Madhavi Ganapathiraju and Narayanaswamy Balakrishnan, "Proceedings Tamil Internet Conference (The Electronic Library: An Indian Scenario)," *Library Philosophy and Practice* 5, no. 2 (2004).

31. Namrata M. Joshi, "Digital Library and Library Networks in India," *Global Journal of Academic Librarianship* 3, no. 1 (2014); Narayanaswamy Balakrishnan, Raj Reddy, Madhavi Ganapathiraju and Vamshi Ambati, "Digital Library of India: A Testbed for Indian Language Research," *TCDL Bulletin* 3, no. 1 (2006).

32. B.D. Kumbar, "Growth and Development of Public Library System in India with Special Reference to Karnataka" (2005).

33. Ajit K. Pyati, "Public Library Revitalization in India: Hopes, Challenges, and New Visions," *First Monday* 14, no. 7 (2009).

34. National Knowledge Commission, *Libraries, Gateways to Knowledge: A Roadmap for Revitalization* (New Delhi: Government of India, 2007).

35. Ajit K. Pyati, "Public Library Revitalization in India: Hopes, Challenges, and New Visions," *First Monday* 14, no. 7 (2009).

36. Bharat Mehra, "Growth Opportunities, and Challenges Facing Indian Librarianship in Developing a Knowledge Society in the 21st Century: Reflections and Insights," Keynote Speech, Souvenir of the 57th Indian Library Association Annual Conference, Mangalore, Karnataka, 2012.

37. Ibid, p. 20.

38. R. Seth, "Storehouses of Knowledge to Educate the Masses: The Indian Library System – A Present Day Scenario," *Frankfurter Buchmesse* 58, no. 9 (2006).

39. Patrick Hayden, *Philosophy of Human Rights: Readings in Context* (St Paul: Paragon House, 2001).

40. Jason Burke, "UN Asks India to Review Gay Sex Ban," *The Guardian* (2013).

41. Soutik Biswas, "India Top Court Reinstates Gay Sex Ban," *BBC News* (2011).

42. Alankaar Sharma, "Decriminalizing Queer Sexualitie s in India: A Multiple Streams Analysis," *Social Policy and Society* 7, no. 4 (2008); Nadita Narayan, *Fundamental Rights of Sexual Minorities and Section 377 of IPC: A Need to Revisit the Provision in the Light of Indeterminacy of the Definition of "Against the Order of Nature"* (Saarbrucken: Lambert Academic Publishing, 2014).

43. Matthew Waites, "Human Rights, Sexual Orientation and the Generation of Childhoods: Analyzing the Partial Decriminalization of 'Unnatural Offences' in India," *International Journal of Human Rights* 14, no. 6 (2010).

44. NDTV, "Is Supreme Court's Verdict on Gay Sex a Violation of Human Rights?" *NDTV* (2013).

45. Bharat Mehra and Lisette Hernandez, "Libraries as Agents of Human Rights Protection and Social Justice on Behalf of Sexual Minorities in India: An Action-Based Manifesto for Progressive Change," in *Perspectives on Libraries as Institutions of Human Rights and Social Justice*, ed. U. Gorham, N.G. Taylor, and P.T. Jaeger (Bingley, UK: Emerald, 2016).

46. Gwynn Guilford, "India's Latest Ban Against Gay Sex Has its Origin in a Five-Century-Old British Power Struggle," *Quartz* (2013).

47. Simon Clarke, "Culture and Identity," in *SAGE Handbook of Cultural Analysis*, ed. Tony Bennett and John Frow (London: SAFE Publications Ltd., 2008).

48. Asia Pacific Forum, "ACJ Reference: Human Rights, Sexual Orientation and Gender Identity, Background Paper," paper presented at the 15th Annual Meeting of the Asian Pacific Forum of National Human Rights Institutions, Bali, Indonesia, August 3-5, 2010.

49. Nita Bhalla, "Activists Cautious Over New Government's Stance on Gay Sex," *Reuters Edition* (2014).

50. Suranjana Tewari, "India's Gays, Lesbians 'Suddenly Afraid' After Court Ruling," *NBCNEWS* (2014).

51. Wendy Doniger and Martha Craven Nussbaum, *Pluralism and Democracy in India: Debating the Hindu Right* (Oxford: Oxford University Press, 2015).

52. Sumata Banerjee, "Civilizing the BJP," *Economic & Political Weekly* 40, no. 29 (2005); Yogendra K. Malik and V.B. Singh, "Bharatiya Janata Part: An Alternative to the Congress (I)?" *Asian Survey* (1992).

53. Walter K. Andersen and Damle D. Shridhar, *The Brotherhood in Saffron: The Rashtriya Swayamsevak Sangh and Hindu Revivalism* (Delhi: Vistaar Publications, 1987).

54. Ali Riaz, *Religion and Politics in South Asia* (New York: Routledge, 2010).

55. Isaac S. Fish, "Gay Cruising in Modi's India," *FP* (2015).

56. Denis LeBlanc, "At Least 587 LGBTI Arrested in India in 2014," *Erasing 76 Crimes* (2015).

57. Chicago Chronicle, "It Is the Govt.'s Responsibility to Protect LGBTQ Rights, Says Harsh Vardhan," *Chicago Chronicle* (2014).

58. DPA, "India's LGBTQ Community Outraged Over Government-Planned Re-education Centers in Goa," *HAARETZ* (2015).

59. Deepshikha Ghosh, "Homosexuality a Natural Gift: Goa Chief Minister's Counter to Minister's Gaffe," *NDTV* (2015).

60. Amartya Sen, *The Argumentative Indian: Writings on Indian History, Culture and Identity* (New York: Picador, 2006).

61. BBC News, "India Outrage Over Goa Minister's Plan to 'Cure' Gays," *BBC NEWS* (2015).

62. ANI, "Misquoted, Never Said Section 377 May Be Scrapped: Gowda," *The New Indian Express* (2015).

63. Audit Bureau of Circulations, "Details of Language Wise Most Circulated Dailies for the Audit Period July-December 2013" (2015).

64. Newswatch.in, 2011.

65. Trust Research Advisory, "India's Most Trusted Brands 2014" (2014).

66. Devdutt Pattanaik, *Shikhandi: And Other Tales They Don't Tell You* (New Delhi: Zubaan/Penguin Books, 2014).

67. Gayatri Reddy, *With Respect to Sex: Negotiating Hijra Identity in South Asia* (Chicago: University of Chicago Press, 2005).

68. The Telegraph, "'Third Sex' Finds a Place on Indian Passport Forms," *The Telegraph* (2005).

69. BBC News, "Pakistani Eunuchs to have Distinct Gender," *BBC News* (2009).

70. NDTV, "Transgenders are the 'Third Gender' Rules Supreme Court," *NDTV* (2014).

71. Lalit Dandona, Rakhi Dandona, Juan Pablo Gutierrez, Anil G. Kumar, Sam McPherson, Stefano M. Bertozzi, and the ASCI FFP Study Team, "Sex Behaviours of Men Who Have Sex with Men and Risk of HIV in Andhra Predesh India," *AIDS: Official Journal of the International AIDS Society* 19, no. 6 (2005).

72. Stefan Baral, Frangiscos Sifakis, Farley Cleghorn, and Chris Beyrer, "Elevated Risk for HIV Infection Among Men Who Have Sex with Sex in Low-and-Middle-Income Countries 2000-2006: A Systematic Review," *PLOS Medicine* 4, no. 12 (2007)

73. Ravi Kumar Verma and Martine Collumbien, "Homosexual Activity Among Rural Indian Men: Implications for HIV Prevention," *AIDS: Official Journal of the International AIDS Society* 18, no. 13 (2004).

74. Bharat Mehra and Lisette Hernandez, "Libraries as Agents of Human Rights Protection and Social Justice on Behalf of Sexual Minorities in India: An Action-Based Manifesto for Progressive Change," in *Perspectives on Libraries as Institutions of Human Rights and Social Justice* (Bingley, UK: Emerald, 2016), 147-82.

75. George Miles, *Foundations for the LPC 2014-2015* (Oxford: Oxford University Press, 2014).

76. Amnesty International and Desmond Tutu, *Freedom: Stories Celebrating the Universal Declaration of Human Rights* (New York: Broadway Books, 2011).

77. Bharat Mehra, "What is the Value of Social Justice in Pakistan's Library and Information Science Professions? Guest Editorial," *Pakistan Journal of Information Management and Libraries* 14, no. 1 (2014).

78. Barun Kumar Sahu, *Unwritten Laws of Indian Bureaucracy* (New Delhi: Pustak Mahal, 2004); Jeff Saperstein and Danial Rouach, *Creating Regional Wealth in the Innovation Economy: Models, Perspectives and Best Practices* (Upper Saddle River, NJ: FT Press, 2002); John Dickinson, *India: Its Government Under a Bureaucracy* (New York: General Books, 2009); Lila Mortezaie and Nader Naghshineh, "A Comparative Case Study of Graduate Courses in Library and Information Studies in the UK, USA, India and Iran: Lessons for Iranian LIS Professionals," *Library Review* 51, no. 1 (2002).

79. Bharat Mehra, Devendra Potnis and Jennifer Morden, "An Exploratory Study of the Nature and Composition of Current Library and Information Science Programs in Indian State Universities," *Perspectives in International Librarianship* 2012, no. 1.

80. Bharat Mehra, "Introduction," Library Trends: Social Justice in *Library and Information Science & Services* 64, no. 1 (2015).

81. Alison M. Lewis, ed,. *Questioning Library Neutrality: Essays from Progressive Librarian* (Duluth, MN: Library Juice Press, 2008).

82. Bharat Mehra and Robert J. Sandusky, "LIS Students as Community Partners in Elective Course: Applying Community-based Action Research to Meet the Needs of Underserved Populations," in *Service Learning: Linking Library Education and Practice,* ed. Loriene Roy, Kelly Jensen, and Alex Hershey Meyers (Chicago: American Library Association, 2009); Toni Samek, *Librarianship and Human Rights: A 21st Century Guide* (Atlanta: Neal-Schuman Publishers, 2007).

83. Bharat Mehra and Rebecca Davis, "A Strategic Diversity Manifesto for Public Libraries in the 21st Century," *New Library World* 116, no. 1/2 (2015).

84. Bharat Mehra, Kevin Rioux, and Kendra S. Albright, "Social Justice in Library and Information Science," in *Encyclopedia of Library and Information Sciences* (2009).

85. Bharat Mehra, "Guest Editor's Introduction," *Qualitative and Quantitative Methods in Libraries Journal,* Special Issue 2014: Social Justice, Social Inclusion (2014).

Bibliography

Amnesty International and Desmond Tutu. *Freedom: Stories Celebrating the Universal Declaration of Human Rights.* New York: Broadway Books, 2011.

Andersen, Walter K., and Damle D. Shridhar. *The Brotherhood in Saffron: The Rashtriya Swayamsevak Sangh and Hindu Revivalism.* Delhi: Vistaar Publications, 1987.

ANI. "Misquoted, Never Said Section 377 May be Scrapped: Gowda." *The New Indian Express.* Last modified June 30, 2015. http://www.newindianexpress.com/nation/Misquoted-Never-Said-Section-377-May-be-Scrapped-Gowda/2015/06/30/article2894768.ece1.

Asia Pacific Forum. "ACJ Reference: Human Rights, Sexual Orientation and Gender Identity, Background Paper." Paper presented at the 15th Annual Meeting of the Asian Pacific Forum of National Human Rights Institutions, Bali, Indonesia, August 3-5, 2010. Accessed June 29, 2015. http://adityabondyopadhyay.webs.com/apps/documents/.

Audit Bureau of Circulations. "Details of Language Wise Most Circulated Dailies for the Audit Period July-December 2013." Accessed April 11, 2015. http://www.auditbureau.org/news/view/17.

Balakrishnan, Narayanaswamy, Raj Reddy, Madhavi Ganapathiraju, and Vamshi Ambati. "Digital Library of India: A Testbed for Indian Language Research." *TCDL Bulletin* 3, no. 1 (2006). Accessed June 29, 2015. http://www.ulib.org/conference/genpub/balakrishnan.html.

Banerjee, Sumanta. "Civilising the BJP." *Economic & Political Weekly* 40, no. 29 (2005): 3116-3119. Accessed April 13, 2015. http://www.jstor.org/discover/10.2307/4416896?uid=2&uid=4&sid=21106443682663.

Baral, Stefan, Frangiscos Sifakis, Farley Cleghorn, and Chris Beyrer. "Elevated Risk for HIV Infection among Men Who Have Sex with Men in Low-and-Middle-Income Countries 2000-2006: A Systematic Review." *PLOS Medicine* 4, no. 12 (2007): e339. Accessed April 16, 2015. http://journals.plos.org/plosmedicine/article?id=10.1371/journal.pmed.0040339.

Barua, Bijoy P. "Raja Ram Mohan Roy Library Foundation and Library Movement in India." Presented at 39th All India Library Conference, Delhi, Indian Library Association, 1994.

BBC News. "India Outrage Over Goa Minister's Plan to 'Cure' Gays." *BBC News*. Last modified January 13, 2015. http://www.bbc.com/news/world-asia-india-30791795.

BBC News. "Pakistani Eunuchs to have Distinct Gender." *BBC News*. Last modified December 23, 2009. http://news.bbc.co.uk/2/hi/south_asia/8428819.stm.

Bhalla, Nita. "Activists Cautious Over New Government's Stance on Gay Sex." *Reuters Edition*. Last modified May 19, 2014. http://in.reuters.com/article/2014/05/19/india-modi-gay-ban-idINKBN0DZ1K420140519.

Bhatt, Rakesh K. *History and Development of Libraries in India*. New Delhi: Mittal Publications, 1995.

Bhatt, Rakesh K. and S. Majumdar. "Libraries through the Ages in India: Sojourn from Palm Leaf to Palmtop." *Libraries in the Early 21st Century: An International Perspective* (Volume 2), 2012, edited by Ravindra N. Sharma, 235-274. Berlin: Walter de Gruyter, 2012.

Bhattacharjee, R. *Public Library Services in India: Systems and Deficiencies – Country Report: India*. International Federation of Library Associations and Institutions, 2002. Accessed November 30, 2008. http://www.ifla.org/VII/s8/annual/cr02-in.htm.

Bhattacharjee, R. "Role of Raja Rammohan Roy Library Foundation in the Promotion of Public Library Movement in India." *Herald of Library Science* 30 (1999): 1-2.

Biswas, Soutik. "India Top Court Reinstates Gay Sex Ban." *BBC News*. Last modified December 11, 2013. http://www.bbc.com/news/world-asia-india-25329065.

Bonham, Mark S. Champions: *Biographies of Global LGBTQQ Pioneers*. Toronto: Bonham & Co. Inc., 2014.

Burke, Jason. "UN Asks India to Review Gay Sex Ban." *The Guardian*. Last modified December 12, 2013. http://www.theguardian.com/world/2013/dec/12/un-asks-india-review-gay-sex-ban.

Chicago Chronicle. "It is the Govt.'s Responsibility to Protect LGBTQ Rights, Says Harsh Vardhan." *Chicago Chronicle*. Last modified July 17, 2014. http://www.chicagochronicle.com/index.php/sid/223864555.

Clarke, Simon. "Culture and Identity." *SAGE Handbook of Cultural Analysis*, edited by Tony Bennett and John Frow, 510-529. London: SAFE Publications Ltd., 2008.

Dandona, Lalit, Rakhi Dandona, Juan Pablo Gutierrez, Anil G. Kumar, Sam McPhersonm Stefano M. Bertozzi, and the ASCI FFP Study Team. "Sex Behaviour of Men Who Have Sex with Men and Risk of HIV in Andhra Pradesh, India." *AIDS: Official Journal of the International AIDS Society* 19, no. 6 (2005): 611-619. Accessed April 16, 2015. http://journals.lww.com/aidsonline/Fulltext/2005/04080/Sex_behaviour_of_men_who_have_sex_with_men_and.10.aspx.

Dickinson, John. *India: Its Government Under a Bureaucracy*. New York: General Books, 2009.

Doniger, Wendy, and Martha Craven Nussbaum. *Pluralism and Democracy in India: Debating the Hindu Right*. Oxford: Oxford University Press, 2015.

DPA. "India's LGBTQ Community Outraged Over Government-planned Re-education Centers in Goa." *HAARETZ*. Last modified January 13, 2015. http://www.haaretz.com/news/world/1.636812.

Dreze, Jean, and Amartya Kumar Sen. *India: Development and Participation*. Oxford: Oxford University Press, 2002.

Dutta, Bimal Kumar. *Libraries and Librarianship of Ancient and Medieval India*. Delhi: Atma Ram, 1970.

Fish, Isaac S. "Gay Cruising in Modi's India." *FP*. Last modified February 6, 2015. http://foreignpolicy.com/2015/02/06/gay_sex_cruising_modi_india/.

Garfield, Eugene. "Current Comments: A Tribute to S.R. Ranganathan, the Father of Indian Library Science. Part 1. Life and Works." *Essays of an Information Scientist* 7, no. 6. (1984): 37-44. Accessed October 31, 2010. http://www.garfield.library.upenn.edu/essays/v7p037y1984.pdf.

Ghosh, Deepshikha. "'Homosexuality a Natural Gift': Goa Chief Minister's Counter to Minister's Gaffe." *NDTV*. Last modified January 13, 2015. http://www.ndtv.com/india-news/homosexuality-a-natural-gift-goa-chief-ministers-counter-to-ministers-gaffe-726530.

Ghosh, Maitrayee. "The Public Library System in India: Challenges and Opportunities." *Library Review* 54, no. 3 (2005): 180-191. Accessed June 15, 2015. http://dx.doi.org/10.1108/00242530510588935.

Guilford, Gwynn. "India's Latest Ban Against Gay Sex Has its Origin in a Five-Century-Old British Power Struggle." *Quartz*. Last modified December 11, 2013. http://qz.com/156409/indias-latest-ban-against-gay-sex-has-its-origin-in-a-five-century-old-british-power-struggle/.

Hada, Kapil Singh, and Ram P. Bajpai. *Integrated Indian Public Library System*. Gurgaon, India: Partridge Publishing India, 2014.

Harris, Gardiner. "India's Supreme Court Restores an 1861 Law Banning Gay Sex." *The New York Times.* Last modified December 11, 2013. http://www.nytimes.com/2013/12/12/world/asia/court-restores-indias-ban-on-gay-sex.html.

Hayden, Patrick. *Philosophy of Human Rights: Readings in Context* (Paragon Issues in Philosophy). St. Paul: Paragon House, 2001.

Jaeger, Paul T., Ursula Gorham, John Carlo Bertot, and Lindsay C. Sarin. *Public Libraries, Public Policies, and Political Processes: Serving and Transforming Communities in Times of Economic and Political Constraint.* Plymouth, UK: Rowman & Littlefield, 2014.

Jagdish, Misra. *Histories of Libraries and Librarianship in Modern India Since 1850.* Delhi: Atma Ram, 1979.

Jambhekar, Neeta. "National Policy on Public Libraries in India." *World Libraries* 5, no. 2 (1995). Accessed November 15, 2015. http://ojsserv.dom.edu/ojs/index.php/worldlib/article/viewArticle/301/257.

Jayaraman, Anandh, Srinivas Sangani, Madhavi Ganapathiraju and Narayanaswamy Balakrishnan. "Proceedings Tamil Internet Conference (The Electronic Library: An Indian Scenario)." *Library Philosophy and Practice* 5, no. 2 (2004): 23-29. Edited by V. Franklin David Jebaraj and M. Deivasigamani. Accessed June 25, 2015. from http://unllib.unl.edu/LPP/jebaraj.html.

Joshi, Namrata M. "Digital Library and Library Networks in India." *Global Journal of Academic Librarianship* 3, no. 1 (2014): 37-44. Accessed June 12, 2015. http://www.ripublication.com/gjal/gjalv3n1_04.pdf.

Jung, Patricia Beattie, and Ralph F. Smith. *Heterosexism: An Ethical Challenge.* New York: State University of New York Press, 1993.

Kabir, Abulfazal. "Ranganathan: A Universal Librarian." *Journal of Educational Media & Library Sciences* 40 (2003): 453-459.

Khan, Shivananda. "Culture, Sexualities, and Identities: Men Who Have Sex with Men in India." *Journal of Homosexuality* 40, no. 3/4 (2001): 99-115.

Knowledge@Wharton. "Public Policy: Why Housing Isn't Enough to Create Sustainable Communities." Philadelphia: Wharton School, University of Pennsylvania. Last modified August 23, 2007. http://knowledge.wharton.upenn.edu/article/indias-rural-poor-why-housing-isnt-enough-to-create-sustainable-communities/.

Kumar, Nirnimesh. "Delhi High Court Strikes Down Section 377 of IPC." *The Hindu: Online Edition of India's National Newspaper.* Last modified July 3, 2009. http://www.hindu.com/2009/07/03/stories/2009070358010100.htm.

Kumar, Krishan, and Jaideep Sharma. "Library and Information Science Education in India: A Historical Perspective." *DESIDOC Journal of Library and Information Technology* 30, no. 5 (2010): 3-8.

Kumbar, B. D. "Growth and Development of Public Library System in India with Special Reference to Karnataka." Accessed June 12, 2015. http://www.nigd.org/libraries/mumbai/reports/article-4.pdf.

LeBlanc, Denis. "At Least 587 LGBTI Arrested in India in 2014." *Erasing 76 Crimes.* Last modified January 6, 2015. http://76crimes.com/2015/01/06/at-least-587-lgbti-arrested-in-india-in-2014/.

Lewis, Alison M, ed. *Questioning Library Neutrality: Essays from Progressive Librarian.* Duluth, MN: Library Juice Press, 2008.

Lifshitz, Sebastien. *The Invisibles: Vintage Portraits of Love and Pride. Gay Couples in the Early Twentieth Century.* New York: Rizzoli International Publications, 2014.

Malik, Yogendra K., and V. B. Singh. "Bharatiya Janata Party: An Alternative to the Congress (I)?." *Asian Survey* (1992): 318-336. Accessed April 13, 2015. http://www.jstor.org/discover/10.2307/2645149?uid=2&uid=4&sid=21106443682663.

Mehra, Bharat. Introduction to *Library Trends: Social Justice in Library and Information Science & Services* 64, no. 1 (2015).

Mehra, Bharat. "What is the Value of Social Justice in Pakistan's Library and Information Science Professions? Guest Editorial." *Pakistan Journal of Information Management and Libraries* 14, no. 1 (2014). Accessed April 15, 2015. http://pu.edu.pk/images/journal/pjlis/pdf/Editorial%20-%20Bharat%20Mehra.pdf.

Mehra, Bharat. Guest Editor Introduction to *Qualitative and Quantitative Methods in Libraries Journal, Special Issue* 2014: Social Justice, Social Inclusion (2014): 1-3. Accessed February 25, 2014. http://www.qqml.net/Special_Issue_2014_Social_Justice_Social_Inclusion.html.

Mehra, Bharat. "Growth Opportunities, and Challenges Facing Indian Librarianship in Developing a KNOWLEDGE SOCIETY in the 21st Century: Reflections and Insights." Keynote Speech, Souvenir of the 57th Indian Library Association Annual Conference, Mangalore, Karnataka, February 23-25, 2012.

Mehra, Bharat and Donna Braquet. "Marriage between Participatory Leadership and Action Research to Advocate Benefits Equality for Lesbian, Gay, Bisexual, and Transgender People: An Extended Human Rights Role in Library and Information Science." In *Leadership in Academic Libraries Today: Connecting Theory to Practice*, edited by Bradford Lee Eden and Jody Condit Fagan, 185-210. Toronto: Scarecrow Press, 2014.

Mehra, Bharat, and Rebecca Davis. "A Strategic Diversity Manifesto for Public Libraries in the 21st Century." *New Library World* 116, no. 1/2 (2015): 15-36.

Mehra, Bharat and LaVerne Gray. "'Don't Say Gay' in the State of Tennessee: Libraries as Virtual Spaces of Resistance and

Protectors of Human Rights of Lesbian, Gay, Bisexual, Transgender, and Queer (LGBTQ) People." LGBTQ Users Special Interest Group, Proceedings of the World Library and Information Congress: 80th International Federation of Library Associations and Institutions (IFLA) General Conference and Council, Lyon, France, August 16-22, 2014. Accessed April 15, 2015. http://library.ifla.org/1011/1/151-mehra-en.pdf.

Mehra, Bharat, Eric Haley, and Dylan Lane. "Culturally Appropriate Information Support Services for Lesbian, Gay, Bisexual, and Transgender (LGBTQ) South Asians: Representing Multiple Shades of Identity Based on Sexual Orientation and Ethnicity." In *Expanding the Circle: Creating an Inclusive Environment in Higher Education for LGBTQ Students and Studies*, edited by John C. Hawley, 317-341. New York: SUNY Press, 2015.

Mehra, Bharat and Lisette Hernandez. "Libraries as Agents of Human Rights Protection and Social Justice on Behalf of Sexual Minorities in India: An Action-Based Manifesto for Progressive Change." In *Perspectives on Libraries as Institutions of Human Rights and Social Justice*, edited by U. Gorham, N. G. Taylor, and P. T. Jaeger, 147-82. Bingley, UK: Emerald, 2016.

Mehra, Bharat, Devendra Potnis, and Jennifer Morden. "An Exploratory Study of the Nature and Composition of Current Library and Information Science Programs in Indian State Universities." *Perspectives in International Librarianship* 2012, no. 1 (2012). Accessed April 15, 2015. http://www.qscience.com/doi/abs/10.5339/pil.2012.1.

Mehra, Bharat, Kevin Rioux, and Kendra S. Albright. "Social Justice in Library and Information Science." In *Encyclopedia of Library and Information Sciences*, edited by Marcia J. Bates and Mary Niles Maack, 4820-4836. New York: Taylor & Francis Group, 2009.

Mehra, Bharat and Ramesh Srinivasan. "The Library-Community Convergence Framework for Community Action: Libraries as Catalysts of Social Change." *Libri: International Journal of Libraries and Information Services* 57, no. 3 (2007): 123-139.

Mehra, Bharat and Robert J. Sandusky. "LIS Students as Community Partners in Elective Courses: Applying Community-based Action Research to Meet the Needs of Underserved Populations." In *Service Learning: Linking Library Education and Practice*, edited by Loriene Roy, Kelly Jensen, and Alex Hershey Meyers, 153-168. Chicago, American Library Association (ALA) Editions, 2009.

Miles, George, editor. *Foundations for the LPC 2014-2015*. Oxford: Oxford University Press, 2014.

Mortezaie, Lila and Nader Naghshineh. "A Comparative Case Study of Graduate Courses in Library and Information Studies in the UK, USA, India, and Iran: Lessons for Iranian LIS Professionals." *Library Review* 51, no. 1 (2002): 14-23.

Narayan, Nandita. *Fundamental Rights of Sexual Minorities and Section 377 of IPC: A Need to Revisit the Provision in the Light of Indeterminacy of the Definition of "Against the Order of Nature."* Saarbrücken: Lambert Academic Publishing, 2014.

National Knowledge Commission. *Libraries, Gateways to Knowledge: A Roadmap for Revitalization*. New Delhi: Government of India, 2007.

National Knowledge Commission. *Report to the Nation 2007*. New Delhi: Government of India, 2008.

NDTV. "Transgenders are the 'Third Gender' Rules Supreme Court." *NDTV*. Last modified April 15, 2014. http://www.ndtv.com/india-news/transgenders-are-the-third-gender-rules-supreme-court-557439.

NDTV. "Is Supreme Court's Verdict on Gay Sex a Violation of Human Rights?" *NDTV*. Last modified December 11, 2013. http://www.ndtv.com/video/player/left-right-centre/is-supreme-court-s-verdict-on-gay-sex-a-violation-of-human-rights/301009.

Newswatch.in. *Indian Readership Survey – World's Largest Survey*. Last modified June 30, 2011. Accessed October 16, 2012. http://mruc.net/images/irs2012q2-topline-findings.pdf.

Parayil, Govindan, ed. *Political Economy and Information Capitalism in India: Digital Divide, Development and Equity*. New York: Palgrave Macmillan, 2006.

Patel, Jashu and Krishan Kumar. *Libraries and Librarianship in India*. Westport, CT: Greenwood Press, 2001.

Patra, Swapan Kumar, and Prakash Chand. "Library and Information Science Research in India:: A Bibliometric Study." *Annals of Library and Information Studies* 53, no. 4 (2006): 219-223. Accessed June 12, 2015. http://nopr.niscair.res.in/bitstream/123456789/6029/1/ALIS%2053%284%29%20219-223.pdf.

Pattanaik, Devdutt. *Shikhandi and Other Tales They Don't Tell You*. New Delhi: Zubaan/Penguin Books, 2014.

PTI. "60% of India's Rural Population Lives on Less Than Rs. 35 a Day." *Firstpost: India News*. Last modified May 3, 2012. http://www.firstpost.com/india/60-of-indias-rural-population-lives-on-less-than-rs-35-a-day-297253.html.

Pyati, Ajit K. "Public Library Revitalization in India: Hopes, Challenges, and New Visions." *First Monday* 14, no. 7 (2009). Accessed June 14, 2015. http://firstmonday.org/ojs/index.php/fm/article/view/2588/2237.

Ranganathan, Shiyali R. *The Five Laws of Library Science*. Bombay: Asia Publishing House, 1963.

Rao, T.S. Sathyanarayana and K.S. Jacob. "The Reversal on Gay Rights in India." *Indian Journal of Psychiatry* 56, no. 1 (2014): 1-2. Accessed April 16, 2015. http://www.ncbi.nlm.nih.gov/pmc/articles/PMC3927237/.

Reddy, Gayatri. *With Respect to Sex: Negotiating Hijra Identity in South India.* Chicago: University of Chicago Press, 2005.

Riaz, Ali, ed. *Religion and Politics in South Asia.* New York: Routledge, 2010.

Sahu, Barun Kumar. *Unwritten Laws of Indian Bureaucracy.* New Delhi: Pustak Mahal, 2004.

Samek, Toni. *Librarianship and Human Rights: A 21st Century Guide.* Atlanta: Neal-Schuman Publishers, 2007.

Saperstein, Jeff and Danial Rouach. *Creating Regional Wealth in the Innovation Economy: Models, Perspectives, and Best Practices.* Upper Saddle River, NJ: FT Press, 2002.

Satija, M.P. "Doctoral Research in Library and Information Science in India: Some Observations and Comments." *Libri: International Journal of Libraries and Information Services* 49, no. 4 (1999): 236-242.

Sen, Amartya. *The Argumentative Indian: Writings on Indian History, Culture, and Identity.* New York: Picador, 2006.

Seth, R. "Storehouses of Knowledge to Educate the Masses: The Indian Library System – A Present Day Scenario." *Frankfurter Buchmesse* 58, no. 9 (2006): 662-628.

Sharma, Alankaar. "Decriminalising Queer Sexualities in India: A Multiple Streams Analysis." *Social Policy and Society* 7, no. 4 (2008): 419-431.

Singh, S.P. "Library and Information Science Education in India: Issues and Trends." *Malaysian Journal of Library & Information Science* 8, no. 2 (2003): 1-17.

Srivastava, Anand P. *Ranganathan: A Pattern Maker.* New Delhi: Metropolitan Book Co., 1977.

Subramanian, Ramesh, and Lea Shaver, eds. *Access to Knowledge in India: New Research on Intellectual Property, Innovation & Development.* London: Bloomsbury, 2011.

Sukula, Shiva Kanaujia. "Indigenous Database Development in Indian Research and Development Library and Information Centres." *Online Information Review* 29, no. 2 (2005): 193-207.

Tewari, Suranjana. "India's Gays, Lesbians 'Suddenly Afraid' After Court Ruling." *NBC News*. Last modified October 12, 2014. http://www.nbcnews.com/news/world/indias-gays-lesbians-suddenly-afraid-after-court-ruling-n221831.

The Telegraph. "Third Sex' Finds a Place on Indian Passport Forms." *The Telegraph*, March 10, 2005.

The World Bank Group. "Data: Rural Population (% of Total Population)." Accessed June 1, 2015. http://data.worldbank.org/indicator/SP.RUR.TOTL.ZS?order=wbapi_data_value_2013%20wbapi_data_value%20wbapi_data_value-last&sort=asc.

Trust Research Advisory. "India's Most Trusted Brands 2014." Accessed April 11, 2015. from http://www.trustadvisory.info/allindia_2014.html.

UN News Center. "UN Issues First Report on Human Rights of Gay and Lesbian People." Last modified December 11, 2011. http://www.un.org/apps/news/story.asp?NewsID=40743#.Up4eNye0adx.

Verma, Ravi Kumar and Martine Collumbien. "Homosexual Activity Among Rural Indian men: Implications for HIV Prevention." *AIDS: Official Journal of the International AIDS Society* 18, no. 13 (2004): 1845-1847.

Waites, Matthew. "Human Rights, Sexual Orientation and the Generation of Childhoods: Analysing the Partial Decriminalization of 'Unnatural Offences' in India." *International Journal of Human Rights* 14, no. 6 (2010): 971-993.

Wani, Zahid Ashraf. "Development of Public Libraries in India." Library Philosophy and Practice (2008). Accessed June 29, 2015. http://digitalcommons.unl.edu/libphilprac/165.

Chapter 6

"What is It We Do Not Know?" - LGBTQ and Library Staff

Ragnhild Brandstedt

Introduction

Sweden has a strong library culture, but there are always areas in need of exploration, development, and improvement. Issues of inclusiveness are aspects that are not yet fully discovered or explored. This chapter describes the process of creating awareness at Mariestad Public Library through collaboration between the public library and LGBTQ (lesbian, gay, bisexual, transgender, queer/questioning) advocates. It presents a project of local action-based research that was conducted in 2012-2013 and describes what has taken place thereafter.

In Sweden, a high degree of awareness of human rights, civil liberties, and gender equality is generally presumed to be well-founded in society. Furthermore, this awareness is expected to be common practice in public libraries which, by extension, means that most library staff and operations have an open attitude towards diversity. Libraries are considered a significant public meeting place and are open to everyone. Legislation such as the Library Act[1] has ensured that a public library is to be found in every municipality throughout the country.

With that being said, it is interesting to note that, although there is legislation that ensures public access to free library service and legislation that protects against discrimination on the basis of sex, gender identification, ethnicity, sexual orientation or age (the Anti-Discrimination Act[2]), there are still areas in society where discrimination, prejudice, and acts of homophobic violence occur. There are also gaps in the knowledge about, and understanding of, LGBTQ-related issues and normativity that, on a sub-conscious level, risk excluding individuals, their actions, and lifestyles, and thus deny the otherwise prevailing rights and services in Swedish society.

RFSL is the Swedish Federation for Lesbian, Gay, Bisexual and Transgender Rights; it is a non-profit organization with no affiliation to any political or religious organizations. Being the country's strongest organization for LGBTQ rights, the organization does extensive work with information dissemination and has educational programs for organizations, institutions, and state and private companies. There are various levels of common interests and collaborations between libraries and the RFSL.

The Swedish Library Association, a non-profit organization which also has no political or religious affiliations, supports all types of libraries and library operations. One of several networks of the association is the LGBTQ Network, which connects library staff members at a number of libraries throughout the country. Mariestad Public Library is a member of the Swedish Library Association.

The importance that education and learning play in the path towards understanding and acceptance, and growing beyond tolerance, should not be understated. A proven method of furthering knowledge and understanding is by working collaboratively, which is a common practice in the sphere of public libraries in Sweden. Collaborations exist between libraries and any number of organizations, as well as with individuals and groups.

Background

Mariestad is a typical small city in central Sweden, with a public library as well as school libraries and a branch library for the University of Gothenburg. Mariestad Public Library is dedicated to continuously working with diversity in a number of different areas. Democratic values are thought to permeate the library's operations in general, including many areas related to diversity such as interculturalism, language diversity, and services to the physically and/or mentally challenged. This is an ongoing process of daily awareness that has been created through education and numerous projects such as "Together we study the city! A report on CityArtLab the summer of 2011" and "Mural 2012,"[3] as well as through interactions with individuals, organizations, and institutions. Strong lobbying groups at local, regional, and national levels have strengthened the position of individuals and groups, both inside and outside library walls. To a degree, an awareness of general norms and gender issues can be found in the selection of media and in recommendations for literature in different situations. This awareness can also be seen in delivering library services and in dealings with the general public.

The areas of focus that appeared on the local library's agenda in 2012 were issues of gender and LGBTQ, as well as social norms. In the course of investigating how these issues were looked upon and dealt with on a strategic level, and perhaps even more importantly, on a daily basis, a different type of challenge was discovered. Through discussions and observations, it became evident that these were delicate issues and that they were rather unfamiliar to library personnel and often not reflected in library operations. In an effort to live up to library standards, focus was placed on the question of how to approach these matters on the local level.

Identifying issues that needed to be addressed was step one. In the case of the Mariestad Public Library, this was something that happened over time through observations of society as a whole as well as observations at the library. Issues were identified ranging from a trickle of almost indiscernible derogatory comments to the lack of books and other media with LGBTQ content, especially in the children and youth sections of the library. For years, there were only a handful of LGBTQ-related books available for children and youth. This is not unique to Mariestad, however, and is due in part to the lack of relevant published materials. Beyond library holdings, there are questions about such things as how we express ourselves when speaking with children. Do we automatically say "your mother and father," or do we choose more neutral language?

So, LGBTQ issues had not been specifically explored in the local library context. What steps would be suitable for a successful approach? Also, how does one implement new information and knowledge throughout library operations? Based on these inquiries, discussions,and research, as well as by examining LGBTQ issues both within and outside of Sweden, the research questions we developed were as follows:

- How does one create a library organization's interest in, and knowledge about, seemingly invisible LGBTQ issues in library operations?
- What steps are involved in strengthening skills and qualifications in the process of furthering development of a norm-critical approach?

As this research was as a small-scale undertaking, there was not adequate time to fully delve into all the research that has been done on LGBTQ issues in reference to library policies or library services around the globe. However, we did at the time draw on a few examples from colleagues at other public libraries. The first was the public library in Hallonbergen, Stockholm, Sweden. Through extensive collaboration with the RFSL organization, Hallonbergen Public Library was awarded the prestigious LGBT-certification in 2012, which ensures a high-quality of services and staff related to LGBTQ issues and inclusiveness. The Rainbow Library in Umeå, also in Sweden, is another model library dealing with these issues. As Maria Broman and Malena Jäder discuss in their Bachelor thesis from 2014, *LGBTQ in the Public Library*,[4] different libraries take different approaches to LGBTQ-related issues such as staff training and displaying LGBTQ-related materials in the library. Broman and Jäder came to the conclusion that training makes a notable difference, regardless of whether it is short or long. Once LGBTQ issues are raised, even in a short training, discussions are initiated and a learning process is set in motion.

Research Outside Sweden

Studies in the United Kingdom and the United States have shown that access to LGBTQ literature and other media in public libraries plays an important role for the LGBTQ community as a whole, and most specifically for youth struggling with identity issues. Elizabeth Chapman at the University of Sheffield, England, has done extensive research on the availability and importance of LGBT-related fiction for young readers, as well as on the importance of a knowledgeable and open-minded staff.[5] Her research sheds interesting light on the situations in a number of public libraries in the United Kingdom. In Ann Curry's article "If I ask, will they answer?"[6] the focus is on public library reference service. The results of these two studies have significant similarities in that both point to the importance of a knowledgeable and open-minded staff regarding LGBTQ identities.

Learning Process

The importance of the learning environment must be considered. It is not surprising to find that a supportive work climate leads to the best results. This is true on an individual as well as an operational level.[7]

The work environment at Mariestad Public Library is not inhibiting in regard to questions of multicultural tolerance and inclusiveness. On the contrary, the work climate is open and permissive, with a staff that takes on great responsibilities for managing library operations and services on both a daily and long-term basis. The absence of intentional planning for LGBTQ services was not due to any reluctance on the part of the employer or employees, but rather was due to a patron population that had remained largely invisible. This means that once these questions were initially raised, the possibilities for change dramatically improved.

David A. Kolb's model of experience-based learning illustrates the cycle of actions that a learning process can entail. This consists of four main steps: concrete experience, reflective observation, abstract conceptualization, and active experimentation.[8] A collective learning experience means, for instance, that a group of employees act together, generate an experience, integrate and interpret these experiences, and finally act anew based on their findings. Kolb's model was an important starting point for the work at Mariestad's library, and has continued to be so.

The LGBT-Certification of Hallonbergen Library

RFSL and Hallonbergen Library in Regional Stockholm implemented a comprehensive training which resulted in the library receiving a LGBT-certification in December 2012. In Cecilia Bengtsson's report, The LGBT-Certification of Hallonbergen Library, she accounts for the collaboration with RFSL.[9] The LGBT certification process is a two-year contract between RFSL and, in this case, Hallonbergen Library. It was comprised of a number of steps including scouring strategic policy documents, web pages, and other materials, as well as considering the appropriate use of language, which was a real eye-opener. These sessions were attended by the entire library staff and consisted of lectures, films, discussions, and workshops. Bengtsson's text describes how a combination of these learning methods and experiences in the various areas mentioned above gradually increased their understanding and knowledge throughout the process.

With a "from the floor" perspective, Bengtsson's report confirms the importance of the work climate in a learning process involving LGBT-issues. "In training examples and group discussion much has been based on personal values and one's own thoughts. It is both brave and important to share these values and thoughts. This requires an open and non-threatening learning environment, as well as trust."[10]

Since 2012, a number of organizations, including Sundbyberg Public Library in Stockholm, have received the LGBTQ certification.[11]

Research Method

Despite the limited scope of the research conducted in 2012-2013, it was important to choose an appropriate method. Collaborative action-based research is a method that is well-tried and proven in library research, as well as in various other fields. It is relatively easy to apply in public library settings and incorporates aspects of both theory and known norms, along with in-depth inquiries into the library's daily practices. The tools used in this particular case were observations recorded in a journal, interspersed with findings such as relevant articles and previous research on the subject, interviews, mentorship, and developing the "action" itself, i.e., an RFSL-seminar/workshop. The mentors who supported this project are from Region West Sweden, Kultur i Väst, consultants Kerstin Wockatz and Eva Fred, as well as researcher Cecilia Gärdén from the University of Borås, Sweden.

Process

As mentioned earlier, focusing on LGBTQ issues leads to greater awareness and more meaningful discussions over time. Centering these conversations on the library context provided library staff with the opportunity to explore various approaches to fulfilling the needs of LGBTQ patrons.

Once the research questions were decided upon, the focus was placed on observations, interviews, and discussions taking place, both before and after the RFSL workshop. Finally, all of the gathered material was analyzed.

Action-Based Research

- Information about action-based research was given at general staff meetings on two occasions well in advance of the planned seminar and workshop with RFSL.
- Information was also disseminated at a meeting between the department head and union representatives.
- The research on LGBTQ and gender issues was tentatively discussed in other contexts such as smaller meetings and informally at coffee breaks.

- Informal small group interviews were conducted with the staff. The goal of this activity was to offer a comfortable environment for questions about the upcoming seminar with RFSL. It was also an opportunity to inform everyone about a soon-to-be-opened LGBTQ-café for young adults in Mariestad, the first of its kind.
- Individual interviews were held with six staff members after the day of the seminar/workshop.

Before the process of action-based research was initiated it was observed that:

- Finding relevant literature at the library was difficult.
- There was a trickle of derogatory remarks about individuals' sexual or gender identity among the staff and library users.
- There were issues with language use and choice of words, for example, the automatic use of gendered assumptions regarding family members such as "your mother and father."
- Exasperation was expressed when the use of "other" as a third choice alongside the genders female/male was suggested for the yearly library survey.
- Many people of all ages are not familiar with the terms LGBT or LGBTQ.
- Teachers and other educators frequently request books specifically for boys or girls.

Between the initiation of the local action-based research and the "action," i.e. the seminar and workshop, it was observed that:

- In general, library employees had a sense of uncertainty about the subject.
- Discussions continuously led to the question of sexual orientation.
- "What is it we do not know?" was a pertinent question posed during the early stage of the research.

- The upcoming seminar and workshop, talks, and marketing information sparked slightly more conversation on the topic of LGBTQ community members.
- There was a slightly increased focus on media purchasing and use of relevant descriptors and subject headings.
- There was a small increase in demand for gender and LGBTQ-related media for children and youth from students in the teaching profession.
- Library staff were concerned about whether the LGBTQ community would feel targeted if a special LGBTQ- or gender-based section at the library was established.

RFSL's Seminar and Workshop

The seminar and an interactive workshop were planned for seventeen individuals, including the library director, librarians, library assistants, photo archivists, building manager, and trainees.

The seminar began with basic information about the concept and terminology of LGBTQ. Discussions evolved around social norms in general and prevailing heteronormativity in society in particular. This included awareness of the consequences these issues can have in the context of library services and the idea of inclusiveness, as well as the potential effects on the individual who, by choice or otherwise, is outside these social norms.

Discussion and interaction with practical examples highlighted such things as how the library staff can:

- meet and serve library patrons with a non-heteronormative approach
- carry out successful meetings with groups such as parents, class visits, and others
- explore and maintain a safe and open work environment
- make well-informed choices in media purchasing
- change and expand marketing strategies to ensure inclusiveness

- plan cultural activities from a broad perspective
- become aware of how to use neutral words and language as a means of expanding inclusiveness

Interviews

Six interviews were performed after the seminar. In an effort to get a more nuanced picture, the interviewees were located in a variety of library departments.

Results

One step in the sought-after increase in competency was to generate an interest in LGBTQ issues. The staff's initial sense of uncertainty was expressed partly as near-silence before the training (the RFSL seminar and workshop), which is apparently not an unusual reaction. When a new field of work or study is introduced, a certain level of apprehension is not uncommon.[12] With this particular topic, a degree of uncertainty and hesitancy was expected. Despite great efforts, it was still found at the meetings, talks, and group interviews which happened at different stages that insufficient information had been provided before the seminar. In the Hallonbergen report, Bengtsson tells of how each individual became involved on a personal level to a degree not often found when otherwise developing work-related skills. This can be an indication of how complex LGBTQ and social norm issues are; for many individuals, this is a delicate area of new information and knowledge that takes time to absorb.

With this in mind, it was not surprising to find that informing the staff about the training was a long process. It was only after the subject had been brought up collectively a number of times in the work environment that talking about it started taking place. Even then, staff were observably tentative and cautious. I found that there were many questions running through the minds of staff, including what the topic actually was, what these words meant, and what was expected of each individual staff member.

Once the day of training was completed, everyone seemed somewhat relieved (see list below). Perhaps this has to do with the fact that the focus was not exclusively on LGBTQ issues but included how society is focused on norms in general and heteronormativity in particular, both spoken and unspoken. It is only when an individual is placed (or places oneself) outside of these social norms that restrictions and boundaries become evident. There seemed to be a new sense of general understanding that these were significant issues for everyone, and particularly for library operations. Spontaneous responses to the interview questions included comments such as:

- It was very interesting... there is so much more to this than I thought.
- I have always considered myself rather open-minded and unbiased, I had no idea I had so many prejudices...
- I feel we already greet everyone in the same way and with the same respect.
- Now I feel more comfortable with the terminology
- Now I better understand what you (Brandstedt) meant when you kept pointing things out about language and how we express ourselves
- I would like a 3-day course, then maybe I will begin to understand – and it's so important that we *do* understand!

All of the persons interviewed replied that RFSL's seminar was both educational and interesting. What it meant to each individual partly depended on their field of work and responsibilities. A heightened awareness can affect areas such as marketing, meeting the public, and how we verbally express ourselves, as well as future media purchasing. The observations at different intervals, the talks and meetings, the RFSL seminar, the subsequent interviews and continued discussion, all reflect the four steps of David A. Kolb's model to experience, reflect, generalize and theorize, and act. This can be seen when looking at the learning process results as a whole. This careful and repetitive approach is verified in the Hallonbergen Library certification report: "The continuous and repetitive process has made possible in-depth study and mutual reflection on these areas."

My initial understanding was that these questions were about how society is formed by social norms and standards, for better and for worse, and furthermore, how these norms control and moderate society and the individuals who challenge them. Since the library continuously works with inclusiveness, tolerance, and multiculturalism, it becomes obvious that these issues and LGBTQ identities are closely connected and that this is merely a continuation of already ongoing diversity efforts.

Conclusion

The action-based research dealt with inclusiveness and diversity in the context of an LGBTQ perspective and revealed a mostly unexplored area. This was both interesting and somewhat discouraging. As stated earlier, Mariestad Public Library is dedicated to hard and continuous work with diversity in a number of different areas, and yet there is a gap. The results that I could discern pointed to the possibility that we have lived in the belief that we are familiar with and cover basically everything that a Swedish public library is expected to cover, within the realm of openness and inclusiveness. Not until the action-based project did we collectively become aware of LGBTQ issues and the importance of a norm-sensitive approach that was made visible by the study. Among the items we now discuss are the tone of discussion in the work place, what types of collaborations could be beneficial to further explore and develop LGBTQ issues in the library, and how to implement new knowledge about marketing and purchasing on a long term basis in an effort to secure quality service for all.

This learning process showed aspects of library services that the staff were interested in learning more about and developing further. This implies that, because these questions were presented and a heightened awareness was detected, the possibilities for change and improvement are good. I also wanted to keep these issues on the table, so to speak, as Sweden's public libraries are an important democratic arena. There remains a great deal of work to be done, but we now have a platform from which to expand library diversity efforts to fully include the LGBTQ community.

Stage Two: Development Over Time

Since 2013, Sweden, along with many other countries, has seen LGBTQ issues rise in the awareness of the general public as well as on the political agenda. This increased awareness plays a significant role in fostering a greater degree of tolerance, understanding, and acceptance in many areas of Swedish society.

What part libraries have played in this development is hard to say without a comprehensive study, which is beyond the scope of this article. However, the public library in Mariestad has made substantial progress in awareness of LGBTQ issues during the past two years. This comes in part from the action-based research of 2012-2013, as discussed in this article. This progress also stems from other factors, including the overall LGBTQ climate in Sweden, as well as from articles and a small number of newly published theses on related issues.

The action-based research at Mariestad Public Library led to the presentation of a paper at the IFLA Congress in Singapore in 2013 titled, "*Identifying and Implementing Diversity: Collaborative Action-based Research at Mariestad Public Library on LGBTQ Issues.*"[13] At previous IFLA congresses, there had been conversations about these issues in an effort to create a Special Interest Group (SIG). In Singapore, discussions continued and expanded, culminating in a petition requesting the formation of a SIG. In December 2013, the IFLA Professional Committee approved the Lesbian, Gay, Bisexual, Transgender, Queer (LGBTQ) Users SIG, which is supported by the Acquisition and Collection Development Section.[14] At the IFLA Congress in Lyon, in 2014, seven LGBTQ-related papers were presented.

In Broman and Jäder's thesis *LGBTQ in the Public Library*, the objective was to determine what ideas and questions form the underlying reasons for how the library personnel wish to work with LGBTQ issues at their local library. Their benchmark is one of queer theory and the effect of a norm-critical approach. One aspect that becomes clear in the interviews that are reported in Broman and Jäder's thesis is that education for the entire library staff is all-important.[15] This coincides with the work done at Mariestad Public Library.

Another area that we have focused on is the library programming that is planned twice a year. Conscious efforts to widen the perspective of the activities have resulted in a more equal spread of events produced by men, women, and others. This also applies to the content of specific programs on the agenda, such as author visits and exhibits. Lectures by authors of books on LGBTQ issues have been very popular. Opportunities for talks, lectures, or other types of programs with or about persons identifying as transgender have also presented themselves. Although these events have not yet taken place, we will continue to engage with the community to develop programs of this type. This is part of an ongoing and developing process. Mariestad is a small town with a population of 25,000 people. This does not imply that there is no need or demand for various types of activities dealing with LGBTQ identities; however, it is a slow process.

Collection Management

Since 2013, there has been an increased awareness in the acquisitions department. Materials in Swedish dealing with LGBTQ issues are not that common, so a close eye is needed to locate them when they become available on the market. Mariestad's library has a long history of putting emphasis on subject headings to enable easy retrieval. In their study, Broman and Jäder looked at the accessibility of LGBTQ materials and the importance of subject headings.[16] This is one of the areas where Mariestad's library staff has increased efforts. Being observant and adding appropriate subject headings is now part of daily cataloging tasks.

LGBTQ materials are now more visible in the library, which has opened up dialogue between staff and library visitors. For example, a slight increase in purchase requests for materials with LGBTQ content has occurred. We have received positive comments on the printed folder "LGBTQ books" which is compiled by local library staff. This is supported by Broman and Jäder who found in their study that having a special section or shelf for LGBTQ materials has a symbolic value. This not only signals the immediate availability of materials, but also that the library is familiar with and actively addresses these issues.[17] When materials are displayed, it can also encourage patrons to approach library personnel with accessibility-related questions. The staff's increased knowledge of, and confidence in, a wider vocabulary (i.e., LGBTQ-related terms) has proven to be very positive in Mariestad.

Another aspect of collection management is the weeding process. Since the LGBTQ selection is limited to begin with, careful consideration in this area is important. As with any subject area, attention is always paid to the availability as well as usage statistics of various titles in the local collection.

Gender, Migration, and Politics

In early 2015, Mariestad's municipality adopted a new strategic policy on gender equality and multicultural issues. A library strategic plan, in accordance with the latest Library Act (SFS 2013:801), is underway. There is also a regional library strategic plan due this year. These documents will play an important role in strengthening the position of various minorities and underrepresented persons. As an example, Library Act §6 states that every municipal library shall be available to one and all and geared to the users' needs.

With a strong increase in migration to Sweden over the last few years, the library sees many new demands and opportunities for expanding information sources, including materials in more languages and opportunities for meeting across cultural borders. This strengthens the library staff's commitment to human rights in their everyday work. When meeting with a patron who speaks a different language, is part of a different culture, or in any way identifies outside of the social norm, staff work to ensure that each user is made to feel welcome at the library. Every encounter with patrons can be regarded as a learning opportunity for the staff. Absorbing new knowledge and improving access to library services is seen as a positive and ongoing process.

Endnotes

1. "Library Act," (Bibliotekslagen 2013:801) RIKSDAGEN.se, accessed July 30, 2015, http://www.riksdagen.se/sv/Dokument-Lagar/Lagar/Svenskforfattningssamling/sfs_sfs-2013-801/.

2. "Anti- Discrimination Act," (Diskrimineringslagen 2008:567) RIKSDAGEN.se, accessed July 30, 2015, http://www.riksdagen.se/sv/Dokument-Lagar/Lagar/Svenskforfattningssamling/Diskrimineringslag-2008567_sfs-2008-567/.

3. Two successful international interactive social arts projects in Mariestad. http://www.mariestad.se/download/18.3e77242813a2d30498a2f28/1366327513108/Rapport+stadslaboratoriet.pdf

4. Maria Broman and Malena Jäder, "LGBTQ in the Public Library" (Bachelor of Science, University of Borås, Sweden, 2014), pp 25-28.

5. Elizabeth L. Chapman, "Provision of LGBT Materials for Children and Young People in English Public Libraries: A Mixed-Method Study," accessed August 29, 2015, https://dub118.mail.live.com/mail/ViewOfficePreview.aspx?messageid=mgCuzYgYJJ5RGcywAhWtamPg2&folderid=flinbox&attindex=0&cp=-1&attdepth=0&n=17547654.

6. Ann Curry, "If I Ask, Will They Answer? Evaluating Public Library Reference Service to Gay and Lesbian Youth." *Reference and User Services Quarterly* 45, no. 1 (2005.): pp 65-75.

7. Henrik Kock, "The Developing of Skills at the Workplace – Conclusions and Reflection," In *Workplace Learning: To Lead and Organize the Developing of Skills*, ed. Henrik Kock (Sweden, Lund: Studentlitteratur, 2010), 161-192. [Title translation by R.K. Brandstedt].

8. David A. Kolb, "Deliberate Experiential Learning." Experienced Based Learning Systems, Inc., accessed July 2015. http://learningfromexperience.com/research_library/deliberate-experiential-learning/.

9. Cecilia Bengtsson, *The LGBT-Certification of Hallonbergen Library* (Stockholm: Regionbibliotek Stockholm, 2013). [Title translation by R.K. Brandstedt].

10. Ibid., 11-12.

11. Q for "Queer" was added in 2013.

12. "Uncertainty Reduction Theory," *WIKIPEDIA.org*, last modified June 12, 2015, https://en.wikipedia.org/wiki/Uncertainty_reduction_theory.

13. Ragnhild Brandstedt, "*Identifying and Implementing Diversity: Collaborative Action-based Research at Mariestads Public Library on LGBTQ Issues*" (Paper presented at the annual IFLA Congress, Singapore, August 2013). http://library.ifla.org/65/.

14. LGBTQ SIG: http://www.ifla.org/node/8253.

15. Broman and Jäder, 22.

16. Ibid., 21.

17. Broman and Jäder, 26.

Bibliography

"Anti-Discrimination Act" (Diskrimineringslagen 2008:567) RIKSDAGEN.se, accessed July 30, 2015, http://www.riksdagen.se/sv/Dokument-Lagar/Lagar/Svenskforfattningssamling/Diskrimineringslag-2008567_sfs-2008-567/.

Bengtsson, Cecilia. *LGBT Certification of Hallonbergen Public Library*. Stockholm: Regionbibliotek Stockholm, 2013.

Brandstedt, Ragnhild. "*Identifying and Implementing Diversity: Collaborative Action-Based Research at Mariestads Public Library on LGBTQ Issues.*" Paper presented at the annual IFLA Congress, Singapore, August 2013. http://library.ifla.org/65/.

Broman, Maria and Malena Jäder. "LGBTQ in the Public Library." Bachelor of Science, University of Borås, Sweden, 2014.

Chapman, Elizabeth L. "Provision of LGBT Materials for Children and Young People in English Public Libraries: A Mixed-Method Study." The University of Sheffield, England, 2015. https://dub118.mail.live.com/mail/ViewOfficePreview.aspx?messageid=mgCuzYgYJJ5RGcywAhWtamPg2&folderid=flinbox&attindex=0&cp=-1&attdepth=0&n=17547654.

Curry, Ann. "If I Ask, Will They Answer? Evaluating Public Library Reference Service to Gay and Lesbian Youth." *Reference and User Services Quarterly* 45, no. 1 (2005.): 65-75.

Kock, Henrik. "The Developing of Skills at the Workplace – Conclusions and Reflection." In *Workplace Learning: To Lead and Organize the Developing of Skills 2010*, edited by Henrik Kock, 161-192. Sweden, Lund: Studentlitteratur, 2008. [Title translation by R.K. Brandstedt].

Kolb, David A. "Deliberate Experiential Learning." *Experienced Based Learning Systems, Inc.* Access date July 2015. http://learningfromexperience.com/research_library/deliberate-experiential-learning/.

"Library Act" (Bibliotekslagen 2013:801) RIKSDAGEN.se, accessed July 30, 2015, http://www.riksdagen.se/sv/Dokument-Lagar/Lagar/Svenskforfattningssamling/sfs_sfs-2013-801/.

Chapter 7

FROM GAY SURFERS TO OLD LESBIANS ORGANIZING FOR CHANGE: DEVELOPING AN LGBT INITIATIVE AT A STATE UNIVERSITY IN FLORIDA

Matthew Knight

In late 2012, the University of South Florida (USF) Libraries firmly committed to developing an LGBT initiative,[1] with the bulk of the materials acquired to be housed in the special collections department;[2] the goal was to expand our collections of historically significant lesbian, gay, bisexual, and transgender materials in monographic, audio-visual, ephemeral, and archival formats. Initially, we intended to concentrate on collecting materials that documented LGBT history, culture, politics, community relations, and public health in the Tampa Bay region; that said, while Tampa Bay remained an important focus, we were also tasked with ensuring that our collections generated national and international interest. All of this sounded wonderful; however, the realities of starting a collection virtually from scratch with such ambitious goals proved to be a valuable learning experience. This chapter will document some of the highlights and lowlights encountered during this process, and will outline future strategies that we plan to implement to achieve our goals. Some aspects that will be covered in this chapter are the necessities of community engagement; the pitfalls—and triumphs—of working with potential donors and development officers; the frustrations of managing a dwindling budget; the challenges of promoting the materials to faculty, students, and community researchers; the problems associated with placing age restrictions on materials; the difficulties in choosing the right public programming for the right price; and the pleasures of establishing powerful relationships and partnerships with outside organizations. On May 10, 2015, a short survey [see Appendix] was sent out to select institutions with LGBT collections, and to the Gay, Lesbian, Bisexual, and Transgender Round Table Listserv [glbtrt-l] of the American Library Association; comments from that survey are included *passim*.

History

While 2012 marked the firm commitment to an LGBT initiative at the USF libraries, there were, in fact, earlier attempts to implement such a program. In 2005, USF professors David Johnson and Sara Crawley were instrumental in acquiring collections and generating support for what was at the time intended to be both a GLBT and a Florida Women's History Initiative. In February 2006, Dr. Crawley made arrangements with Edie Daly for the first materials to be donated to the library's special collections department.[3] Edie, who calls herself an Old Lesbian Feminist, returned to Florida in 1981 and quickly became a force of nature in both the women's and LGBT movements. She opened a women's bookstore on Madeira Beach in 1981, and the next year co-founded a lesbian feminist organization called Women's Energy Bank [WEB], which held monthly "salons" for more than twenty-four years. At these gatherings WEB hosted speakers, held concerts, and organized bowling outings. WEB also published a monthly journal called *Womyn's Words* for more than thirty years. Two boxes of archival materials from WEB and a full run of *Womyn's Words* constituted this first donation to the USF library. According to Edie, "Lesbian voices have been silenced for too long in the past and this university's willingness to make these original materials available marks a milestone in documenting our history and recording our contributions to our communities." In that spirit, in 2006 Edie called for the GLBT Initiative to be named LGBT in honor of those women who marched on Washington, D.C. in 1997 and also struggled against male-dominated pride march committees. "We insisted," said Edie, "that our own struggle as women be acknowledged; that our differences and uniquenesses as lesbians be acknowledged and the men acquiesced...and put Lesbian "L" first in the acronym which has now become LGBTQ." As a result, the USF Libraries changed the name and, on April 18, 2006, the inaugural collection was celebrated at an event co-sponsored by the Florida Women's History Initiative and the Florida LGBT Initiative.

At the same time that Dr. Crawley was facilitating the donation from Edie Daly, Professor David Johnson was working to secure an invaluable collection of photographs from Tampa Bay photographer Rex Maniscalco. Rex was attempting to document the history of the Tampa Bay LGBT community in what he termed the "Rainbow in Sunshine Project." While accumulating images for this project, Rex acquired a series of nearly 500 photographs taken by Bobby Smith from the 1940s to the 1970s. Bobby worked for *Southern Photo and News* from 1948-1989, and she and her partner Kay were a butch/femme couple who founded the inter-denominational Metropolitan Community Church in Tampa in the 1960s. Many of Bobby's photos in Rex's possession were taken at a gay bar on Madeira Beach called Jack's Place; a nudist camp called the Sunshine Beach Club in Lutz, Florida; as well as in Jimmy White's Tavern and the Knotty Pine, gay bars in downtown Tampa. Rex also had numerous boxes of his own photographs documenting the LGBT community, beginning in the 1980s. Dr. Johnson managed to acquire permission from Rex to donate both the Bobby Smith photographs and his own photos before Rex passed away in April 2009.

The Edie Daly and Rex Maniscalco collections proved to be a wonderful start to the LGBT initiative, and other small but notable collections followed. Edie Daly helped secure a collection from feminist and lesbian activist Lee Ann "Oak" Wojkowski and David Johnson acquired eleven boxes of material from Donald L. Bentz in 2007 that documented many LGBT organizations and events in the Tampa Bay area from the 1990s to the early 2000s. As important as these collections were, however, the initiative began to lose steam after 2009. Despite having more than $60,000 earmarked for the LGBT initiative, for example, the money was never spent and eventually was moved to other projects. Two lone highlights occurred in 2011 when graduate student Cyrana Wyker selected many of the Bobby Smith photographs for digitization, thereby establishing an online presence for the LGBT Initiative, and the records of Equality Florida[4] and the National Center for Lesbian Rights[5] in St. Petersburg were donated to USF. Without a firm commitment to the initiative from the special collections department, however, these records sat unprocessed in storage. By this time, William Garrison, the Dean of the USF Libraries, was beginning to lose patience with the lack of progress, and realized that the initiative needed to be revitalized.

In late 2012, Dean Garrison generously donated more than 400 books—predominantly novels—to the USF special collections department, thereby launching the Queer Literature Collection. With this donation came the need to establish a policy for what the USF Libraries LGBT initiative would collect, as well as to set a plan of action in motion with clear, achievable goals. It was suggested internally that the USF Libraries' LGBT initiative should first and foremost expand its collections with acquisitions that document the history of LGBT life in Florida, particularly the Tampa Bay area. Items with a national and international focus, however, would also be collected when they provided more complete coverage of LGBT history and concerns for USF students, faculty, and staff, as well as the community at large. Next, a three-pronged approach was developed in terms of preferred items to collect: monographs, archival materials, and oral histories. Lastly, in order to best promote the reinvigorated USF Libraries' LGBT initiative, lectures, symposia, and online and physical exhibits were deemed a necessary step. As for an action plan, the initial goal in early 2013 was to double the overall LGBT holdings by the end of the year; process all previously donated materials and have their finding aids made accessible online via Encoded Archival Description (EAD); increase the collection of LGBT oral histories; begin to actively promote the LGBT collections through exhibits, presentations, and outreach; engage with the faculty, staff, and students served by the USF Tampa Library in regards to the LGBT collection, in order to encourage research and development of the collection as an academic resource; and, since Edie Daly and other early supporters had become disillusioned with the lack of progress in the initiative by this time, and had fallen out of contact with the library, bridges needed to be repaired within the larger community.

And yet, notwithstanding good intentions and strategic approaches, it is often a serendipitous meeting or two that works to move events forward. To that point, it was at the Tampa International Airport one afternoon in early 2013 that Dean Garrison was approached by an anonymous collector who mentioned that he had two large research collections that he felt might bolster our newly revitalized LGBT initiative: a Gay Surfer Collection[6] and an Asian Male Nude Collection.[7] These two collections were the result of more than fifteen years of research, and consisted of roughly forty-five linear feet of material. Dean Garrison met with Professors Johnson and Crawley to discuss the potential acquisition, and the decision was made to accept the materials in their entirety. Because they had not examined the collection first, however, the library was placed in the awkward position of having promised to house materials that no representative had properly examined or evaluated. Thus, whereas this acquisition marked a major step toward reaching the goal of expanding our collections by 100%, it also marked a distinct period in our evolution: the USF Libraries' LGBT Initiative officially accepted pornography.[8] At almost the same time in 2013, former graduate student Cyrana Wyker, now a Ph.D. candidate at Middle Tennessee State University, agreed to have the oral histories she would be collecting for her doctoral residency, the "Tampa Gay, Lesbian, Bisexual, and Transgender Oral History Project," donated to the USF Libraries' Oral History collections. These narratives planned to touch on "drag culture, bar culture, local and state activism, 'coming out,' gay businesses, and politics from the 1950s to the present"[9] in Tampa Bay, and would, when completed, more than double the existing oral histories available online at the time.

Both of these opportune meetings have borne great fruit for the LGBT initiative. Our anonymous benefactor has, since his initial gift, donated more than 400 books on the history of the nude, male photography, gay fiction, and assorted LGBT issues. Further, he began—and continues—to donate materials that supplement our LGBT Ephemera collection, and has recently contributed research collections on gay bathhouses and sex in advertising in 2015. Perhaps most importantly, he remains a vocal advocate for our initiative in the community, and continues to increase awareness of our importance to LGBT issues locally and beyond. For her part, Cyrana Wyker has removed from obscurity and fully processed the eleven boxes of Rex Maniscalco photographs donated back in 2009, so that an online finding aid can now be used to isolate particular themes, events, and individuals from the Tampa Bay LGBT community over the past three decades. In addition, she has transcribed, edited, and deposited fourteen oral histories into the USF Oral History collections online.

Cyrana is not the only graduate student who has been essential to the success of the revived LGBT initiative, however. Once it was determined in 2013 what goals we wanted to achieve, USF library school Master's student Kevin Arms joined the department and was tasked with numerous labor-intensive, but crucial, assignments. First, he fully processed the Equality Florida and National Center for Lesbian Rights collections and published finding aids online. Next, he completed processing and publishing the Gay Surfer and the Asian Male Nude Collections, while also starting the LGBT Ephemeral collection from random donations to the initiative. When St. Pete Pride and the USF Pride Alliance donated their materials, Kevin fully processed those collections as well. Further, he created a physical exhibit of materials which we placed in our lobby display case for LGBT History Month in October 2013, and selected materials for a "show and tell" event for USF faculty, students, and the community held that same month. Library school student Todd Ciardiello took over the mantle when Kevin graduated, and has processed and catalogued hundreds of books, periodicals, and ephemeral materials for the initiative. Given budget shortfalls for faculty and staff at the USF

Library, having student workers like Cyrana, Todd, and Kevin, who are sensitive to LGBT issues and professional in their duties, has been a rare, but privileged opportunity for USF Libraries special collections to advance this initiative.

By the end of 2013, nearly all the previous year's goals had been achieved: the LGBT collections—monographs, archives and oral histories—more than trebled; events were well-attended and word about the collections was getting out; and all previously unprocessed LGBT materials were completed and had published EAD finding aids available online. However, two initial goals were not yet met: faculty and student research in the collections was still minimal, and some key figures in the community had not yet been successfully engaged or, in the case of Edie Daly and others, re-engaged. The latter issue was addressed in December 2013 when Edie visited the department and listened to our renewed commitment to the LGBT initiative. Within weeks, we had the complete WEB library in our possession, as well as a collection of papers from Old Lesbians Organizing for Change (twenty-two Hollinger boxes worth of material), and Edie and her partner Jackie[10] generously purchased a high-end scanner for the department to facilitate the digitization of LGBT items for our online collections. Connections to numerous other potential donors also arose through Edie's networks. One of these individuals, Eunice Fisher, donated invaluable archival items related to the Human Rights Task Force and the Gay and Lesbian Community Center of Tampa Bay, as well as her book, *Christian and Lesbian: A Life in Progress*, which explores her lesbian activism and deep Christian faith. This type of community goodwill has continued to the present day, and hundreds of monographs and numerous archival and ephemeral collections have been donated. Further, librarian Joe Floyd has continued to purchase books, e-books, and databases for the circulating collections to complement the LGBT materials assembled in USF Libraries' Special Collections. Yet, despite more than doubling our collections in 2013, thanks to generous donations and aggressive outreach, and increasing acquisitions by another fifty percent in 2014, use of the collections remains lower than we would like. Hopefully, there are stories that can be told so that other institutions who choose to establish similar initiatives can learn from some of our experiences.

Difficulties, Drawbacks, and Lessons Learned

What's in a Name?

This first issue may seem like a given, but it is imperative to establish consensus among all key players regarding what materials will be collected, and what the overarching goal of any initiative will be. Difficulties usually arise when a name is sought for the initiative or for a specific collection, and complications may continue as time goes by. For example, what began as the "Florida Women's History Initiative" and the "Florida LGBT Initiative" in the USF Libraries' Special Collections has now become a much more expansive "USF Libraries LGBT Initiative," and this has made a tremendous difference to the quantity, quality, and overall use of our collections. That said, the monographs are still cataloged as part of the "Queer Literature Collection," while archival collections are listed by the name of the donor. Thus, a researcher may not immediately know that the "Eunice Fisher Collection" is part of the overarching term "USF Libraries LGBT Initiative," and there is no comprehensive and sophisticated web presence to bring every LGBT-related collection together. We do have a separate "LGBT Initiative" webpage that describes all of the relevant materials in special collections, but this is not a top-level page on the library's website, and is not easily discoverable. Moreover, with many databases and e-books being purchased to complement the LGBT initiative in special collections, to say nothing of the occasional physical book being added to the circulating collection, a patron could be forgiven for becoming confused as to where and what this LGBT Initiative is. This is an ongoing issue that is mainly solved through outreach and education; however, these difficulties can be anticipated when LGBT collections are not housed in one single location under one title. Therefore, if you are just starting out, do try to think of the patrons' or users' needs first. At USF, we are working on revamping our web presence to facilitate patrons' experiences, and hope that many issues can be resolved in the coming months.

What Do You Collect? What Don't You Collect?

Back in 2006, faculty, students, and especially community members were unsure what materials would be accepted into the LGBT collections; in fact, there are records from 2006-2011 detailing significant donations that were refused because they did not relate directly to Tampa Bay.[11] We have since determined that while it is vital to "think and act locally," each location in America is merely part of a larger whole, and issues and concerns of the wider LGBT community should have a place in our collections for researchers to access—denying patrons access to important research material based on lack of geographical significance is a flawed approach. In order to avoid past mistakes, therefore, it was determined that all materials chosen for the LGBT Initiative will be assessed according to the following criteria: utility in teaching, learning, or research; scholarly value; uniqueness/rarity of the item[s]; potential for digitization and exhibition; and, in the case of archival collections, the historical and ephemeral value of the collection as a whole. This is a similar approach taken by other successful LGBT initiatives, for example, Emory University's MARBL LGBT collection. That being said, it has been our experience that community members often underestimate the research value of their materials, especially ephemera. Therefore, we encourage all potential donors to pay us a visit so that special collections librarians can make a proper evaluation. For example, a significant collection of nearly 100 lesbian books from the '60s, '70s, and '80s was saved after a chance meeting at an antiquarian book sale: "You are interested in this kind of junk?" asked the woman after witnessing a purchase, "Well, I am about to throw out my life's collection." On the other hand, when donations are accepted *in toto* with the agreement that no materials may be deaccessioned or discarded, institutions may inadvertently get themselves into the business of collecting hardcore pornography, which often does not adequately fulfill the assessment criteria listed above. There are exceptions to every rule, however, and each collection, book, or ephemeral item should be judged on its own merits. If materials fall outside of the scope of the collecting policy listed above, they are returned to the donor or discarded per the terms of the donation agreement.

What about Access to the Materials?

This is a particularly thorny issue. Since the USF Libraries LGBT Initiative has most of its collections located in special collections, there are added barriers to access for researchers: materials are only accessible Monday to Friday, 9:00am-5:00pm; patrons need to be buzzed into the reading room, create an account with us, and then request the material; some collections have been declared age-restricted by their donor, so no one under the age of eighteen may access these items; and, finally, many community members are not aware that USF Libraries' Special Collections is open to all researchers and not restricted to students and faculty. Further, given that the Queer Literature collection began with a donation of novels, many patrons have asked why they were placed into special collections and not made more readily available in the circulating collection. Adding this extra barrier to patrons might be seen as hindering those who may be questioning or desirous of more private and less intrusive transactions than those in a special collections reading room under security cameras. We at USF are comfortable answering these questions, but are simultaneously aware of the validity of the concerns put forward—especially as they relate to ease of access. This may be an issue that each individual institution will need to work out for itself; do the wishes of a donor trump the access problems for the LGBT community and interested researchers, for example?

Are the L, G, B, and T Treated Equally?

This is likely the most crucial aspect to consider when trying to build a balanced LGBT initiative from the ground up. Limited budgets require intense advocacy in the local community to encourage donations, which can unintentionally lead to an imbalance in collections. For example, an evaluation was done in early 2013 which determined that the LGBT materials in special collections were composed of 80% gay male literature and materials, 10% lesbian literature and materials, 5% bisexual literature and materials and 5% transgender literature and materials. This was not entirely shocking; after all, the Queer Literature collection began with mainly gay male literature, and the Gay Surfer Archive and Asian Male Nude Collection alone accounted for close to ninety Hollinger boxes. Yet, as Cyrana Wyker, who has collected many LGBT oral histories around Tampa Bay, noted when discussing her work:

> It is easy to convince prominent community members, particularly wealthy ones, that their voices are important, that their experience matters, and that being immortalized in the archive is worthwhile. The many other individuals, that often get overlooked or perhaps don't understand the significance of the archive, are a lot more difficult to convince to participate. What happens then, in my opinion, is that the experience of gay white men becomes the narrative for all LGBT(Q) experience... The records of formal organizations and wealthy community members are most certainly invaluable to an archive but so are those of the working class, ethnic minorities, and sexual subcultures (consensual, of course) such as BDSM, and those who have had a different historical experience than middle to upper class white men.

Graduate student Kevin Arms came to the same conclusion in March of 2013, encouraging special collections faculty to strive to increase the balance between communities: "We have a preponderance of materials related to the 'G' in LGBT…Collection development areas could include more Lesbian, Bisexual and Transgendered (sic) items, books and collections so that the overall initiative is more representative of the community it serves. There are only a handful of instances and one collection that expressly deal with Lesbians, and we have very little, if anything, for bisexual and transgendered study outside of the materials presented in Equality Florida's records." As a respondent to our survey noted: "Make certain that the community has the buy-in for the institution and what we are trying to accomplish and that we are doing due diligence to make sure that we are collecting a wide scope of the community's history and not just the 'easy' to get records." In that regard, we knew we needed to add much more depth to the initiative to be true to our mission and to the local, national, and international LGBT community.

We have been extremely successful in some areas since early 2013: our lesbian collections have grown exponentially, thanks to donors and supporters like Edie Daly, and to aggressive collection development and strategic purchases. We now have one of the largest collections of *Lesbian Connection,* for example, and a large collection of many other lesbian periodicals from the 1960s to the present courtesy of the WEB library. But the bisexual and transgender materials have been harder to come by; as a respondent to a survey we conducted with other like-minded institutions said, "It is important to allow time for Bi and Trans history because it is difficult to locate but necessary for a robust collection. Ask for help often and from the folks who want to help!" This advice has borne fruit, as a chance encounter by one of our donors at an LGBT event led to us acquiring the papers and autobiographies of a local activist and transgender female, Janice Josephine Carney. This same donor aggressively pursues potential donors at high-profile LGBT events, and has sent many wonderful collections our way. We still have a long way to go for a perfect balance, certainly, but the USF Libraries LGBT Initiative is committed to making it happen.

Does Anyone Come to Use These Collections?

The good news is that use of USF Libraries LGBT materials in special collections increased more than a hundred-fold between 2013 and 2014; the bad news is that this amounted to less than 120 LGBT items being paged over the course of the year.[12] Additionally, when items are used in display cases or events, they are "checked out," leaving the number of physical patron requests lacking, at least in terms of our ambitious goals. There are many issues at play here: the relatively low number of courses offered at USF that have an LGBT component; the lack of awareness on campus and in the community about our initiative; and a lack of knowledge about what we have in our collections. According to our survey, other institutions have similar issues in the latter regard: said one respondent, "We have a dynamic Women's and Gender Studies program. My only wish is that they would suggest that students see us first when considering research topics, instead of deciding on a topic and come hoping we can provide adequate archival resources." This could easily have been said by library faculty and staff here at USF. While we have labored to facilitate engagement with faculty, staff, students, and the community about our LGBT materials, it is clear that we need to work harder to encourage research and exploration of our resources for both academic and community researchers. We do hold a yearly lecture during LGBT History Month in October, and while past events have gone over extremely well, with both the USF and wider Tampa Bay community in attendance, perhaps we need to consider expanding our event agenda. The head of special collections also co-presented "Getting in the Stacks: Using Archival Sources to Better Understand LGBTQ+ Histories and Intersectional Identities," with Ph.D. candidate Keegan Shepherd at the 2015 Florida Collegiate Pride Coalition, which was well-regarded and showcased many of our LGBT materials to attendees from across Florida. An online exhibition has also just been launched by librarian Andy Huse, which documents the "witch hunt" against suspected communists and homosexuals at USF by the Florida Legislative Investigation Committee (perhaps better known as the Johns Committee) in the early 1960s.[13] Additionally, the special collections department has networked with faculty and staff in the departments of the Arts, History, Sociology, Anthropology, Psychology, Health and Medicine, and Political Science to promote the LGBT collection, but one meeting or phone call is not enough. Faculty and students need to be reminded again and again what materials we have, and this outreach needs to be expanded.

Do You Have the Support of Administration and Colleagues?

Since arriving in 2008, William Garrison, the Dean of USF Libraries, has been committed to building the LGBT Initiative. As mentioned above, he earmarked more than $60,000 for the cause, but the Director at the time chose not to spend the money and it was eventually distributed elsewhere. It is crucial to achieve unanimous buy-in from all major players when establishing this type of initiative. Looking beyond this lack of action in the past, there are still frequent cases of faculty and staff expressing their strong opinions about having certain LGBT materials in the library. "If we have all this gay porn, does that mean we can collect straight porn too?" is one frequent comment, and incredulity about "filth" and "useless materials" is not uncommon. But this is certainly not unique to USF; one respondent to the survey from a public library with an LGBT collection was told by a branch manager that, "For each LGBT program/topic we have, she reserves the right to have one Christian program/topic." Another comment was, "There seems to be a level of discomfort in straight collection development staff—not knowing what LGBTQ books are 'good,' wondering if they will be judged for buying LGBTQ titles, etc." These minor complaints are simple to dodge, however, and education of straight staff is ongoing and, speaking personally, extremely rewarding; yet it is the backing at the highest level that is most crucial, and USF Libraries is lucky and proud to have that support. That said, widespread support across campus and the community is an ongoing struggle, and must be constantly sought out with diligence and strategic approaches.

What is Your Budget?

Technically, as a state university, we have a set budget for collections each fiscal year. Faculty are able to request what they need, or wish for, but often we are unable to honor these requests. Of course, with electronic resources taking up so much of the total budget—if not all of it—physical collections are difficult to build. For that reason, we need to rely heavily on donations and foundation funds. The former is handled by special collections for the most part, but the latter depends in large part upon the library's development officer. At the USF Libraries, we have found this to be a blessing and a curse; it is truly a blessing when the development officer brings in a check for an LGBT fund, but it can be an unmitigated disaster when potential donors of materials are preyed upon for money at the expense of donating their materials, or collections are accepted without an eye to their value in order to advance a financial agenda. It is a delicate dance, surely, and one that we recommend be joined by at least one librarian to ensure that the mission of the initiative or program is upheld above all. Despite a few pitfalls, however, development, the dean, and special collections have successfully worked together to set up an LGBT Undergraduate Research Award, have established an LGBT endowment, and have reached out to numerous entities and individuals in the community with positive results of gifts in kind and financial contributions.

What about Community Outreach?

Community outreach is an area that we feel needs improvement. Since 2013, we have been involved in a somewhat systematic attempt to engage the community, but have likely missed some potential supporters. Our initial plan was to reach out to prominent members of the LGBT community and utilize their networks to spread the word about our initiative. This, coupled with attendance at meetings and events, has been our main focus, but we clearly need to be more vocal and visible in the community. Other institutions have similar approaches, and one in particular developed an ingenious strategy for supplying metadata: "We have been using old grassroots style outreach to date. Creating connections with older community members and allowing them to help us expand our networks. We have also engaged the community to help us identify photos and documents in order for them to feel like they are a part of the process. So far it's been amazingly successful." This method of engagement with the materials and the personal history of community members is a strategy that we plan to employ in the future in order to increase knowledge of our initiative and expand the knowledge base we can tap to further our mission.

Do You Collaborate with Outside Organizations?

Collaborations with the Tampa International Gay and Lesbian Film Festival, Metro Wellness and Community Centers, Equality Florida, St. Pete Pride, Watermark, National Center for Lesbian Rights, PNC Bank, USF's Committee on Issues of Sexual Orientation and Gender Identity, USF Pride Alliance, USF's Office of Multicultural Affairs, and others, have paid significant dividends and increased both awareness and goodwill toward the initiative. These connections to the community are vital, not only for the mutual benefit they provide, but because they can help to build a more balanced collection as well. As Cyrana Wyker mentioned, getting to know as much about local LGBT issues as possible can drive discussions about the myriad subjectivities, behaviors, identities, sexual practices, and the like that fall under the umbrella of LGBT. That said, there is still much to be done at the organizational level in the Tampa Bay area, and much more that could have been done better.

Conclusion

Since its revival in 2012, the USF Libraries LGBT Initiative has remained committed to its mission, and we have had our share of minor and major triumphs as outlined above. Our initiative is really the only one of its kind in Florida: the Stonewall Archive in Fort Lauderdale is less research-focused, although a distinct treasure, and the GLBT museum in Orlando is smaller and more geared toward digitizing physical objects—so we take our role as a repository for the community very seriously. Our story is a young but interesting one, we hope, and if there are any details which emerged in the foregoing discussion that may help a similar institution in their commitment to LGBT issues, then this can be counted a successful excursion. For USF, our task is just beginning:

we need to increase our physical collections; continue to engage the community; bolster our online LGBT materials and exhibitions; and offer more events to strengthen the initiative and the LGBT community. For now, however, we continue to learn from our mistakes and follow up on our successes—never sitting back, but always moving forward and enjoying the challenges that face us.

Endnotes

1. At the USF Library, the LGBT initiative is distinguished from a general collection in a number of ways. First, the library administration and the institution at large are in full support of the venture; this benefits budget allocations for collection development, fund-raising efforts, and faculty outreach, and helps garner community support. The initiative also hosts (and plans to host) lectures, symposia, and "show and tell" events, featuring local activists, scholars, and community members. Another part of the initiative is an oral history project that has already gained tractions and momentum moving forward. Lastly, the initiative includes physical collections, both archival and monographic.

2. USF Libraries' Special Collections is open to all visitors and researchers; there are no access restrictions.

3. A deed of gift transferring legal ownership rights for the materials to the University accompanies all collections. Donations may be considered charitable gifts, to the extent provided by law. Collection appraisals for charitable gift purposes are the responsibility of the donor. The Special and Digital Collections Department welcomes donations to its LGBT collection from private or institutional entities. Prospective donations are assessed by the Department according to collection area guidelines, Library and University strategic goals, evidence of research value, collection condition, and available resources to house, preserve and provide access to those items. Reasons for refusal include: content outside the scope of the collection, poor physical condition, or unnecessary duplication of material in the collection.

4. The Equality Florida collection at USF is comprised of many items, including correspondence, budgets, ephemera, program logs, annual reports, director reports, news articles, research materials on a wide variety of topics, and some audio/visual materials. Also included within the collection are files dedicated to many projects that Equality Florida has worked on in the past, such as the St. Petersburg Human Rights Ordinance and the Tampa Human Rights Ordinance, the Safe Schools Summit, and even meetings between members of clergy of different denominations in the Equal Partners in Faith conferences.

5. Stemming from an original parent organization within Equality Florida, the NCLR became its own stand-alone organization supported by the National Office in 2000. This donated collection contains corporate documents that include annual reports, major gift campaigns, and grant materials of the organization. Additionally, there are documents regarding the aforementioned projects, both those done solely by NCLR as well as those done in cooperation with Equality Florida.

6. This collection contains numerous magazines, news clippings, and other ephemera relating to the gay surfer image in printed form. Beginning in 1936, the collection documents the increasingly visible appearance of surfers and surfing's connection with gay men and women through nude photographs, all male physique magazines, and eventually to overtly gay lifestyle publications and advertisements.

7. Containing magazines, news clippings, photographs, ephemera, and audio/visual materials, this collection documents the historical rarity of the Asian male nude and the transition to the more common proliferation of materials found in later years. The collection illustrates the historical reality of this racial stereotype and the rarity of the nude Asian male in depictions of gay imagery in art as well as in Western pornography.

8. Materials in the Gay Surfer Archive and the Asian Male Nude Collection have been marked and catalogued as "Age Restricted" at the donor's request. No patron under eighteen years of age may view these materials.

9. See https://cyranabwyker.wordpress.com/projects/residency/.

10. Edie and Jackie Mirkin, together for 18 years, were married in California in 2008. Their stories are included in *Without Apology*: the second collection of life stories based on interview transcripts in the Old Lesbian Oral Herstory Project edited by Arden Eversmeyer and Margaret Purcell, 2012.

11. Efforts have been made to try to re-engage those potential donors to gauge their interest in donating to the revitalized initiative, but often the materials—or individuals—are long gone.

12. USF Libraries' Special Collections uses Aeon as its registration and request manager; this system allows simple calculations of collection use and patron type.

13. http://exhibits.lib.usf.edu/exhibits/show/witchhunt/.

Appendix: Survey for LGBT Institutions

The following survey was sent out to selected institutions known to have LGBT initiatives and/or collections, and was posted to the GLBT listserv. There were 10 responses.

1. How long has your institution had an LGBT initiative and/or solid commitment to collection development in LGBT areas?
2. What is your official title, and are you in charge of LGBT collection development? Part of a team?
3. What do you call your collection? Do you have separate names for monographic collections vs. archives? Was there any debate about what to call the collection[s]?
4. Do you work with Development when soliciting donations/support for collections?
5. If you answered yes to the above, could you describe your experience with Development officers? Have they helped or hindered in your efforts to build LGBT collections? Please be honest—all responses are anonymous!

6. What is the most important thing, in your opinion, to building a quality LGBT collection at your institution?
7. Do you feel you have full support from administration for your efforts? Feel free to expand.
8. What types of materials--if any—will you decline to add to an LGBT collection. Why? Conversely, what are the most important items you wish to add?
9. How do you reach out to community members for support? Has it been successful?
10. What other resources do you utilize to build your LGBT collections?
11. Please describe your budget situation, and strategies you use to successfully build collections if money is tight.
12. What advice would you give to a librarian who has been tasked with building an LGBT collection basically from scratch?
13. Are your collections primarily circulating? In a special collections/archives area? Both? Has this caused issues?
14. Can you share some of your spectacular successes; and, if you've had them, your failures building collections?
15. Do you feel that faculty have adequately supported your efforts? Explain.
16. What glaring omission does this survey make that you would like to discuss. Please feel free to talk about any issues that you feel important in the discussion of building LGBT collections. Thank you!

Chapter 8

GLOBAL PROMOTION OF LGBTQ LIBRARY RESOURCES AND SERVICES THROUGH SOCIAL MEDIA

Rachel Wexelbaum

Introduction

People around the world do not have equal access to traditionally published LGBTQ information resources. Censorship, legalized persecution of LGBTQ people, poverty, lack of native-language publishing industries, and cultural differences in information sharing all contribute to global LGBTQ information inequities. At the same time, the number of people with smart phones and wireless Internet is outstripping the number of people who live within reasonable distance of a physical library.[1] LGBTQ information seekers use social media and Web 2.0—often without intervention from librarians—to research information needs and exchange knowledge and resources in online communities of like-minded people.

Wikipedia, YouTube, blog feeds, Twitter, Facebook, GoodReads, LGBTQ social media apps, and other media channels currently serve as alternatives to library resources and services for LGBTQ information seekers around the world. While social media and Web 2.0 appear to increase access to LGBTQ information, the authority, validity, objectivity, and safety of these unregulated information resources varies widely. As content creators predominantly come from those nations with the widest economic, cultural, and linguistic reach, the artifacts that LGBTQ information seekers locate may not provide answers relevant to their local realities. At the same time, LGBTQ content creators from nations most in need of such information may jeopardize their safety by posting their work online, or may lack an appropriate venue for their work. Public and academic librarians who wish to provide outreach to LGBTQ information seekers should join their online communities and connect a diverse population of local and global users to legitimate, relevant LGBTQ information resources and services.

The State of LGBTQ Library Resources and Services around the World

LGBTQ library resources and services in most countries remain an unknown entity. The availability of traditionally published native language LGBTQ materials varies widely in countries where governments sanction the marginalization of LGBTQ people. If librarians in those countries are collecting LGBTQ resources, they must be careful about how they make these resources accessible, how they promote these resources to users, and how they address such resources and services in international surveys. People living in countries that criminalize LGBTQ existence in person or in print may generate "born digital" LGBTQ content such as blogs, podcasts, Facebook groups, Twitter accounts, and Wikipedia content, thus bypassing the library completely for LGBTQ information.

A young queer person with access to a physical library in his or her town may hesitate to approach a reference desk and ask for a book about queer people. The phenomenon of LGBTQ library anxiety would definitely take place in countries that criminalize LGBTQ existence. Librarians in countries that criminalize LGBTQ existence may hesitate or flat out refuse to add LGBTQ-affirming materials to their collections due to state-sanctioned prejudice or fear for their own safety. In countries with limited native-language publishing output, libraries must often pay more for translations of global bestsellers and award winning titles; this is especially so if they purchase access to electronic versions of these titles.[2]

A complete global directory of LGBTQ collections does not exist. The most comprehensive list reveals that at least forty independent LGBTQ-specific library collections exist around the world, the vast majority of which are in English-speaking countries.[3] More than half of these collections exist as independent archives or museums, and twenty per cent exist in higher education institutions. While some public libraries collect LGBTQ-specific materials, and may even have a special section in the library for LGBTQ materials, not all of them promote their LGBTQ holdings to the public. In fact, the movement to "de-segregate" LGBTQ collections in public libraries, to integrate LGBT fiction with the rest of the fiction for example, often makes it difficult for interested library users to locate LGBT books in libraries.[4] If curious queers in disadvantaged or hostile environments have Internet access, they will most likely attempt to search for LGBT information, books, and films on their own.

Most research literature on LGBT library resources and services—as well as library resources and services for marginalized populations—comes from "first world" English-speaking countries. While homophobia, lesbophobia, biphobia, and transphobia still exist in these countries, their laws protect freedom of expression and the civil rights of all individuals. This manifests as libraries having the privilege of providing access to library resources and services to all individuals in their communities without fear of professional censure, imprisonment, torture, or execution. Scandinavian countries and the Netherlands also enjoy such privilege. Little if any published material exists on LGBT library resources and services in southern and eastern Europe, the former Soviet Union, the Middle East (including Israel), Africa, or Asia.

In 2013, the International Federation of Library Associations and Institutions (IFLA) stated that, "substantial discussions of issues related to library services for LGBTQ community members have not taken place at IFLA." This resulted in the launch of the LGBTQ Users Special Interest Group, supported by the Acquisition and Collection Development Section, in December 2013.[5] Although the Gay, Lesbian, Bisexual, and Transgender Round Table (GLBTRT) of the American Libraries

Association (ALA) has had a profound influence on LGBT library practices in the United States and other countries, no federal or state laws of any nation mandate that libraries must acquire LGBT resources or provide services specifically for LGBT patrons.

LGBT Library Resources and Services as Legal and Ethical Obligation

The Office of the United Nations High Commissioner for Human Rights (OHCHR) identified "five core legal obligations of states with respect to protecting the human rights of LGBT persons." These include "1) protect individuals from homophobic and transphobic violence, 2) prevent torture and cruel, inhuman and degrading treatment of LGBT persons, 3) decriminalize homosexuality, 4) prohibit discrimination based on sexual orientation and gender identity, and 5) respect freedom of expression, association and peaceful assembly."[6] LGBT people, even in countries with advanced civil rights protections, face microaggressions,[7] discrimination, abuse, health disparities, and unsafe physical spaces around the world.[8]

In the IFLA Internet Manifesto 2014, Section 3, "The role and responsibilities of library and information services," states at the very top of the list that libraries have the responsibility of "serv[ing] all of the members of their communities, regardless of age, race, nationality, religion, culture, political affiliation, physical or mental abilities, *gender or sexual orientation, or other status* [emphasis added]."[9] While librarians may want to take on this responsibility, they may also find themselves walking a tightrope between compliance and subversion against the state.

Countries that suppress or criminalize LGBTQ expression or existence may not support libraries that provide resources and services that support *all* people in their communities. As nations strive to create "safe" cyberspace for children in state-funded environments such as schools and libraries, such policies can also restrict or eliminate access to LGBTQ content—particularly in areas where LGBTQ existence is perceived as a threat to minors.[10] Websites with URLs that end in two-letter country code Top-Level Domains (ccTLDs) represent the state and its norms.[11] This includes library websites, as the vast majority of libraries around the world receive local, state, and/or federal funding in order to exist. Depending on the state's control of education, freedom of the press, and freedom of expression, libraries will develop collections and services that represent national and local interests, thus making a statement about national identity. For this reason, librarians around the world who wish to provide resources and services to LGBTQ people must resist and work with non-traditional information resources outside of traditional library environments.

LGBTQ Mobile Device Ownership, Internet Access, and Social Media Preferences

Rapid Expansion...But in Libraries?

As of November 2014, the number of global Internet users passed 3 billion—nearly half of the world's population.[12] As of January 2015, the number of active mobile connections surpassed the total world population.[13] According to Cisco's Global Mobile Data Traffic Forecast 2011-2016, over 10 billion mobile devices will be connected to the Internet by 2016, with the most rapid expansion taking place in the Middle East, Africa, Asia, and Eastern Europe.[14] This explosion of mobile access to the Internet worldwide has expanded public access to information and education. In some developing countries, Millennials believe that they can learn independently through a mobile device to supplement or replace traditional schooling.[15] Libraries worldwide remain behind in addressing the needs of mobile users, whether through the creation of mobile versions of their online resources and services or the effective employment of social media to promote library resources and services.[16]

In 2014 IFLA published its "Internet Manifesto." In Section 1.3, it states:

> 1.3 Library and information services should be essential gateways to the Internet, its resources and services. Their role is to act as access points which offer convenience, guidance and support, whilst helping overcome barriers created by differences in resources, technology, and skills.[17]

At the same time, according to the live IFLA World Report, eighty-six of the world's nations—nearly half —do not provide adequate Internet access to their users. Less than forty per cent of public and research libraries in those nations offer Internet access to users.[18] Included in this count are South Africa, Russia, and China. Even in nations where nearly all libraries provide Internet access in libraries, no legal obligation exists to provide free unlimited Internet access for patrons.[19] This reality creates more barriers for LGBTQ patrons—particularly those who may prefer locating LGBTQ information online.

LGBTQ Internet Access and Ownership of Mobile Devices

The majority of studies conducted on LGBTQ Internet users have taken place in the United States. At the same time, it may be safely assumed that, around the world, LGBTQ populations may be more likely than cisgender heterosexual populations to have access to the Internet and mobile devices. LGBTQ individuals are often early adoption of emerging technologies, online spaces, and social media.[20]

LGBTQ people, including those living in countries historically unfriendly to LGBTQ populations, perceive the Internet as a "safe space."[21] Those who have access to the Internet through personal smartphones, tablets, or laptops create social media accounts and join a wide variety of LGBTQ social, academic, and professional networks. Those who cannot afford mobile devices may visit Internet cafés and, if unfettered by government-mandated filtering or the blocking of particular sites altogether, will attempt to reach out to other LGBTQ people through more indirect means. LGBTQ social media users may depend on pseudonyms and a wide variety of IP addresses to use LGBTQ social media or create LGBTQ content. This includes LGBTQ Wikipedia contributors from countries where LGBTQ identity and expression remains illegal.

In the Wikipedia community, LGBTQ contributors maintain anonymity through their own actions and the loyalty of fellow Wikipedians. Some LGBTQ Wikipedia contributors do not create user profiles, and simply log in to Wikipedia to make edits; the IP addresses from devices used are recorded in the "View History" page of every entry. Some LGBTQ Wikipedia contributors from countries that criminalize LGBTQ existence may choose to create user profiles with names that do not reflect their true gender identity or ethnicity. These people are "known" in the LGBT Wikimedia community: out of respect for their privacy and safety LGBT Wikimedians will not "out" them in any forum or publication. In discussions where these LGBT Wikimedians cannot be present, participants will only refer to these people by their Wikipedia username.

Social Media Preferences

Global data on social media preferences does not make specific mention of LGBTQ media preferences. At the same time, it appears that a greater percentage of LGBTQ individuals around the world have access to the Internet, mobile devices, and online spaces.[22] For this reason, we might be able to assume that LGBTQ social media preferences in different countries may mirror those of the mainstream populations. Librarians must take generational differences into account, as those who have used social media and mobile technologies since childhood may prefer different media channels than older generations. English language proficiency may also play a role in social media preferences for LGBTQ populations in non-English speaking countries. Finally, if governments monitor individual Internet activity through well-known mainstream social media sites such as Facebook and Twitter, LGBTQ populations may seek out alternative social media channels.

The most comprehensive data collected on LGBTQ social media use has come from American market research companies.[23] Community Marketing Inc. (CMI) has conducted a marketing research survey on LGBTQ people in China. They gathered this data through collaboration with an organization called Shanghai LGBT Professionals, "a non-profit network for gay and lesbian employees and platform for dialogue and cooperation with companies across China on LGBT inclusion."[24] Shanghai LGBT Professionals had partnered with twenty LGBTQ-friendly organizations in China to conduct their survey. Approximately 8,000 individuals from different regions of China completed the survey. The majority of respondents were young adults, since they were most likely to be out and involved in China's increasingly visible LGBTQ community. While the number of participants was small, and primarily from educated, affluent backgrounds, it was an enormous accomplishment considering that China still does not have civil rights laws to address discrimination or harassment on the basis of sexual orientation or gender identity, and that Internet monitoring and censorship is a government-approved practice. The majority of Chinese young adults surveyed had smartphones, and information access through these devices is very important to them. This population enjoys using LGBTQ mobile apps and reading LGBTQ websites and blogs,[25] a pattern of online information consumption that is similar to American LGBTQ individuals surveyed by CMI.[26]

Some studies exist on LGBTQ media preferences for advertising in other countries, which may prove informative to librarians in those countries who wish to promote their LGBTQ resources and services to LGBTQ populations. In general, however, more research is needed on LGBTQ social media preferences in other regions of the world.

LGBTQ Information Seeking through Social Media

In the past, physical spaces such as bars, cafés, bookstores, and libraries have played a role in building LGBT community and providing LGBT-related information resources to all interested people. In the twenty-first century, when queer existence remains illegal in eighty countries,[27] librarians can still provide access to reliable, authoritative information on LGBT health issues, law, immigration, and relationships—as well as leisure reading and media with significant LGBT characters and content—in online environments. Roughly half of LGBT youth use the Internet to gather information and seek connection with others during their "coming out" process.[28] Social media channels present an exciting opportunity for librarians around the world to reach out to LGBT individuals and organizations, to determine their information needs, and to promote their LGBT-related resources and services.

Historically, LGBTQ populations have been early adopters of online spaces, as well as pioneers in digital content creation.[29] LGBTQ individuals can participate in online activities through pseudonyms and alternate identities if they wish. The Internet also provides LGBTQ individuals with opportunities to meet and exchange information with other LGBTQ people from around the world. While language, national social media preferences, and government Internet filtering and website blocking often impact the reach of LGBTQ individuals in particular countries to all the world's information resources, access to local or national LGBTQ online social networks still benefits LGBTQ individuals. Global organizations that serve LGBTQ populations of minority religions and cultures also create online presences to bring people together and provide support.

Social media has provided LGBTQ populations with spaces that they perceive as "safe" for coming out and finding support.[30] Around the world, LGBTQ individuals use social media to locate information about sexual health, transitioning, safe ways to come out, and legislation that affects LGBTQ individuals. They also use social media to find friends, sexual partners, significant others, social groups, and political groups. Last but not least, LGBTQ individuals may employ social media to look for LGBTQ books and media for entertainment—or to find forums where they can discuss books and films.

As of 2015, no official directory of LGBTQ online spaces exists. Online spaces are often ephemeral and may be accessible only on certain platforms. No one has noted the national origins of the social media administrators or content creators, so no clear picture exists of LGBTQ-specific social media activity around the world. In 2013, a poster on the LGBTQ wedding site PrideZillas.com shared a list published by gaydatingsites.net of the 100 most frequently "liked" LGBTQ Facebook pages published in English. Twenty percent of those pages focus on LGBTQ populations in countries such as Scotland, Denmark, the United Kingdom, South Africa, and Russia. They also focus on global populations such as Latinos/as, Arabs, Muslims, Jews, and Buddhists.[31]

I decided to search on Facebook for other LGBTQ Facebook pages published in Spanish, French, German, Russian, Turkish, Arabic, and Chinese.[32] I used the native language terms for gay, lesbian, bisexual, transgender, and LGBT. Facebook pages in Spanish, French, and German included pages focused on particular nationalities, ethnicities, and cultures who spoke those languages. The most popular page categories varied; community pages were most popular for Spanish speakers and French speakers, while the most popular pages for German speakers were for events, a magazine, and a community organization. There were significantly fewer German LGBTQ Facebook pages than there were for French and Spanish; this could result from the fact that fewer German speakers exist than Spanish or French speakers, or because German LGBTQ social media users may prefer other social media channels to connect. There were very few Arabic language LGBTQ Facebook pages; the most popular were for movies, community groups, and a book store. Turkish language searches for LGBTQ pages, surprisingly, retrieved Facebook pages for the International Lesbian Gay Transgender Association (IGLTA), International Gay & Lesbian Travel, and Lesbian and Gay Inter-University Organizations. No LGBTQ Facebook pages existed for Russian or Chinese speakers, at least none that used globally recognized queer terminology.

Slight cultural differences exist in regard to LGBTQ-specific social networking sites. I conducted searches through the Google search engines of the United States, Mexico, France, Germany, Russia, Saudi Arabia, Turkey, Hong Kong, South Africa, and Israel to find out which

LGBTQ, gay, and lesbian social media sites they used. The searches revealed that several English LGBTQ-specific social networking sites consistently appear in the first top ten results from each country, but native language searches for in those sites retrieve very different results. In only two countries studied—Germany and Russia—were native language LGBTQ, gay, and lesbian social media sites as plentiful as those in English. When social media sites had apps for mobile devices, those often proved more popular than the web-based media, particularly in countries where LGBTQ existence and expression is at risk.

Use of Social Media to Promote LGBTQ Information

Research on LGBTQ individuals and their Internet and social media use often has a bias toward and privileges LGBTQ people on the "right side" of the digital divide. Those using the Internet and social media often own at least one mobile device that allows them to do so. In nations that put LGBTQ individuals at risk, they may not use libraries for Internet access if they perceive that librarians collude with the government or if they perceive libraries as unsafe spaces. As libraries place more of their collections, resources, and services online, they should also continue to collect physical LGBTQ resources whenever possible and communicate through local LGBTQ social media channels that those resources exist at the library.

Most published research about LGBTQ social media use addresses undergraduates and sexual minority youth, as well as gay and bisexual men.[33] Studies on the use of social media to connect with others for friendship, romantic relationships, or sex are common,[34] along with the use of the Internet and social media to locate health information.[35] Libraries are slowly transitioning from a focus on collection development to a focus on community development, which includes reaching out to vulnerable populations through social media.[36]

LGBTQ-friendly librarians working and living in unsafe environments for LGBTQ information and people must develop creative strategies to serve patrons in need of LGBTQ-related information. While some information professionals promote information resources at HIV/AIDS related events and community organization gatherings, others infiltrate social media and other Web 2.0 tools to make LGBTQ-related information accessible to all, not just to local audiences but to the world at large. Librarians can employ the same social media strategies as organizations that provide health information to LGBTQ populations.[37] Librarians can also communicate information about LGBTQ books, magazines, or online resources through YouTube and share those videos through Twitter, a more global social media channel than Facebook.[38] Perhaps the best strategy librarians can use to promote LGBTQ library resources and services through social media is to have people from the LGBTQ community take on the role of "library promoters." Librarians can "befriend" LGBTQ community leaders, ask to visit centers of LGBTQ activity, and engage in dialogue about LGBTQ library resources and services to determine whether or not people have access to the LGBTQ information or resources that they would like. They can also generate interest in reading clubs or the use of library space for support groups. The LGBTQ community, if they have reached a certain comfort level with the librarian, may discuss their social media use, their media preferences, and what the library could do to fill information or Internet access gaps for their community. If librarians must make a report to their compliance-focused director, they do not have to state that this feedback came specifically from the LGBTQ community. Instead, they can simply state that the feedback and requests came from *the community*. Data such as this would might also come in handy to explain declines in gate counts and circulation, and may spur a library to provide more online resources and services for all users.

Challenges to Serving LGBTQ Populations through Social Media

LGBTQ populations living in unsafe physical environments, including countries that monitor Internet use and LGBTQ-related activities, may not speak openly about their online information needs or preferences.

In these environments, locating LGBTQ participants for research studies could prove to be difficult and might not be supported by local or state grants. For these reasons, the majority of studies conducted on LGBTQ Internet and social media use have taken place in spaces that protect LGBTQ civil rights, freedom of expression, or both.[39]

Social media trends, particularly among marginalized communities, change over time. This is especially true for youth who may not want to be associated with social media channels that older family members use. In places where governments may monitor native language social media channels, such as in China and Russia, LGBTQ populations will seek alternatives. English, French, or German fluency can open many doors for them if their wish is to connect to and share information with people around the world. If LGBTQ individuals wish to focus on connecting with local communities, they can create an online space using a locally popular social media channel to do so, using "code words" to relay the fact that the site is for LGBTQ socialization. The group may shift their space from one media channel to another if they feel that they are under scrutiny, or if younger or more tech-savvy members find a different media platform that better meets their needs.

Internet censorship of LGBTQ individuals and content is very real. During the writing of this article, Lane Rasberry posted to the LGBT Wikimedia Outreach listserv that Wikipedians in Azerbaijan had been kidnapped and tortured for publishing "political propaganda" on Wikipedia.[40] LGBT Wikipedians from countries that criminalize LGBTQ existence and information sharing must contribute to Wikipedia using pseudonyms and roaming IP addresses. As libraries around the world provide space for Wikipedia parties, it is possible that librarians may find themselves taking stands on civil rights issues in their countries that they would not have imagined.

In 2012, Facebook estimated that they had eighty-three million "fake" accounts. When they made this information public, their stock prices plummeted.[41] For this reason, Facebook decided to implement its "real-name policy" for user profiles. According to the real name policy, a "real name" is "your real name as it would be listed on your credit card, driver's license, or student ID."[42] This policy has caused disproportionate harm to LGBTQ individuals, especially transgender people who may not have had formal name changes made with their governments, closeted youth and other vulnerable individuals, and drag queens. While Facebook insists that their real name policy "keeps our community safe," it endangers LGBTQ people who may not have a safe place to engage in LGBTQ-related communication using their real names. While Facebook Chief Product Officer Chris Cox issued an apology to the LGBTQ community, making the claim that "we're going to fix the way this policy gets handled so that everyone affected here can go back to using Facebook," the real name policy has led Facebook to deactivate the user profiles of Native Americans and other groups.[43] Facebook's faux pas inspired disgruntled users to migrate to the up-and-coming Ello, a more intimate social media channel that allows people to use pseudonyms.[44] While it is possible that Ello may gain popularity with the mainstream in the future, at the time of this writing it lacks the user-friendly features and user protections that most regular social media users have come to expect.[45]

Future Research and Future Action

Around the world, more research is needed on LGBTQ social media use and librarians' best practices for promoting library resources and services to LGBTQ populations in their own countries. IFLA has created a special interest group to address the needs of LGBTQ library users around the world; they are well-positioned to serve as the voice of these library users and to reach the ears of IFLA and other international organizations that provide funding for research. Entities in countries that persecuted LGBTQ existence and expression would often support research and publishing initiatives related to HIV/AIDS education and prevention. Library-related research on LGBTQ populations, their information seeking behaviors, and information needs could easily fall under this umbrella. This research on LGBTQ populations could also fall under the umbrella of mobile education and provision of library resources and services to populations at a distance for the purposes of education and the well-being of youth.

Libraries that do not provide Internet access to their patrons should assess whether or not its absence contributes to a decline in the use of library resources and services. Librarians can determine whether this is the case by conducting casual face-to-face interviews with people in the community, or by leaving anonymous paper surveys with a locked submission box in strategic locations. Data collected from interviews or surveys should provide evidence of community members' information-seeking preferences. If local or national governments wish to support libraries, library directors around the world must petition for Internet access so that those without mobile devices or Internet access at home or school can learn and grow. Libraries can also serve as centers for online education, which may encourage governments to fund Internet access.

Language barriers remain in our global world. Those fluent in major European languages—particularly English—are privileged with greater access to LGBTQ culture and global community, as well as the most widely distributed research on LGBTQ populations and LGBTQ library resources and services. Those LGBTQ individuals and communities that are primarily fluent in languages with a smaller global reach face a systemic information divide, which includes reduced access to social media channels. At the same time, these groups might not come forward to announce their existence to the world if that existence is as risk in their countries. The Wikimedia Foundation has advice and best practices for reaching minority language groups and encouraging them to add content to Wikipedia; these practices could also be applied to library outreach.[46]

One trend in libraries involves supporting content creation.[47] In places where libraries may not have money for LGBTQ print books, or sufficient access to LGBTQ ebooks due to cost or language barriers, librarians can support ebook publishing, Wikipedia edit-a-thons, blogging, podcasting, or digital storytelling on a secure, password-protected hosting site and server where access is limited to interested library users, or a mobile app with cloud storage specifically designed for this purpose.

This could potentially to encourage LGBTQ individuals to use the library, provide security for individuals under threat, and support native language LGBTQ cultural development.

To find out how best to reach and support LGBTQ communities through social media, librarians must go into those communities and develop relationships with LGBTQ community leaders. The community leaders may be the ones to take on the duties of providing information about the library to the community through their social media channels. The community leaders could share information about library-sponsored events or new resources and services that would be of interest to LGBTQ users, and provide contact information for the library (or the particular librarian) in case anyone has any questions.

Librarians around the world should assess their library spaces—physical and online—and ask themselves whether or not these spaces are *safe spaces* for education, expression, and community building for their most vulnerable users. The building of safe space does not only benefit the LGBTQ population—it helps everyone. If libraries currently use social media to reach out to their users, user satisfaction surveys may inform librarians as to whether or not patrons feel comfortable commenting, posting, or sharing through library social media channels. It is possible that library social media may push racist, heteronormative, ableist messages which librarians may not be aware of. In the article "Progressive LGBTQ Reference: Coming Out in the 21st Century," Mehra and Braquet published excellent lists of what librarians need to learn and commit to in order to create safe spaces for LGBTQ people in libraries;[48] these best practices can also guide librarians in providing a rationale, content, and plan for social media communication with the LGBTQ community. In response to the arrest and torture of the Azerbaijani Wikipedians, libraries around the world should have serious discussions about the ways libraries, their online spaces, and Wikipedia itself could serve as global "safe spaces" for expression and education.

Librarians around the world face multiple challenges in keeping their libraries welcoming and relevant in the 21st century. They must ask difficult questions, such as how they can acquire resources on limited budgets, and why those who need information the most may not walk through their doors or visit their webpages. In an increasingly globalized world, librarians working for states that enforce censorship and criminalize the existence of racial, ethnic, religious, cultural, economic, sexual, and differently-abled minorities may find themselves walking a tightrope between compliance and social justice.

Endnotes

1. This is particularly the case for people living in rural or economically disadvantaged communities without access to transportation. According to the Pew Internet & American Life Project report "How Americans Value Public Libraries in Their Communities", people of color, the physically disabled, and the unemployed in the United States are more likely to report that it is difficult to visit a library than white, able, employed people. Similar patterns may emerge in other countries, particularly those that have fewer libraries to serve the population to start off with. For more information on the number of libraries per people in the population, see the 2010 IFLA World Report.

2. A visit with the director of the public library in Uppsala, Sweden in November 2013 revealed that Swedish public libraries have a more expensive pay-per-view platform for ebooks in Swedish; this may also be the case for libraries in other non-English speaking countries where the number of speakers falls below a certain number and those ebooks, originally published or translated into that native language, would not have a broad global audience. Also, nations around the world still add a high VAT to ebooks; see the latest International Publishers Association report *VAT/GST on Books & E-Books: An IPA/FEP Global Special Report*, July 20, 2015. Retrieved from http://www.internationalpublishers.org/images/VAT2015.pdf.

3. "Libraries and the LGBTQ Community," Wikipedia, https://en.wikipedia.org/wiki/Libraries_and_the_LGBTQ_community.

4. In the United States, librarians have discouraged the labeling and segregation of LGBT books for fear of stigmatizing patrons and

violating their privacy. In Canada, the United Kingdom, and Sweden, however, separate shelving and labeling of LGBT materials for easy access has become a common practice. Compare Naidoo's article "Over the Rainbow and Under the Radar: Library Services and Programs to LGBTQ Families" to Cooper's "Rainbow Flags and Donor Tags: Queer Materials at the Pride Library," Ederholt and Lindgren's "The Rainbow Library at Umeå City Library and The Swedish Network for LGBTQ Issues at Libraries," and Chapman's "Provision of LGBT-Related Fiction to Children and Young People in Public Libraries," which addresses both sides of this debate in public libraries in the UK.

5. International Federation of Library Associations and Institutions (IFLA), "IFLA approves creation of LGBTQ Users SIG." Dec. 24, 2013. http://www.ifla.org/node/8253?og=8291.

6. Human Rights Office of the High Commissioner. *Born Free and Equal: Sexual Orientation and Gender Identity in International Human Rights Law* (New York: United Nations, 2012), 5. http://www.ohchr.org/Documents/Publications/BornFreeAndEqualLowRes.pdf.

7. "Microaggressions are the brief and commonplace daily verbal, behavioral, and environmental indignities, whether intentional or unintentional, that communicate hostile, derogatory, or negative racial, gender, sexual-orientation, and religious slights and insults to the target person or group" from Derald Wing Sue, *Microaggressions in Everyday Life: Race, Gender, and Sexual Orientation* (Hoboken, NJ: John Wiley & Sons, Inc., 2010), 5.

8. Aengus Carroll and Lucas Paoli Itaborahy, *State-Sponsored Homophobia: A World Survey of Laws: Criminalisation, Protection and Recognition of Same-Sex Love*, 10th edition, (Geneva: International Lesbian, Gay, Bisexual, Trans and Intersex Association [ILGA], 2015), http://old.ilga.org/Statehomophobia/ILGA_State_Sponsored_Homophobia_2015.pdf.

9. International Federation of Library Associations and Institutions (IFLA), "Internet Manifesto 2014," http://www.ifla.org/publications/node/224.

10. EUR-Lex, "Protecting Children in the Digital World," EUR-Lex, Dec. 6, 2011, http://eur-lex.europa.eu/legal-content/EN/TXT/

?qid=1432327937782&uri=URISERV:si0023 ; "Protection of minors and human dignity in audiovisual and information services (2006 recommendation)." EUR-Lex, Feb. 19, 2007. http://eur-lex.europa.eu/legal-content/EN/TXT/?qid=1432327937782&uri=URISERV:l240 30a ; Title XVII—Children's Internet Protection Act (CIPA). http://ifea.net/cipa.pdf.

11. Lukasz Szulc. Banal Nationalism and Queers Online: Enforcing and Resisting Cultural Meanings of .tr. *New Media & Society* 17, no. 9 (2014): 2-3.

12. Internet Live Stats, "Number of Internet Users," Internet Live Stats, 2015, http://www.internetlivestats.com/internet-users/#byregion.

13. Simon Kemp, Digital, *Social & Mobile in 2015: We Are Social's Compendium of Global Digital Statistics*, PowerPoint presentation available made available by We Are Social. http://wearesocial.net/blog/2015/01/digital-social-mobile-worldwide-2015/.

14. CISCO, *Cisco Visual Networking Index: Global Mobile Data Traffic Forecast Update 2014-2019 White Paper*. 2015, https://ec.europa.eu/futurium/en/content/cisco-visual-networking-index-global-mobile-data-traffic-forecast-update-2014-2019-white.

15. GSMA & Master Card Foundation, *Shaping the Future—Releasing the Potential of Informal Learning through Mobile*, Vol. 1, 2012.http://www.gsma.com/mobilefordevelopment/wp-content/uploads/2012/05/mLearning_Report_230512_V2.pdf.

16. International Federation of Library Associations and Institutions, "Trend Report: Mobile Becomes the Primary Platform for Access to Information, Content, and Services," 2015, http://trends.ifla.org/literature-review/mobile-becomes-the-primary-platform-for-access-to-information-content-and-services.

17. "Internet Manifesto 2014."

18. This statistic was calculated by the author from the interactive maps provided by the International Federation of Library Associations and Institutions' 2010 World Report: http://db.ifla-world-report.org/home/index.

19. Beyond Access, *Providing Internet Access through Public Libraries: An Investment in Digital Inclusion and Twenty-First Century Skills,* Issue Brief (Nov. 2012), http://www.ifla.org/files/assets/clm/WSIS/libraries_public_access.pdf.

20. Anthony M. Haag and Franklin K. Chang, "The Impact of Electronic Networking on the Lesbian and Gay Community," *Journal of Gay & Lesbian Social Services* 7, no. 3 (1998): 83-94.

21. Cultural Politics, LGBTQueering Cyberspaces. 2015, http://culturalpolitics.net/digital_cultures/LGBTQ.

22. Community Marketing, Inc., "1st China LGBT Community Survey®," 2014, http://www.communitymarketinginc.com/documents/temp/CMI_China-LGBT-Community-Survey-2014_EN.pdf; Community Marketing, Inc., "Gay & Lesbian Consumer Index Study" (New York: Green Book, 2010); Experian Marketing Services, *The 2013 LGBT Report: Vivid Insights for Reaching Lesbian, Gay, Bisexual and Transgendered Consumers Year-Round* (Schaumburg, IL: Experian Information Solutions, Inc. 2010), 11-14; Pew Research Center, "A Survey of LGBT Americans: Attitudes, Experiences and Values in Changing Times," Pew Research Center, June 13, 2013, http://www.pewsocialtrends.org/2013/06/13/a-survey-of-lgbt-americans/.

23. Ibid.

24. Community Marketing, Inc. "1st China LGBT Community Survey®," 2014.

25. Eddie Chong, "Social Media as Social Capital of LGB Individuals in Hong Kong: Its Relations with Group Membership, Stigma, and Mental Well-Being," *American Journal of Community Psychology* 55, no 1/2 (2015): 228-238; Community Marketing, Inc. "1st China LGBT Community Survey®," 2014.

26. Community Marketing, Inc. "Gay & Lesbian," 2010; Experian Marketing Services.

27. Carroll and Paoli Itaborahy, *State-Sponsored Homophobia,* 2015.

28. Gay Lesbian Straight Education Network, "Out Online: The Experiences of Lesbian, Gay, Bisexual and Transgender Youth on the Internet," http://www.unh.edu/ccrc/pdf/OutOnline.pdf.

29. Haag and Chang, "The Impact of Electronic Networking," 83-94.

30. Eddie Chong, "Social Media," 228-238; Shelley Craig, "Connecting Without Fear: Clinical Implications of the Consumption of Information and Communication Technologies by Sexual Minority Youth and Young Adults," *Clinical Social Work Journal* 43, no. 2 (2015): 159-168; Jesse Fox and Katie M. Warber, "Queer Identity Management and Political Self-Expression on Social Networking Sites: A Co-Cultural Approach to the Spiral of Silence," *Journal of Communication* 65 (2015): 79-100; Haag and Chang, "The Impact of Electronic Networking," 83-94.

31. As of September 2015, the original page no longer exists. The information is available through a Facebook post published by Omar Kuddus: https://www.facebook.com/okuddus/posts/644259152261043.

32. This informal study was conducted in my home, located in the United States, on June 11, 2015 using a personal laptop with a Windows operating system and Mozilla Firefox as my browser and unfiltered Internet access. I used Facebook as well as Google to search for Facebook pages and popular LGBTQ social networking sites. Those attempting to replicate this study may find that their results may differ if conducted in restricted Internet spaces or in countries where languages other than English are spoken.

33. Please refer to the bibliography of this chapter.

34. Please refer to the bibliography of this chapter.

35. Shelley Craig, "Connecting," 159-168.

36. Bharat Mehra and Donna Braquet, "Progressive LGBTQ Reference: Coming Out in the 21st Century," *Reference Services Review* 39, no. 3 (2011): 401-422; Bharat Mehra, Cecilia Merkel and Ann Peterson Bishop, "The Internet for Empowerment of Minority and Marginalized Users," *New Media & Society* 6, no. 6 (2004): 781-802.

37. According to reports from Business Insider and Forbes, while the distribution of Twitter users around the world changes, the United States lags behind Kuwait, Saudi Arabia, Japan, the United Kingdom, the Netherlands, and other countries in Twitter use.

38. Taylor & Francis, *Use of Social Media by the Library: Current Practices and Future Opportunities*, Taylor & Francis Group, Oct. 2014.

39. Searches in Google Scholar and academic databases available through the St. Cloud State University Library have shown that most national surveys, books, journal articles, masters' theses, and dissertations cover LGBT library users and library spaces as observed in the United States, Canada, the United Kingdom, Australia, New Zealand, and Sweden. In addition to researchers in those countries, LGBT social media usage studies are advancing in China, Hong Kong, Japan, Korea, and Turkey. It is possible that more studies exist of LGBT library users, library spaces, and social media use in other countries, but may not be available online or in English.

40. Message from the LGBT Wikimedia listserv, May 26, 2015.

41. Cadie Thompson, "Facebook: About 83 Million Accounts are Fake," USA Today, August, 3, 2012. http://usatoday30.usatoday.com/tech/news/story/2012-08-03/cnbc-facebook-fake-accounts/56759964/1.

42. To view the real name policy as it exists today, visit Facebook's "What Names Are Allowed on Facebook?" page: https://www.facebook.com/help/112146705538576.

43. Lil Miss Hot Mess, "Facebook's 'Real Name' Policy Hurts Real People and Creates a New Digital Divide," *Guardian,* June 3, 2015, retrieved from http://www.theguardian.com/commentisfree/2015/jun/03/facebook-real-name-policy-hurts-people-creates-new-digital-divide.

44. Sergio Quintana, "Social Media Users Saying Goodbye to FB, Hello to Ello," ABCNews 7. Sept 28, 2014, http://abc7news.com/technology/social-media-users-saying-goodbye-to-fb-hello-to-ello/327645/.

45. Jon Swartz, "My Short, Uneventful Flirtation with Ello," USA Today, Oct. 2, 2014, http://www.usatoday.com/story/tech/columnist/2014/10/02/goodbye-ello-secret-yo-silicon-valley-hype /16442777/.

46. Wikimedia Outreach, "GLAM/Model projects/Engaging a Different Language or Cultural Community," https://outreach.wikimedia.org/wiki/GLAM/Model_projects/Engaging_a_different_language_or_cultural_community. Through GLAM, Wikipedia has developed projects to create wikis that embrace entire towns or cities; see "JoburgpediA" for a terrific example of this: https://en.wikipedia.org/wiki/Wikipedia:GLAM/JoburgpediA.

47. David Lee King, "Content Creation, Media Labs, and Hackerspaces," David Lee King blog, Dec. 15, 2011, http://www.davidleeking.com/2011/12/15/content-creation-media-labs-and-hackerspaces/; Jennifer Schaffner and Ricky Erway, *Does Every Research Library Need a Digital Humanities Center?* (Dublin, OH: OCLC, 2014), http://www.oclc.org/content/dam/research/publications/library/2014/oclcresearch-digital-humanities-center-2014.pdf.

48. Mehra and Braquet, "Progressive LGBTQ Reference," 401-422.

Bibliography

Abu Zayyad, Ziad Khalil. "Human Rights, the Internet and Social Media: Has Technology Changed the Way We See Things?" *Palestine-Israel Journal of Politics, Economics & Culture* 18, no. 4 (n.d.): 38-40.

American Libraries Association. (ALA). "LGBT Collections." Gay, Lesbian, Bisexual, and Transgender Round Table, April 2011. http://www.ala.org/glbtrt/popularresources/collection.

———. "Out in the Library: Materials, Displays and Services for the Gay, Lesbian, Bisexual, and Transgender Community." Accessed March 4, 2017. http://www.ala.org/advocacy/intfreedom/iftoolkits/glbttoolkit/glbttoolkit.

Bennett, Shea. "Want to Reach Lesbian, Gay and Bisexual Internet Users? Use Facebook (Not Twitter)." *Adweek.com*, September 23, 2014. Accessed March 4, 2017. http://www.adweek.com/socialtimes/lgbt-social-media-study/501776.

Beyond Access. Providing Internet Access Through Public Libraries: An Investment in Digital Inclusion and Twenty-First Century Skills. Issue Brief (Nov 2012). http://www.ifla.org/files/assets/clm/WSIS/libraries_public_access.pdf.

Beyond Access. "Public Libraries around the World." http://beyondaccess.net/wp-content/uploads/2013/07/Beyond-Access_Library_Map_EN_201304.png.

Braquet, Donna and Bharat Mehra. "Contextualizing Internet Use Practices of the Cyber-Queer: Empowering Information Realities in Everyday Life." *Proceedings of the American Society for Information Science and Technology* 43, no. 1 (2006): 1-10.

Browning, Bill. "Politics at Lightning Speed." *The Gay & Lesbian Review* (May-June 2009): 20-21.

Carroll, Aengus and Lucas Paoli Itaborahy. *State-Sponsored Homophobia: A World Survey of Laws: Criminalisation, Protection and Recognition of Same-Sex Love*. 10th ed. Geneva, Switzerland: International Lesbian, Gay, Bisexual, Trans and Intersex Association (ILGA), 2015. http://old.ilga.org/Statehomophobia/ILGA_State_Sponsored_Homophobia_2015.pdf.

Chapman, Elizabeth. "No More Controversial than a Gardening Display? Provision of LGBT-Related Fiction to Children and Young People in U.K. Public Libraries." *Library Trends* 61, no. 3 (2013): 542-568.

———. "Provision of LGBT-Related Fiction to Children and Young People in Public Libraries." Master's Thesis, the University of Sheffield, England, 2007. http://dagda.shef.ac.uk/dispub/dissertations/2006-07/External/Chapman_Elizabeth_MALib.pdf.

Chan, Michael. "Mobile Phones and the Good Life: Examining the Relationships among Mobile Use, Social Capital and Subjective Well-Being." *New Media & Society* 17, no. 1 (2015): 96-113.

Choi, Junho, Jaemin Jung and Sang-Woo Lee. "What causes Users to Switch from a Local to Global Social Network Site? The Cultural, Social, Economic, and Motivational Factors of Facebook's Globalization." *Computers in Human Behavior* 29 (2013): 2665-2673.

Chong, Eddie. "Social Media as Social Capital of LGB Individuals in Hong Kong: Its Relations with Group Membership, Stigma, and Mental Well-Being." *American Journal of Community Psychology* 55, no. 1/2 (2015): 228-238.

CISCO. "Cisco Visual Networking Index: Global Mobile Data Traffic Forecast Update 2014-2019 White Paper". 2015. https://ec.europa.eu/futurium/en/content/cisco-visual-networking-index-global-mobile-data-traffic-forecast-update-2014-2019-white.

Community Marketing, Inc. "1st China LGBT Community Survey®." 2014. http://www.communitymarketinginc.com/documents/temp/CMI_China-LGBT-Community-Survey-2014_EN.pdf.

———. "Gay & Lesbian Consumer Index Study." New York: Green Book, 2010. http://www.greenbook.org/marketing-research/gay-lesbian-consumer-index-study.

Connaway, Lynn Silipigni and Kevin M. Randall. "Why the Internet is More Attractive than the Library." *The Serials Librarian* 64 (2013): 41-56.

Cooper, Danielle Miriam. "Rainbow Flags and Donor Tags: Queer Materials at the Pride Library." *InterActions: UCLA Journal of Education and Information Studies* 10, no. 2 (2014). http://escholarship.org/uc/item/0300930c.

Craig, Shelley. "Connecting Without Fear: Clinical Implications of the Consumption of Information and Communication Technologies by Sexual Minority Youth and Young Adults." *Clinical Social Work Journal* 43, no. 2 (2015): 159-168.

Cultural Politics. "LGBTQueering Cyberspaces." 2015. http://culturalpolitics.net/digital_cultures/LGBTQ.

EUR-Lex. "Protecting Children in the Digital World." EUR-Lex, Dec. 6, 2011. http://eur-lex.europa.eu/legal-content/EN/TXT/?qid=1432327937782&uri=URISERV:si0023.

———. "Protection of Minors and Human Dignity in Audiovisual and Information Services (2006 Recommendation)." EUR-Lex, Feb. 19, 2007. http://eur-lex.europa.eu/legal-content/EN/TXT/?qid=1432327937782&uri=URISERV:l24030a.

Ederholt, Christer and Maria Lindgren. "The Rainbow Library at Umeå City Library and the Swedish Network for LGBTQ Issues at Libraries." Conference paper presented at the International Federation of Library Associations and Institutions Conference in Lyon, France, 2014. http://library.ifla.org/1019/1/151-endholt-en.pdf.

Experian Marketing Services. *The 2013 LGBT Report: Vivid Insights for Reaching Lesbian, Gay, Bisexual and Transgendered Consumers Year-Round*. Schaumburg, IL: Experian Information Solutions, Inc., 2013.

Fox, Jesse and Katie M. Warber. "Queer Identity Management and Political Self-Expression on Social Networking Sites: A Co-Cultural Approach to the Spiral of Silence." *Journal of Communication* 65 (2015): 79-100.

Gay Lesbian Straight Education Network. *Out Online: The Experiences of Lesbian, Gay, Bisexual and Transgender Youth on the Internet*. New York: Gay Lesbian & Straight Education Network. http://www.unh.edu/ccrc/pdf/OutOnline.pdf.

Go-Gulf. "Smartphone Users around the World—Statistics and Facts." Jan. 2, 2012. http://www.go-gulf.com/blog/smartphone/.

GSMA & Master Card Foundation. *Shaping the Future—Releasing the Potential of Informal Learning through Mobile*. Volume 1. 2012. http://www.gsma.com/mobilefordevelopment/wp-content/uploads/2012/05/mLearning_Report_230512_V2.pdf.

Gudelunas, David. "There's an App for That: The Uses and Gratifications of Online Social Networks for Gay Men." *Sexuality & Culture* 16 (2012): 347-365.

Haag, Anthony M. and Franklin K. Chang. "The Impact of Electronic Networking on the Lesbian and Gay Community." *Journal of Gay & Lesbian Social Services* 7, no. 3 (1998): 83-94.

Human Rights Office of the High Commissioner. *Born Free and Equal: Sexual Orientation and Gender Identity in International*

Human Rights Law. New York: United Nations, 2012. http://www.ohchr.org/Documents/Publications/BornFreeAndEqualLowRes.pdf.

International Federation of Library Associations and Institutions. (IFLA). "Annual Statistical Survey." Jan. 23, 2015. http://www.ifla.org/node/8106.

———. "IFLA approves creation of LGBTQ Users SIG." Dec. 24, 2013. http://www.ifla.org/node/8253?og=8291.

———. "Internet Manifesto 2014." http://www.ifla.org/publications/node/224.

———. "IFLA World Report 2010." http://www.ifla-world-report.org/.

———. "Trend Report: Mobile becomes the primary platform for access to information, content, and services." 2015. http://trends.ifla.org/literature-review/mobile-becomes-the-primary-platform-for-access-to-information-content-and-services.

International Publishers Association. *VAT/GST on Books & E-Books: An IPA/FEP Global Special Report*. July 20, 2015. http://www.internationalpublishers.org/images/VAT2015.pdf.

Internet Live Stats. "Number of Internet Users." 2015. Internet Live Stats. http://www.internetlivestats.com/internet-users/#byregion.

Kemp, Simon. Digital, "Social & Mobile Worldwide in 2015." We Are Social, 2015. http://wearesocial.net/blog/2015/01/digital-social-mobile-worldwide-2015/.

Levy, Karyne. "Facebook Apologizes for 'Real Name' Policy that Forced Drag Queens to Change Their Profiles." *Business Insider*, Oct. 1, 2014. http://www.businessinsider.com/facebook-apologizes-for-real-name-policy-2014-10.

"Libraries and the LGBTQ Community." Wikipedia. https://en.wikipedia.org/wiki/Libraries_and_the_LGBTQ_community.

"Lil Miss Hot Mess. Facebook's 'Real Name' Policy Hurts Real People and Creates a New Digital Divide." *Guardian,* June 3, 2015. Retrieved from http://www.theguardian.com/commentisfree/2015/jun/03/facebook-real-name-policy-hurts-people-creates-new-digital-divide.

Lipman, Victor. "Top Twitter Trends: What Countries are Most Active? Who's Most Popular?" *Forbes,* May 24, 2014. http://www.forbes.com/sites/victorlipman/2014/05/24/top-twitter-trends-what-countries-are-most-active-whos-most-popular/.

Mehra, Bharat and Donna Braquet. "A 'Queer' Manifesto of Interventions for Libraries to 'Come Out' of the Closet! A Study of 'Queer' Youth Experiences during the Coming Out Process." *Libres* 16, no. 1 (2006): 1-29.

———. "Progressive LGBTQ Reference: Coming Out in the 21st Century." *Reference Services Review* 39, no. 3 (2011): 401-422.

Mehra, Bharat, Cecilia Merkel and Ann Peterson Bishop. "The Internet for Empowerment of Minority and Marginalized Users." *New Media & Society* 6, no. 6 (2004): 781-802.

Mitra, Rahul. "Resisting the Spectacle of Pride: Queer Indian Bloggers as Interpretive Communities." *Journal of Broadcasting & Electronic Media* 54, no. 1 (2010): 163–178.

Naidoo, Jamie Campbell. "Over the Rainbow and Under the Radar: Library Services and Programs to LGBTQ Families." *Children & Libraries* 11, no. 3 (2013): 34-40.

Norman, Mark. "OUT on Loan: A Survey of the Use and Information Needs of Users of the Lesbian, Gay and Bisexual Collection of Brighton and Hove Libraries." *Journal of Librarianship and Information Science* 31, no. 4 (1999): 188-196.

Pew Research Center. "A Survey of LGBT Americans: Attitudes, Experiences and Values in Changing Times." Pew Research Center, June 13, 2013. http://www.pewsocialtrends.org/2013/06/13/a-survey-of-lgbt-americans/.

———. "Cell Phones in Africa: Communication Lifeline." Pew Research Center, April 15, 2015. http://www.pewglobal.org/2015/04/15/cell-phones-in-africa-communication-lifeline/.

———. "Emerging Nations Embrace Internet, Mobile Technology." Pew Research Center, Feb 13, 2014. http://www.pewglobal.org/2014/02/13/emerging-nations-embrace-internet-mobile-technology/.

———. "How Americans Value Public Libraries in Their Communities." Pew Research Center, Dec. 11, 2013. http://libraries.pewinternet.org/2013/12/11/section-3-perceptions-of-public-libraries/.

Reporters without Borders. *Enemies of the Internet 2014*. Reporters without Borders. http://12mars.rsf.org/wp-content/uploads/EN_RAPPORT_INTERNET_BD.pdf.

Schaffner, Jennifer and Ricky Erway. *Does Every Research Library Need a Digital Humanities Center?* Dublin, OH: OCLC, 2014. http://www.oclc.org/content/dam/research/publications/library/2014/oclcresearch-digital-humanities-center-2014.pdf.

Smith, Cooper. "These are the Most Twitter-Crazy Countries in the World, Starting with Saudi Arabia." *Business Insider*, Nov. 7, 2013. http://www.businessinsider.com/the-top-twitter-markets-in-the-world-2013-11.

Sue, Derald Wing. *Microaggressions in Everyday Life: Race, Gender, and Sexual Orientation*. Hoboken, NJ: John Wiley & Sons, 2010.

Swartz, Jon. "My Short, Uneventful Flirtation with Ello." *USA Today*, Oct. 2, 2014. http://www.usatoday.com/story/tech/columnist/2014/10/02/goodbye-ello-secret-yo-silicon-valley-hype/16442777/.

Szulc, Lukasz. Banal Nationalism and Queers Online: Enforcing and Resisting Cultural Meanings of .tr. *New Media & Society* 17, no. 9 (2014): 1530 - 1546.

Taylor & Francis. *Use of Social Media by the Library: Current Practices and Future Opportunities*. London: Taylor & Francis Group, 2014.

The World Bank. "Mobile cellular subscriptions (per 100 people)." The World Bank, 2015. http://data.worldbank.org/indicator/IT.CEL.SETS.P2.

Title XVII—Children's Internet Protection Act (CIPA). http://ifea.net/cipa.pdf.

Thompson, Cadie. "Facebook: About 83 Million Accounts are Fake." *USA Today*, August, 3, 2012. http://usatoday30.usatoday.com/tech/news/story/2012-08-03/cnbc-facebook-fake-accounts/56759964/1.

Wikimedia Outreach. "GLAM/Model projects/engaging a different language or cultural community." Page last modified on October 24, 2012. https://outreach.wikimedia.org/wiki/GLAM/Model_projects/Engaging_a_different_language_or_cultural_community.

Wikipedia. "Wikipedia: GLAM/JoburgpediA." Page last modified on June 2, 2015. https://en.wikipedia.org/wiki/Wikipedia:GLAM/JoburgpediA.

ABOUT THE CONTRIBUTORS

Noriko Asato is Associate Professor of Library & Information Science Program, University of Hawai'i at Mānoa. She teaches Asian Studies Librarianship, Asian Informatics, and coordinates the LIS Internship Program. She has an MLISc from UHM, a Ph.D. from Purdue University and graduate degrees in Asian Studies and Education from the University of Wisconsin. Her recent publications include *Handbook for Asian Studies Specialists: A Guide to Research Materials and Collection Building Tools* (Libraries Unlimited, 2013), *Toshokan to Chitekijiyu: Kankatsu Ryoiki, Hoshin, Jiken, Rekishi [Libraries and Intellectual Freedom: Domain, Policies, Incidents, History]*(Kyoto Institute for Library and Information Science Study Group, 2013), and "Librarians' Free Speech: The Challenge of Librarians' Own Intellectual Freedom to the American Library Association 1946-2007," *Library Trends* 63 (2014): 75-105.

Ragnhild Brandstedt has an M.S. in Library and Information Science, graduating from University of Boras, Sweden in 2000. Her main area of interest is developing library operations and collaborations, with special interests in studies of diversity and gender. For the past five years Brandstedt has been involved in processes focusing on inclusiveness and tolerance. This includes projects such as the international social art project Mural 2012, outreach programs, and building networks with professionals and others in various fields. Brandstedt's action-based research on LGBTQ issues has been presented at the 2013 IFLA Congress in Singapore and in various contexts in Sweden. She also took part in the formation of the *Lesbian, Gay, Bisexual, Transgender and Queer/Questioning Users Special Interest Group* of IFLA. She is currently the Library Director of the Mariestads Public Library in Sweden.

Elizabeth L. Chapman (Liz) recently completed her Ph.D. at the University of Sheffield, UK, focusing on the provision of LGBTQ* fiction to children and young people in English public libraries. She now divides her time between working for Sheffield Libraries and lecturing in Education Studies at Sheffield Hallam University. She is Section Editor for Equality and Diversity for the *Journal of Radical Librarianship*, and previously edited *Public Library Journal*. As a bi woman, she has a strong commitment to LGBTQ* inclusion in libraries.

Lisette Hernandez (lisette.hernandez@mail.wvu.edu) received her Master's degree in Information Sciences from the University of Tennessee's School of Information Sciences in 2015. She currently holds a Resident Librarian position in the West Virginia University's Evansdale Library. Lisette is researching ways to assist rural libraries and plans to sit on a committee servicing the LGBTQ student population on her campus.

Louis Kamwina Nsapo holds a degree in Documentation and Libraries and another in Archives from the Higher Institute of Statistics of Kinshasa, a Certificate in Access for Documentary Computer Technician Functions from the Pan African Institute for Development (IPD-AC, Douala-Cameroon), and an Advanced Diploma in Human Rights and Social Communication from the University of Kinshasa UNESCO Chair. He is currently a doctoral student in Human Rights and Communication and also works as a librarian at the Protestant University of Congo.

Matthew Knight completed his M.A. in Celtic Languages & Literatures from Harvard University in 2005 and received an M.A. in Library and Information Science from the University of South Florida in 2009. As Assistant Director of Special Collections at the University of South

Florida Tampa Library, Matthew curates the Queer Literature Collection and the LGBT archival materials and also organizes all LGBT programming. Apart from the LGBT collections, Matthew works extensively with the Dion Boucicault Theatre Collection, the Alvin P. Yorkunas Collection, and the Anglo-Irish Literature collection for his research.

Lucas McKeever is the Head of Technical Services at Elmwood Park Public Library near Chicago, IL. Since 2013, he has been an active coordinator of the LGBTQ Users Special Interest Group of the International Federation of Library Associations and Institutions (IFLA). Additionally, he has served on the Rainbow Book List Committee of the GLBT Round Table of the American Library Association and has been named an American Library Association Emerging Leader. Previously, Lucas was the director of the Gerber/Hart Library and Archives, an organization committed to documenting and preserving facets of LGBTQ life in the Midwestern United States.

Bharat Mehra (bmehra@utk.edu) is Associate Professor in the School of Information Sciences at the University of Tennessee. His research examines diversity and intercultural communication, social justice in library and information science (LIS), critical and cross-cultural studies, and community informatics or the use of information and communication technologies to empower minority and underserved populations to make meaningful changes in their everyday lives. Mehra has applied conceptual frameworks in LIS with interdisciplinary approaches to expand the profession's traditional definition, scope, extent, representation, and relevance in the 21st century. He has collaborated with racial/ethnic groups, international communities, sexual minorities, rural librarians, small businesses, and others, to represent their experiences in shaping the design and development of various community-based information systems and services.

Rae-Anne Montague is Director of Outreach Programs at Hawai'i Pacific University. Her interests include community engagement, inquiry, and social justice. She has developed and provided leadership for several LIS initiatives including WISE (Web-based Information Science Education), LAMP (LIS Access Midwest Program), and *E Noelo I Ka 'Ike* (To Search for Knowledge), a project designed to increase awareness and understanding of Hawaiian resource materials. Montague is a proud Illinois graduate who has been involved in the ALA GLBT Round Table, the IFLA LGBTQ Users SIG, and many other progressive groups.

Gregory Toth is currently the Metadata and Discovery Manager at Senate House Library, the central library of the University of London, England, UK. He has previously worked in a variety of academic and national libraries where he used different taxonomies. Originally he is from Hungary and has been living in the UK for more than a decade. He is a feminist and advocate of equality.

Andrew B. Wertheimer is Associate Professor in the Library and Information Science Program at the University of Hawaii at Manoa, where he served as Program Chair for five years. He has also taught at San José State University as well as three Japanese universities (Tsukuba, Keio, and J. F. Oberlin). Wertheimer has a Ph.D. from the University of Wisconsin-Madison School of Library and Information Studies with a doctoral minor in Print Culture Studies. He also has an M.L.S. from Indiana University and a B.A. in Journalism and Asian Studies from the University of Wisconsin-Eau Claire. He is on the American Library Association's Council and the editorial board of *Library Quarterly*. His research focuses on the history of ethnic print cultures, libraries, and professional education and ethics for the information professions.

Rachel Wexelbaum is Collection Management Librarian and Associate Professor at St. Cloud State University. She is her campus LGBT Resource Center faculty liaison and is the LGBTIQ Studies selector. Rachel is a senior editor and book reviewer for the Lambda Literary Foundation, and serves on the Harrington Park Press Advisory Board for Library & Information Resources. Rachel has also served as the

LGBT Studies peer reviewer for *Resources for College Libraries*. In 2016 she became the official reviewer of LGBTIQ academic non-fiction published by the University of Minnesota Press. Rachel has developed curricula for and taught "Introduction to LGBTIQ Studies" and "Critical Thinking in Academic Research on LGBTIQ Issues." Based on her teaching experience and own research, she is aware of the challenges that students and faculty face when researching LGBTIQ topics. Currently she is doing research on safe spaces in higher education, how academic libraries aid in the retention of LGBTIQ students, and LGBTIQ student perceptions of safety in academic libraries. She is also a trained safe space facilitator. In 2014 Rachel won the LGBT Faculty/Staff/Administrator Leadership Award at her institution for her support and advocacy for LGBTIQ curriculum, students, and colleagues. Rachel is the editor of *Queers Online: LGBT Digital Practices in Libraries, Archives and Museums* (Library Juice Press, 2015), in which she contributed chapters on LGBTIQ ebook publishing, LGBTIQ presence in Wikipedia, and online censorship. She is the lead author of the article "Gifted and LGBTIQ: A Comprehensive Research Review" (*International Journal for Talent Development and Creativity*, August 2014). She has also contributed chapters to *Serving LGBTIQ Library and Archives Users: Essays on Outreach, Service, Collections, and Access* (ed. Ellen Greenblatt, McFarland & Company, 2011) and *Out Behind the Desk: Workplace Issues for LGBTQ Librarians* (ed. Tracy Nectoux, Library Juice Press, 2011).

INDEX

A

academic librarians. *See* librarians, academic
academic libraries. *See* libraries, academic
ACRL. *See* Association of College and Research Libraries
action-based research, xvi, 171, 176-179, 182
activism, xiv, 7, 13, 193, 195
Adoption of Children Act of 2005 (United Kingdom), 22, 23
Al Hussein, Zeid Ra'ad, xiv
ALA. *See* American Library Association
American Library Association, xv, xvii, xviii, 1-2, 3, 4, 7, 11
Anti-Discrimination Act, 172
archival content, 78, 85
archives, xiii, xvi, 77, 78, 84, 89, 127
Arms, Kevin, 194, 199
Asato, Noriko, 239
Association of College and Research Libraries, 5

B

Baker-McConnell papers, xv, 13
Baker, Jack, xv, 1, 2, 3, 4, 13-14
Bentz, Donald L., 191
Berman, Stanford, xv, 103, 104, 113
Berninghausen, David, 5
Bharatiya Janata Party, 131-132
BJP. *See* Bharatiya Janata Party
Bodies that Matter, xiii

Brandstedt, Ragnhild, 239-240
Butler, Judith, xiii

C

card catalogs. *See* library card catalogs
Casement, Roger, 80-81
cataloging practices, xiii, xvi, 103, 184
Chapman, Elizabeth L., 240
Chartered Institute of Library and Information Professionals, 25, 26, 39
Chartered Institute of Public Finance and Accountancy, 23
CILIP. *See* Chartered Institute of Library and Information Professionals
CIPFA. *See* Chartered Institute of Public Finance and Accountancy
Classification Decimale Universelle, 107
classification systems, xvi, 102, 103, 114, 184
collective memory, 78
Colon Classification System, 128
coming-out narratives, 101
content analysis, xvi, 126, 132-139
Crawley, Sara, 190-193
cultural memory, xv
Cutter, Charles, 102

D

Daly, Edie, 190-192, 195, 200

DDC. *See* **Dewey Decimal Classification**
Delmas, Bruno, 78
Democratic Republic of the Congo
archival collections, xv, 77-78, 86-89
attitudes towards homosexuality and the lesbian, gay, bisexual, transgender, queer/questioning community, xv, 77, 84-85
effects of colonialism, xv, 78-81
laws, 78-85
number of lesbian, gay, bisexual, transgender, queer/questioning people in, 85
politics and government, 78-85
social conditions, xv, 77-78, 84-85
Dewey Decimal Classification
bias in, xvi, 102, 104, 105
history of, 105-107
importance of, 102
relationship to Universal Decimal Classification, 105-109, 112-113
Dewey, Melville, 105
discrimination, xiv, 125, 127, 132, 145, 171-172, 209, 212, 216
Discrimination and Violence against Individuals Based on Their Sexual Orientation and Gender Identity, xiv
Drabinski, Emily, 104
DRC. *See* **Democratic Republic of the Congo**

E
EEO. *See* **Equal Employment Opportunity (ALA)**
EEO Subcommittee. *See* **Equal Employment Opportunity Subcommittee (ALA)**
Equality Act of 2010 (United Kingdom), 22, 23
Equal Employment Opportunity (ALA), 9
Equal Employment Opportunity Subcommittee (ALA), 12

F
Federation Internationale de Documentation, 106, 107, 112-113
FID. *See* **Federation Internationale de Documentation**
Fisher, Eunice, 195
Five Laws of Library Science, 128
Florida LGBT Initiative, 191, 196
Florida Women's History Initiative, 191, 196
Freedom to Read Foundation (ALA), 6

G
Garrison, William, 192, 193, 202
Gay, Lesbian, Bisexual, and Transgender Round Table (ALA), xii, xvii, 25, 190

Gay, Lesbian, Bisexual, Transgender, Ally Programs Office (University of Minnesota), 13
Gay Liberation Task Force, 2, 5, 11
Gender Identity Research and Education Society, 34
Gender Recognition Act of 2004 (United Kingdom), 22
Gender Recognition Certificate, 22
Gittings, Barbara, 7, 11-12
GLBTA. *See* Gay, Lesbian, Bisexual, Transgender, Ally Programs Office (University of Minnesota)
GLBTRT. *See* Gay, Lesbian, Bisexual, and Transgender Round Table (ALA)
GLTF. *See* Gay Liberation Task Force
GRC. *See* Gender Recognition Certificate

H
Hai-siatu, 87
Hallonbergen Public Library, 174-176
Haykin's Subject Headings, 103
Hernandez, Lisette, 240
Hodgin, T. Ellis, 6
Hopp, Ralph, 2
Horn, Zoia, 6
human rights, xiv, 103, 125, 129, 130-131, 185, 212

I
ICA. *See* International Council on Archives.
ICT. *See* information and communication technology
IFC. *See* Intellectual Freedom Committee (ALA)
IFLA. *See* International Federation of Library Associations and Institutions
IFLA Internet Manifesto of 2014. *See* International Federation of Library Associations and Institutions Internet Manifesto of 2014
IIB. *See* Institut International de Bibliographie
India
 attitudes towards homosexuality and the lesbian, gay, bisexual, transgender, queer/questioning community, xvi, 125, 127, 129-132
 effects of colonialism, 127
 laws, xvi, 125-126, 127, 129-132
 politics and government, xvi, 125-126, 131-132
 role of libraries, xvi, 126, 127-129
 rural conditions, 126, 128, 129, 139-144, 148-149
 social conditions, xvi, 125-126, 139-144
 urban conditions, 126, 128, 129, 139-140, 144-148

Indian Library Association, 128, 129
information and communication technology, 126, 128
information science. *See* library and information science
information seeking behavior, 101, 216-219
Institut International de Bibliographie, 106
intellectual freedom, 1-2, 3, 6, 11
Intellectual Freedom Committee (ALA), 3, 4, 5, 6
International Conference on Bibliography, 106
International Council on Archives, 78
International Federation of Library Associations and Institutions, xi, 183, 211, 212, 214, 222
International Federation of Library Associations and Institutions Internet Manifesto of 2014, 212, 214
internet access, 213-215
intersectionality, xi, xiii-xv
Iyer, Harish, 132

J
Jean-Nickolaus Tretter Collection in GLBT Studies. *See* Jean-Nickolaus Tretter Collection in Gay Lesbian Bisexual Transgender Studies (University of Minnesota)
Jean-Nickolaus Tretter Collection in Gay Lesbian Bisexual Transgender Studies (University of Minnesota), xv, 13
Johnson, David, 190, 191

K
Kaler, Eric, 13
Kamwina Nsapo, Louis, 240
Keeney, Phillip, 6
Knight, Matthew, 240-241
Kolb, David A., 175-176
Krug, Judith, 7, 11

L
La Fontaine, Henri, 105-106
LAGAR. *See* Lesbian and Gay Archives Roundtable (SAA)
Laich, Katherine, 7-8
LC Classification. *See* Library of Congress Classification
Leroy C. Merritt Humanitarian Fund, 6, 11
Lesbian and Gay Archives Roundtable (SAA), xii
lesbian, gay, bisexual, transgender, queer/questioning, xi, 2, 21-22, 101, 125
Lesbian, Gay, Bisexual, Transgender, Queer/Questioning Users Special Interest Group (IFLA), xi-xiv, xvii, 183
lesbian, gay, bisexual, transgender, transsexual, questioning, queer,

intersex, two-spirited and allies, 85
LGBT library certification, 176
LGBTQ. *See* lesbian, gay, bisexual, transgender, queer/questioning
LGBTQ Users SIG. *See* Lesbian, Gay, Bisexual, Transgender, Queer/Questioning Users Special Interest Group (IFLA)
LGBTTQQI2SA. *See* lesbian, gay, bisexual, transgender, transsexual, questioning, queer, intersex, two-spirited and allies
librarians, academic, 114, 210
librarians, public, 1, 32-36
librarians, radical, xvi, 103-104
Libraries: Gateways to Knowledge, 128
libraries, public
   in India, 127-129, 140-19
   in Sweden, xvi, 171
   in the United Kingdom, xv, 22-23, 24-27, 38-39, 175
   in the United States, 27, 175
   provisioning for lesbian, gay, bisexual, transgender, queer/questioning adult users, 24-26, 173
   provisioning for lesbian, gay, bisexual, transgender, queer/questioning children and young users, xv, 27-32, 38-40, 173, 175
   Ranganathan's vision for, 128
   reading recommendations for lesbian, gay, bisexual, transgender, queer/questioning children and young users, 59-76
Library Act (Sweden), 171, 185
library and information science, xi, xiii, xiv, 104
Library and Information Science programs, 26, 39, 104, 128 *See also* Master of Library and Information Science
Library Bill of Rights (ALA), 5
library card catalogs, 101, 109
library collaborations, 139-148, 171, 172, 204-205
Library of Congress Classification, 102, 103, 104
library patrons
   children, xv, 27-31
   current policy, xv
   engagement of, xvi
   equal access for, xv, xvi, xviii
   lesbian, gay, bisexual, transgender, queer/questioning, xiv-xv, xvi, xviii, 24-31, 59-76
   resource allocation for, xvi, 31-32, 39-40
   vulnerable users, xvi
   young people, xv, 27-31
library services
   bias in, xiii, xvi, 22-23, 28-31
   equality in, xii, xv, xvi, xviii, 101
   for lesbian, gay, bisexual, transgender, queer/questioning adult users, xv, xviii, 173, 210-212
   for lesbian, gay, bisexual, transgen-

der, queer/questioning children and young users, xv, xviii, 27-31, 173, 175, 210-212
  need for staff training for, xv, xvi, 25, 32-38, 104, 174, 176, 180-183
  shortcomings of, xiii, 22-23, 101-102
library users. *See* library patrons
LIS. *See* library and information science
LIS programs. *See* Library and Information Science programs
London Libraries Consortium, 30

M

Madras Public Library Act of 1948 (India), 127
Maniscalco, Rex, 191, 194
Manuel du Répertoire Bibliographique Universel, 106
Mariestad Public Library, xvi, 171, 172-174, 182
Master of Library and Information Science, 26, 27 *See also* Library and Information Science programs
Master Reference File, 107
MBGLTACC. *See* Midwest Bisexual, Lesbian, Gay, Transgender, and Ally College Conference
McConnell, Michael
  archival papers, xv, 13
  court case, xv, 1-3, 12
  dealings with the American Library Association, xv, 1, 2-10, 11, 12
  job offer and rescission from University of Minnesota Saint Paul Library, xv, 1, 2, 4, 10
  relationship with Jack Baker, xv, 1, 2, 13-14
  suggestions for gay librarians, 4-5, 13-14
  upcoming book from the University of Minnesota Press, 13
McKeever, Lucas, 241
Mehra, Bharat, 241
Midwest Bisexual, Lesbian, Gay, Transgender, and Ally College Conference, xii
Minnesota Civil Liberties Union, 2-3
Minnesota Library Association, 4
mobile device ownership, 213, 214-215
Montague, Rae-Anne, 241-242
Montana State University Library, 6

N

National Knowledge Commission, 128
Ngole, Jean-Brettant, 87

O

Office for Intellectual Freedom (ALA), 6, 7

INDEX 253

Office for Library Personnel Resources (ALA), 12
OIF. *See* Office for Intellectual Freedom (ALA)
OLPR. *See* Office for Library Personnel Resources (ALA)
Orlando night club shooting (2016), xviii
Otlet, Paul, 105-106

P
PAMAI. *See* Program of Action for Mediation, Arbitration, and Inquiry (ALA)
Parsekar, Lakshmikant, 132
PASLBR. *See* Program of Action in Support of the Library Bill of Rights (ALA)
PLG. *See* Progressive Librarians Guild
Principle of Intellectual Freedom (ALA), 4
Professional Knowledge and Skills Base (CILIP), 26, 36
Program of Action for Mediation, Arbitration, and Inquiry (ALA), 6-7, 11
Program of Action in Support of the Library Bill of Rights (ALA), 3, 5, 6, 10, 11
progressive change, xvi
Progressive Librarians Guild, xii
public librarians. *See* librarians, public
public libraries. *See* libraries, public
Public Libraries and Museums Act (United Kingdom), 23, 30

Q
QLA. *See* Queer Library Alliance
Quality Assurance Agency Subject Benchmark for Library and Information Management, 26
queer advocacy, xii
queer identity, xi, xiii, xv, xvii, 24
Queer Library Alliance, xi-xiii
queer representation, xi, xiv
queer rights, xiv

R
Rainbow Library, 174
radical librarians. *See* librarians, radical
Ranganathan, S. A., 110, 128
Répertoire Bibliographique Universel, 106
Report on the McConnell Case (ALA)(1972), 7-8
Report on the McConnell Case (ALA) (1973), 8-9
Report on the McConnell Case (ALA) (1975), 9-10
RFSL. *See* Swedish Federation for Lesbian, Gay, Bisexual and Transgender Rights

S
SAA. *See* Society of American Archivists
same-sex marriage
  court cases, xvii, 1
  in Ireland, 22
  in the United Kingdom, 22
  in the United States, xvii, 1, 2-3
  legal aspects, xvii, 1, 2-3, 13, 22
SCMAI. *See* Staff Committee on Mediation, Arbitration, and Inquiry (ALA)
SCRIM. *See* Standing Committee on Review, Inquiry, and Mediation (ALA)
Section 28 (United Kingdom), 22, 25, 38
Section 337 (India), 125-126, 130-131
Singh, Rajnath, 131
Smith, Bobby, 191, 192
social attitudes, 2, 23, 26
social justice, xiv, 103, 104, 127, 129, 149
social media, xvi, 13, 88, 135, 137, 139, 144, 209-210, 213-225
Social Responsibility Round Table (ALA), 2, 4, 6, 7-9
Society of American Archivists, xii
SRRT. *See* Social Responsibility Round Table (ALA)
Staff Committee on Mediation, Arbitration, and Inquiry (ALA), 7-11

Standing Committee on Review, Inquiry, and Mediation (ALA), 11
subject headings. *See* classification systems
Sundbyberg Public Library, 176
Sweden
  attitudes towards homosexuality and the lesbian, gay, bisexual, transgender, queer/questioning community, xvi, 171-172
  laws, 171-172
  politics and government, 171-172
  role of libraries, xvi, 171, 183-185
  social conditions, xvi, 172-174
Swedish Federation for Lesbian, Gay, Bisexual and Transgender Rights, 172
Swedish Library Association, 172, 176-182

T
Task Force on Gay Liberation (ALA), xvii, 4, 5, 7
Tawadkarover, Ramesh, 131
Tenure in Libraries: A Statement of Principles of Intellectual Freedom and Tenure for Librarians, 3-4
Times of India, xvi, 126, 132-133
Toth, George, 242

U
U of M GLBTA Programs Office. *See* University of Minnesota Gay,

INDEX

Lesbian, Bisexual, Transgender, Ally Programs Office
UDC. *See* Universal Decimal Classification
UDC Consortium. *See* Universal Decimal Classification Consortium
UDC Revision Committees. *See* Universal Decimal Classification Revision Committees
UIUC GSLIS. *See* University of Illinois at Urbana-Champaign Graduate School of Library and Information Science
UN High Commissioner for Human Rights. *See* United Nations High Commissioner for Human Rights
UN Human Rights Council. *See* United Nations Human Rights Council
United Kingdom
  attitudes towards homosexuality and the lesbian, gay, bisexual, transgender, queer/questioning community, 22, 23-24
  laws, 22, 25
  politics and government, 22-23, 25
  role of libraries, xv, 22-26
  social conditions, 22-24
United Nations High Commissioner for Human Rights, xiv, 129, 212
United Nations Human Rights Council, xiv
Universal Decimal Classification
  bias in, xvi, 105, 110-112, 114
  everyday usage of, 109-110
  examples of, 107-109
  facets in, 105
  history of, 105-107
  importance of, 104-105, 114
  innovative aspects of, 106, 114
  international nature of, 104-105, 112
  number building in, 107-109, 110-112, 114
  relationship to Dewey Decimal Classification, 105-109, 112-112
  revision of, 112-113, 114
Universal Decimal Classification Consortium, xvi, 107
Universal Decimal Classification Revision Committees, 112
University of Illinois at Urbana-Champaign Graduate School of Library and Information Science, xii, xiii
University of Minnesota Gay, Lesbian, Bisexual, Transgender, Ally Programs Office, 13
University of Minnesota Saint Paul Library, xv, 1, 2
University of South Florida Libraries
  Asian Male Nude Collection, 192, 194, 199

budgetary considerations, 202-203
collaborations, 204-205
collection usage statistics, 200-201
community engagement, 203-204
development of queer academic collections, xvi, 189-190, 192-194, 195-196
Gay Surfer Collection, 193, 194, 199
history of, 190-196
lesbian, gay, bisexual, transgender, queer/questioning initiatives, xvi, 189-190
lessons learned, 196-204
online presence, 192, 201
oral history collections, 193, 194
photography collections, 194
Queer Literature Collection, 192, 199
use of survey data, 190, 207-208
users. *See* library patrons
USF Libraries. *See* **University of South Florida Libraries**

V
Vardhan, Harsh, 131
Vincent, John, 22, 24-25

W
WEB. *See* **Women's Energy Bank**
Web 2.0, 209, 220
web sites, 213
Wertheimer, Andrew B., 242
Wexelbaum, Rachel, 242
Wojkowski, Lee Ann "Oak", 191

Women's Energy Bank, 190
Womyn's Words, **190**
Wyker, Cyrana, 192, 193, 194, 199, 204

Y
Yogyakarta Principles, 130-131
Youth Chances Survey (United Kingdom), 24, 34-35

www.ingramcontent.com/pod-product-compliance
Lightning Source LLC
Chambersburg PA
CBHW051352290426
44108CB00015B/1982